'A PIG ON THE WALL'
OF DAWLISH

This book is dedicated to my parents
Bill and Olive Gregory

Dave Gregory

ISBN: 0-9546672-0-4

Published by Dave Gregory

© Copyright Dave Gregory 2003

Graphic Design and Artwork: Dawn Gregory

Cover Design: Dawn Gregory

Printed in Great Britain by Livesey Limited,
Shrewsbury

ACKNOWLEDGEMENTS

I have received some tremendous help and advice whilst researching and producing this book. Accordingly, I would like to place on record my thanks to all those who have generously given of their time and knowledge.

I am especially indebted to Ken Jones, Helen Sample, the late Fred Briscoe and all those people who gave interviews on tape.

I am grateful for the resources and support of the Shropshire Archives Library Castle Gates, Shrewsbury, and the Ironbridge Gorge Museum Library at Coalbrookdale.

My thanks also go to my daughter, Dawn, for her skills and hard work. Without her efforts this book would not have been produced.

PHOTOGRAPHS

Some of the photographs in the book have been kindly supplied by:

Shropshire Archives Library, pp 111, 134, 140.
Ironbridge Gorge Museum Trust Library, pp 16, 25-26, 35, 40, 41, 51, 57, 69, 90-91, 105, 107, (see Front Cover also), 122, 127, 146.
Alan Woolley, pp 48, 121, 166.
Denzil Skelton, pp 5, 101.

Some photographs are shown by kind permission of the Telford Journal, pp 74, 112, 131-132, 164.
Contemporary photographs taken by the author.

Every effort has been made, where appropriate, to trace the origins of photographs used. Should anyone concerned not have been consulted, the author wishes to apologise.

BIBLIOGRAPHY

*'Victoria County History' - Volume XI - Shropshire Archives Library
Tape transcriptions of Dawley citizens - Ironbridge Gorge Museum Library
The author's own tape recordings of Dawley citizens

FOR FURTHER READING

'Captain Webb and 100 years of channel swimming' by Margaret A Jarvis (published by David and Charles Limited), 1975, from which some of the facts in Chapter 14 were obtained.

WHAT THE BOOK'S ALL ABOUT

I've tried to paint a picture of Dawley life during the first half of the twentieth century, in a way that I hope readers will find both interesting and entertaining. The picture has been coloured with the contrasting experiences of many Dawley people including some born near the turn of the twentieth century, others who grew up during the 1920's and 1930's, and a boy whose formative years were the 1940's and early 1950's.

Such a unique environment didn't appear overnight, so I have dipped into the pages of Dawley's earlier history just enough to help the reader appreciate how the recent past was shaped by what had gone before. The High Street, the outlying villages, local personalities and traditions, well-known buildings, industry, transport, churches, schools, shopping, leisure pursuits and links with nearby towns all form a part of the inimitable tapestry of the Dawley area that existed before the place became enveloped within the New Town of Telford.

We start with a tour of the district, as it was in the late 1940's and early 1950's, then trace the area's origins and development, before having a good look at how things were as the twentieth century progressed.

People will, of course, have their own memories and experiences of growing up and living in Dawley and district. I hope this book will trigger some of them off, but it would be good to think readers who hail from other parts of Shropshire or beyond, will find the book provides an interesting insight into the way in which a small town's provincial culture was developed.

Dave Gregory
2003

A ROUGH IDEA OF HOW THE
DAWLEY DISTRICT LOOKED IN THE 1940s

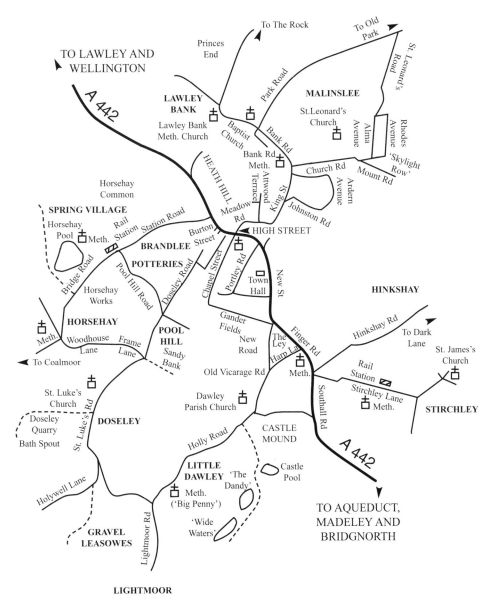

(Not to scale. Not all roads etc. are shown.)

CONTENTS

INTRODUCTION

Why should anyone have ever heard of Dawley?

Anyone outside the Wrekin area of East Shropshire, that is. Surely it was just a small, ordinary-looking provincial town standing partly on a hill? If it was busy at all, it was busy minding its own business, as if the rest of the world had nothing to do with it.

Motorists who simply passed through the town's one main street along the A442 road could not, any more than could a cockney barrowboy from Bow, have any idea what a uniquely special place this was. They couldn't possibly know it was full of people of various social persuasions all of whom possessed a worldly wisdom and quirky sense of humour not found anywhere else within the civilised realm. A passing stranger would be unable to appreciate that Dawley was a fantastic place in which to live, and especially grow up. The town had practically everything any reasonable person could need - a full range of small shops, two cinemas, two railway stations and enough churches and public houses for all those who wanted them. It had a neat municipal park, a football team, plenty of wide-open spaces, a gaggle of surrounding 'satellite' villages, a fascinating history, and it afforded inspirational views of distant hilly countryside. An outsider taking the trouble to walk along the winding High Street would soon realise that here lived a people who possessed their own distinctive dialect (their own language some would say), a curious fusion of seventeenth century rustication and earthy coalfield slang. These people were extraordinary.

There couldn't be anywhere else in the world where men would unfailingly greet one another with the words '*ow bist owd jockey?*' ('how are you, old friend?', roughly translated).

Locals would stand in little knots on the pavement regaling each other in this native tongue, and expound solutions to just about every problem under the sun. Why didn't the government turn to Dawley people for sage advice before reaching important decisions? It would surely prevent a lot of crucial mistakes from being made if they did!

If two strangers met at the North Pole, and each discovered that the other came from Dawley, an immediate, sub-conscious rapport would develop between them so that they would instinctively know that their new-found companion was '*orreet*' (alright) and could be trusted. You could give him your entire collection of cigarette-cards, or your sweet coupons to look at, and positively know they would be returned in tact. You knew they would share the same outlook on life, the same philosophy, and the same opinion on most things from the state of the roads in Dawley to the effect of the lack of rain on this year's runner beans. An outbreak of '*ow bist, owd jockey*' would seal the relationship as surely as the handshake of two stockbrokers on a share deal. It was the same kind of bond as that enjoyed between Yorkshire people, except that nobody else knew about Dawley.

These were the feelings of a young boy born in the town and who journeyed through his formative years there during the late 1940's and early 1950's. He was conscious of Dawley's 'specialness' even then. As he grew older, he experienced an over-whelming compulsion to discover what had made it that way, what had gone on there decades even centuries before his own arrival, to shape its distinctive environment and beget the endearing qualities of its population. There were so many things requiring explanation, and this book will show the fruits of his adult researches into the area's momentous past, and try to place twenty first century Dawley within the context of its history.

First, we must discover the Dawley that greeted the fifth and sixth decades of the twentieth century. That was the seeming age of innocence before the region became entangled, like a surprised fly in the expansive web of Telford New Town, and ceded at least some of its identity to this new creation.

With his friends, the boy would spend countless hours drifting around the locality on innumerable bicycle safaris, taking in the sights, the curiosities, the characters - in fact the whole conglomeration that was Dawley and district at the time of his youth. Let's start the journey then, and part the curtains to reveal the peculiar kaleidoscope shaken out by that unstoppable pair of architects - history and nature - by the time the 40's and 50's had arrived.

A BOYHOOD TOUR OF THE DAWLEY DISTRICT

Chapter One

A BRIEF ENCOUNTER WITH DAWLEY 'HIGH STREET'

There is only one place at which to begin a tour of the Dawley district - 'the Street'. Everybody called it 'the Street' even though it was two streets really. The main part was the dog's leg 'High Street' containing the bulk of the shops and where you could pretty well rely on meeting most of the population, especially on a Saturday morning. If you weren't there for shopping purposes, you were simply standing around available for a natter with whoever might pass by. Since ninety nine point nine per cent of the street's habitues were local, it was a fair bet that the passer-by would be someone you knew. A stranger would be detected at twenty paces or more, eyed suspiciously for a second then promptly ignored. It was hard to believe from this how friendly Dawley people really were, they simply needed to get to know you first.

The High Street stood on a welcome plateau beyond the summit of Dun Cow Bank. A local hostelry bearing the name 'Dun Cow' was perched near the hill-top. Did they serve speciality meat dishes there so that customers would be asked '*how would you like your cow dun sir/madam - medium, rare, well dun?*' The northern end of 'High Street' gave way to a shorter row of buildings known for some reason as 'Burton Street', even though Dawley seemed to have nothing to do with the Staffordshire town of Burton at all.

Anyway, let our cycle tour begin at the top end of 'Burton Street' and then cruise along 'High Street' before heading for further delights of the Dawley 'empire.'

To begin with, behind a three foot stone wall and only just qualifying for a 'Burton Street' address, stood a ramshackle wooden shed of a building which was William ('coffin') Wilkes's undertaker's yard. Wooden planks lay all over the place, and frenzied knocking sounds emerged from the workshop as Mr. Wilkes and others set about erecting a dignified work of art out of a seeming sow's ear of a pile of materials. He didn't seem to have much competition thereabouts, and his future appeared secure so long as enough Dawley people managed to die at fairly regular intervals without creating an undue workload.

Next, was the Police Station, a quite large building that seemed wholly over-adequate for the number of criminals in Dawley. It was reputed to have a lock-up for those members of society who couldn't be trusted to return next morning and apologise for being so drunk and inconsiderate the night before. Most people had no truck with the Police Station at all. It was merely an obligatary facility which every town had to have, yet ought to be left to get on with its own (secretive) business of keeping the town's low-life under control without hindering the rest of the population. The 'Royal Exchange' pub gave way to a side road into an open area called Blews Hill. Here in the 1950's, in a small brick building, an Italian gentleman consistently produced ice-cream of such distinction that he won medals for it. In grateful thanks, he once served free samples to all and sundry in an open-air event which people talked about for years afterwards. Mr. Moruzzi had truly become a naturalised Dawley man.

The narrow Dawley 'High Street'. A cafe sign now pinpoints the former post office on the left.

On the opposite side of the road, the home of Mr. & Mrs. Tom Jones stood back at a respectable distance from the traffic. Alderman Tom Jones was a revered owner of local, small mines. He was thus an expert on Dawley's geology, but also a Justice of the Peace, a Methodist local preacher whose sermons were laced with such down-to earth humour that you felt you should ask forgiveness for laughing so much in chapel, and a generally admirable character. This short and quite tubby man would pause and chat to anyone as he emerged from his Morris Oxford car wearing flat cap, square-shouldered grey coat, and wellies, in any given part of the district. The Jones's comfortable residence had 'The Cosy' cinema for a near neighbour.

'The Cosy' practically defied description. How many towns had a cinema called 'The Cosy' anyway? It was unique in more than name. It too, stood back from the road so that you had to walk across about fifty yards of open space to reach its hallowed entrance. Much of the smallish building was of black, corrugated iron with a pointed roof, and the picture house was

fronted by a plaster facade. It was the cheaper and more down market of Dawley's two cinemas. You entered a rather cramped foyer through an outer door and faced an even more cramped little box that was the ticket office. Only slim ladies needed to apply for the job of ticket seller. Rolls of 'deck-chair' tickets hung from its ceiling and the lady would rip one off in exchange for your nine pence. You then opened a door on either side of the foyer and were immediately plunged into a world of absolute darkness, like entering a ghost train, unsure of where you were or what would happen next. Relief was at hand as a torch with a red lens, like a giant cigarette suddenly moved towards you from the depths of the sloping gangway. A body then attached itself to the torch, your precious ticket was examined and this passport entitled you to a cryptic, torch lit descent of the aisle until a suitable middle row was pointed out to you. If the usherette was not too busy, the torch would be shone along the row for a couple of seconds giving you a rough idea of where you were heading. Left to your own devices and trying not to be too distracted by the screen, you then managed to scramble into a vacant seat. During the mid-fifties, a certain number of double seats were put in for those young couples whose main interest lay beyond the cogent magnetism of the film. On nights of particularly heavy rain, the deluge would hit the metal roof like an endless flow of six-inch nails, with a consequent drowning of the on-screen dialogue. Sometimes, a critical moment in the on-screen drama would be interrupted with a sudden display of upside-down numbers, in descending order, plopping across the screen until all went dark. A sound like a plug being released from a giant sink emanated from the loudspeakers. There would be much whistling and stamping of feet among the cinema's frustrated patrons. Rows of angry heads turned towards the projection room amid cries of *'put another shillin' in the meter, Gilbert'*. At length, calm was restored as a shaft of white light, like a miniature search light beam thrust itself through the projection hole, and the actors resumed the story apparently none the worse for the undignified interruption. Communal applause and cheers would greet their return.

'Burton Street's' little shops were only on one side of the road. They included a newsagent's, a bread shop which also sold those little round pikelets many of which seemed more inclined to fall off the toasting fork and on to the fire at Sunday tea-times, and a pet shop. Opposite, stood the red brick Old Folk's Rest Room.

'Burton Street', Dawley

The 'Elephant and Castle' public house stood four square on the dividing line between 'Burton Street' and the main High Street, gazing down the latter with a solemn glare that ensured no one would pass it without at least a glance. It was in an outhouse at the back of the pub where in 1950, the resourceful landlord charged a couple of old pennies to allow the male population to stand and watch the F.A Cup Final on a diminutive T.V. set. When Jackie Milburn opened the scoring against Arsenal in the first few minutes, the cheers of the Dawley crowd could probably be heard

half a mile away! This was no 'big screen bonanza' of the twenty first century, but merely an assembly of lads and dads straining to see the action on the small, black and white screen of a free standing receiver.

The most striking feature of this 'top end' of the High Street was the elegant (in an unexciting Victorian way) brick facade of the old Market Hall. It had a tall clock tower as its centrepiece, and some lower, rounded arches into which shops had been subsumed following the market's closure. The market had never functioned during the boy's life-time or for a very long time before his birth, so he had been told. He had also heard a story about a particularly devout trader. Apparently, if he hadn't managed to put his horse, wagon and goods away by the stroke of midnight on a Saturday, he would leave everything just where it stood, and retire immediately to bed in fear of eternal damnation should he have been found actually working on the Sabbath! All else about the market's history was a mystery to the boy.

In the 1940's, one of the shops under the Market Hall's arches was run by Miss Mary Jones, a neat and pleasant young lady who wore glasses and kept an equally neat and pleasant shop, which somehow smelled agreeably of quality stationery and writing ink. In the window she displayed attractive rows of sheet music featuring the popular tunes of the day, including 'White cliffs of Dover' (with a picture of Vera Lynn on the front cover), and 'This is the Army Mr. Jones'. Dawley obviously had to be entertained while many of its young men were busy fighting a world war. The adjoining shop was where people carried their accumulators, quite heavy glass containers with a handle at the top, for periodic recharging to power their wireless sets. Another feature of the Market Hall area was the main bus stop for those travelling towards Wellington, the nearest town of any size. The stop was moved to the pavement in front of the hall in the early 1950's. Previously, it had been sited near a bend close to the top of the Dun Cow Bank. The management of the 'Midland Red' bus company belatedly decided that the prospect of a heavy, 'Leyland' lorry burying its nose in the back of one of its prized, red conveyances was no longer tolerable, and the bus stop was duly moved.

The street boasted numerous shops on either side and collectively, provided for most people's needs. Some of them were run by eminent personalities within the life of the town. Colin Evans had a drapery store but was also a stalwart of the Dawley Parish Church.

Harold 'Chippy' Wright kept a successful fish and chip shop, not surprisingly, but was also a prominent urban district councillor, lay preacher, and chairman of the Rest Room Committee. A visit to his shop was an interesting experience. There would always be a long queue, usually spilling out onto the pavement - you could gamble your pocket money on that. When at length, you reached the white, enamelled counter, and decided to lean on it (for there was still a long way to go before getting served), your slumbers were frequently disturbed by sharp back and forth movements beneath your elbows. These resulted from the activities of a white coated, thin lady called Mrs. Fry (honestly!) as she constantly fed huge potatoes onto a cast - iron mesh plate and pulled down a lever to transform bulky spuds into myriad chips which fell into a bucket below, to await cooking. To while the time away, you could read the name of the manufacturer of the chip-fryer 'Samuel Albiston, Zoar Street, Bilston' twenty four times. Alternatively, you could watch the master craftsman Mr. Wright himself at work. He constantly tested the condition of the sizzling chips by reaping a sample amount from the scalding depths using a long handled mesh feeder, and bravely pinching a few of the little gems between thumb and forefinger. Environmental Health Officers had not yet been invented! Only when the colour and texture of the chips were just so, would Mr. Wright allow them the privilege of being served to his customers, the length of the queue having no bearing on his decision, whatsoever. Anyone brought up on chips from that shop would be equipped for life to recognise a good chip when he met one. On summer Friday evenings, tired holiday-makers en-route from the North West to the West Country would annually include a stop at 'Chippy' Wright's oasis on their itinerary, before driving into the night, duly fortified.

Nearby, Mrs. Jones had a fishmonger's. Fresh fish was a relatively cheap and popular meal in those days. The biggest day of Mrs. Jones's year was Good Friday when long queues would develop, while the good lady dressed in white coat and dark beret would, together with her assistant Jean, trundle endless boxes of whole cod, hake and who knows what from a back room. They carved them into slices on the counter, and then duly weighed them and wrapped them in 'The Wellington Journal and Shrewsbury News'. The fish ended up in grateful shoppers' bags, to be consumed with Good Friday lunch, according to a well-worn tradition.

Practically opposite the fish shop stood Dawley High Street Methodist Church. It was the strangest looking building, made of blue brick and having an Italianate tower. To attend worship, you had to scale a steep flight of stairs before entering the main body of the church, then climb again if you wanted to occupy one of the last ten rows of wooden pews. The church was perched on something called the Lightmoor Fault, and people often said that that must be a potentially dangerous state of affairs.

Dawley High Street Methodist Chapel - now replaced by Dawley Christian Centre

Bemrose's was a typical chemist's shop, sporting tall bottles of coloured liquid (blue or red) in one of its windows. The shop smelled reassuringly 'medicinal' as soon as you walked inside its somewhat darkened precincts. The avuncular Mr. Bemrose had the air of a traditional family doctor, and was frequently required to dispense advice as well as pharmaceuticals. He was surely never more nonplussed than when an enthusiastic Dawley woman, having noticed an advertisement proclaiming *'Glaxo builds bonny babies'*, naively enquired of him *'oo 'as to take it, me or me 'usband?'* A young Edith Pargeter (later better known as author Ellis Peters) had also helped behind the counter at Bemrose's during the 1930's.

The post office was situated roughly in the middle of the shopping area, and rather like the chemist's, it seemed a solid, reliable sort of place where important needs could be met in a sympathetic atmosphere.

Stamps could be bought, postal orders encashed, letters posted, and even telegrams transmitted. The post office seemed an 'official' type of emporium that provided a conduit between Dawley and the outside world. Whatever the transaction, it was accompanied by a few moments of homely chat with the face behind the grill. However, why the production of a mere piece of paper caused such a frenzied outbreak of violent thumping by an otherwise sane member of staff using a rubber stamp, remained a mystery. Every document placed on the counter, whether by staff member or unsuspecting customer, came in for the treatment. It could not be allowed to leave the post office without being officially clouted with several staccato blows from the boisterous implement.

Amongst the several shops along the lower end of the street, was the squat little bread and cake shop run by the Watts family. Here, on winter Saturdays, the boy would purchase a 'penny loaf', a miniature lump of bread costing the said sum of one old penny, as a special treat on the way home from a visit to the matinee at 'The Cosy'. The diminutive loaf would be warmed in the oven at home, then consumed with copious amounts of butter at teatime.

In summer, it would be a special joy to carry a large, glass dessert-bowl to Lago's shop, and have it filled with vanilla ice-cream to be shared out subsequently around the table at home.

Slaney Jones's iron-mongery was an institution in the town. Mr. Jones kept his wares in a plethora of small, wooden drawers each labelled as to its contents. He could, faster than any present-day computer, locate the precise drawer for a three-quarter inch brass screw, or left-handed threddle-dangler, or anything else for that matter. If, by some mis-chance, he hadn't got what you wanted, he would say he could soon get it for you, and you knew he meant it. He also had a glass-roofed building next door where chinaware was sold. For a few summers, an elderly gentleman sold freshly-picked strawberries in the space between the two buildings - a throw- back to the days of the market, perhaps.

Frank Bache's tiny newsagent's and fancy goods shop was also nearby. The amiable Frank would have no truck with modern methods of window display. As each carton of new merchandise arrived at the shop, he would split open the top and simply tip the contents onto the existing heap of stock already pressed against the front window. Customers would gaze at the confused array of items through the window as if appraising one of those perspex fairground gift-machines where you had to try and plunge a small grab onto the required item. At Bache's, you often had to invite Frank onto the pavement and point out the selected item, whereupon he would return to the counter and immerse his hand into the pile and find what you wanted.

The street opened out at the 'bottom end', so that a rather uninspiring, concrete memorial to Dawley's most celebrated hero, Captain Matthew Webb, stood at its centre. Webb had distinguished himself as a phenomenal and world-renowned swimmer during the nineteenth century. We will tell his story in detail in a later chapter of the book.

The cream painted 'Lord Hill' Hotel and public house provided a quietly impressive backdrop to the monument, and also straddled the confluence of 'High Street', 'King Street' and 'New Street.'

Some 'High Street' shops-what's there now

'YESTERYEAR'	2003
Clayton/Yates, *Butcher*	'Wrekin Housing Trust' Shop
Frank Bache, *Newsagent*	Adjoining 'Stars' Newsagency
Ball Brothers, *Grocery*	'Super Savers'
'Variety' Phillips, *Furniture*	
Herbert Slaney-Jones, *Hardware*	'Tribe' Unisex Hair Salon
Watts's, *Cake Shop*	'Ice Dreams'
Post Office	'Dawley Diner' Cafe
George Bullock, *Stationery*	Tim Vanes, Optician
Jarvis, *Fishmonger*	Co-op Pioneer, Supermarket
Phillips, *Grocery*	
Harold Wright, *Chip shop*	'Second Hand City'
Mrs. Jones, *Fishmonger*	Barnetts Unisex
Smiths, *Grocery*	'Electro Tek'
Norgrove, *Butcher*	'Sandwich Factory'
Evans & Son, *Draper*	'Abacus' Day Nursery
Gas showroom, *old Council Offices*	Cafe
Dockley/Jack/Basil Lewis	Mason's
Frank Morgan, *Newsagent*	Key Stores

Chapter Two

GOING SOUTH : THE FIRST TOUR
A CYCLE RIDE FROM DAWLEY TO LITTLE DAWLEY AND DOSELEY

Following a dalliance in the heart of town, let's accompany the boy on a cycle tour of some of the district's outlying villages. He bravely decided to leave the street by descending Dun Cow Bank. At the top of the hill, he passed by Maud Fenn's sweet shop (immortalised as the place where he had bought his first ever off the ration sweets), and Ernie Williams's garage and petrol station. Ernie and his wife Lydia, who looked after the attached shop, were two large people yet gentle giants, who would do anyone a favour. Ernie once helped a motorist whose car had suffered a flat tyre nearby, by lifting the rear of the vehicle and holding it off the ground while the grateful owner swiftly changed the wheel! Passing the 'Dun Cow' hotel on the left, and the row of moving heads above the bowling green wall, the bike descended the short, steep hill. It felt like gliding down the side of the globe as vistas of distant south Shropshire hills lay on the horizon, threatening to distract the rider from the business of keeping to a civilised speed. A little used Town Hall building stood half way down the slope.

At the bottom, the road levelled out briefly to pass a council-owned field on the right, an ideal place for grazing council horses, and hosting countless informal games of football and cricket. The horses were merely spectators of course. A pine clad hill stood unassumingly to the left, yet a pine wood near the centre of Dawley struck the boy as being a bit out of character. At the beginning of the rocky road leading to the hill, stood a low, brick building. It housed the famous 'muck druggan' a sort of cesspit on wheels, which one of the horses from

the field had the honour of hauling around the district under the supervision of one Jack Hadley. Many of the older Dawley houses and cottages were still without modern toilets, and so weekly collections had to be made and disposed of. As might be imagined, much local folklore grew up about Mr. Hadley and 'Noah', his redoubtable accomplice, and some of this will be revealed later.

The notorious Portley Corner then had to be negotiated. Over the years, the sudden half-hidden, left-hand bend at the bottom of the short slope had claimed its share of victims. Motorists unused to the route were sometimes caught unawares, like ships trapped in a sudden squall, as the bend abruptly revealed itself just when the driver was convinced the road would go straight ahead. It was a living example of the 'Ha Ha effect', and the boy himself had witnessed the aftermath of several accidents there. These included a heavily laden lorry, which had veered off the road, demolished a lamp-post (whose steel re-inforcers had wrapped themselves around the back axle), and embedded itself into the side of a startled cottage. Then there was the jeep, which became so disorientated that it drove straight into the window of a house at the beginning of the next street. The fog-lamp of a 'Ribble' coach was also seen to scrape the road surface in a shower of sparks as its driver manfully kept his charge on the road, thus maintaining his non-stop journey to Cheltenham.

The bicycle made an ultra-cautious crossing of the road junction with 'New Road', right on the apex of the infamous bend, then continued past the pre-war council houses of that road. Mrs. Matthews's lonely clothing shop stood about halfway down on the opposite side, near some cottages and backed by another hill dressed with pine-trees. Then, came a sharp right turn into 'Old Vicarage Road' close by Mrs. Thompson's general grocery store. Joe Brown's Manor Farm lay to the left (where today stands 'Manor Gardens'), and two thatched, black and white cottages of the 1650's slumbered nearby on the right before Holy Trinity Church was reached. Up to that point, the three-quarter mile journey from Portley Corner to the Parish Church had embraced a changing canvas of property styles - some distinctly pre-twentieth century - and woodland and open spaces suggesting a history that needed exploration. Opposite the church were more dark-brick cottages, plus a larger old house (the old vicarage), and a little lane leading to yet more cramped looking old dwellings and tree-covered hills. There seemed to be a separate settlement here within, yet partly independent of the town of Dawley. Curiously, Dawley's Parish Church was located there, and not in the main part of town.

Soon, a T-junction was reached at the end of a high stone wall that enclosed part of the churchyard. A sharp right turn put the traveller on the road to Little Dawley, at first passing the sloping churchyard, and a view of the large, dark stone church building standing atop a small hill. A host of gravestones decorated the slope and other parts of the church's surroundings. On the opposite side of the road stood the towering presence of the Castle Mound, thickly covered with trees. A broad, rough track ran from the road and down a slope beside the Castle Mound to arrive at a group of pools with ugly, bare mounds on either side. On one such grey hump stood a dilapidated brick tower-like structure. The lads wrongly speculated that this was probably the remains of the Dawley Castle they had vaguely heard about, and wondered what had happened to the rest of it.

The main Little Dawley road, known for some reason as 'Holly Road', carried on for half a mile past a mixture of old, mostly terraced cottages. There was also the occasional detached house, some open fields, two public houses ('The Red Lion' and the 'Unicorn'), and a farm. A final row of cottages, a shop and a large, Methodist Chapel announced the arrival of the small village of Little Dawley.

The boy reasoned that if 'Little Dawley' was meant to be a replica of 'proper Dawley', it didn't seem to bear much resemblance to the larger place.

Apart from Reynolds's general store, there was a small bakery opposite the Methodist Chapel, where warm loaves would be dropped by hand from the upper floor to a waiting van driver who would then load them in the required order before delivering around the district. Near the corner was a little post office run by kindly and elderly Mrs. Williams, from an end-terrace cottage. The boy had, under his parents' supervision, once opened a savings account there and received a blue savings box so that valuable pennies of pocket money could be dropped in weekly, until an eventual fortune was accumulated.

Traditionally, the boy's parents had attended the main chapel at Little Dawley, and that was where he and his brother received their early Christian upbringing, except during severe winters when they were allowed to attend Dawley High Street Sunday School as 'temporary scholars'. Three times on a Sunday they would trek the four mile round trip to Little Dawley and back. Sunday School met at 10 a.m. and 2.30 p.m., and evening worship commenced at 6 p.m. ending at any time after seven o'clock, depending on the long-windedness of the preacher. The walk along field paths was a delight on warm, May Sundays when the breeze picked up the scent of hawthorn blossom which wafted into the nostrils, while blackbirds and others proclaimed the springtime in nearby hedges. On summer afternoons, when the hot sun interacted with the previous day's cow pats on the road near the chapel, the resultant aroma was not entirely disagreeable, and served as an evocative reminder of Little Dawley's semi-rural character.

At a road junction, the left turn led down a hill between tree-covered mounds to the village of Lightmoor. That place seemed to consist of a redundant, small brick chapel called 'Fat Bacon', some brick stables, a row of old terraced cottages with long gardens, a small railway station, some waste ground, and a few mature, detached houses on the far side of the railway line. The waste ground had many lonely pathways running between bushes, ideal for energetic young bikers pretending to be the Sheriff's posse pursuing the bad men across the dusty trail.

The right-turn at Little Dawley descended more gradually between sloping, green fields and beside a bungalow and a remarkable, half-timbered cottage. Ahead, lay views of green undulating countryside, while a tree-covered hill towered above the field to the right. A sprinkling of cottages and yet another chapel lay in the dip beyond a railway line. These formed an intimate little community known as Gravel Leasowes, which stood strangely aloof and quiet. Beyond it, and seemingly built on the switchback contours of a field, stood the dull-brick dwellings of 'Holywell Lane'. Again, there seemed no reason for such a curious string of buildings to be standing in so detached a location, or arranged in such

higgledy-piggledy fashion.

Doseley railway bridge, and the 'Cheshire Cheese' pub.

The main road continued to the level crossing at Doseley Halt before passing between some mature, solitary houses and arriving at Doseley Quarries. This appeared not so much a quarry as a huge space where hundreds of giant concrete drainage pipes were stored. A diversion along the track between the pipes led to a secluded, narrow pathway between trees and to one of the 'seven wonders of Dawley' - the Bath Spout. Here, you cupped your hands beneath a rusty, v-shaped, cast-iron channel to receive a helping of cool and refreshing spring water.

Back at the main road again, the voyage of exploration would continue past St. Luke's Church, Doseley, and under the high railway bridge which had a striking echo-effect whenever anyone shouted rude words as they passed under it. After the bridge, came the 'Cheshire Cheese' public house (a strange name for a Shropshire pub), and a rocky lane running alongside it, leading to a long row of brown-brick cottages that seemed to belong to a previous century. Each one was still occupied and, although there appeared to be no sign to say so, people called it

'Sandy Bank Row'. The cluster of cottages had been assembled seemingly in the middle of nowhere, and was a little community cast adrift among fields and away from the remainder of civilisation. The unmetalled lane then climbed steeply through a veritable tunnel of trees and between rough stone walls. At the summit of the hill you could either carry straight on towards Little Dawley again, or leave the lane by turning left along a narrow dirt-track between railings (always referred to as 'the pailings'). The track ran for about two hundred yards across the top of a hill. To the right, stood the playing field of nearby Pool Hill School. The view to the left was altogether different. A grassy slope fell steeply away towards a large, flat field at the bottom. It would not be unusual for the school football to balloon over the railings, so that the nearest player to the touch-line would have had the unenviable task of climbing both fences and disappearing down the slope in frustrated pursuit. From the pathway vantage point were open views of the distant scene, including Sandy Bank Row, Doseley Pipe Works, the 'Doseley Dodger' railway line, Horsehay and its dominant engineering works, an open-cast coal site, and the strange wasteland of Brandlee. As if to compensate for the harshness of the main vista, the more distant landscape of mildly undulating fields, and the commanding presence of the Wrekin combined to create a rural frieze which agreeably adorned the horizon.

At the far end of 'the pailings' stood Pool Hill School, a strange looking, gothic style building in dark brick with a tower and small turrets, and rooms of all shapes and sizes. It seemed unable to decide whether it was some sort of fortress or a Dickension seat of learning. For a school, its design was curiously abnormal. A brick outbuilding stood in front of it and was used in the boy's time as the domestic science department. He used to assume that it was separated from the main building in case some callow pupil managed to misuse a gas cooker and propel the entire school population towards an early appointment with its Maker. In the segregated playgrounds, were separate shelters for boys and girls in times of inclement weather. At the edge of the junior boys' territory was a small mound that everybody said had been the site of an air-raid shelter. The boy had once seen a dead mole lying there. If the creature was responsible for the mound, it had every reason to be dead by the end of its exertions! Both primary and junior departments were in the same building and later, 'the huts' were built next to the playing fields, to be occupied by eleven plusses who were supplemented with pupils from other junior schools in the area on reaching the same age.

The short journey back home entailed cycling along an alleyway known as 'the gulley' that sliced between a tall, brick wall behind some old private houses, and a bungalow on the opposite side. A bumpy, unmetalled road then took the rider past a wooden bungalow, a small cottage on the opposite side, the gas works and home again.

Parts of the Little Dawley area, including Gravel Leasowes still retain their rural appearance.

Chapter Three

NORTH OF THE HIGH STREET: THE SECOND TOUR

KING STREET, MALINSLEE, PARK ROAD, LAWLEY BANK, BANK ROAD, DAWLEY BANK, ROUGH GROUNDS

The boy had been born in 'Portley Road' just off 'High Street', and moved to the newly built 'Windsor Road' some 13 years later. Both places were located on the southern side of the High Street so that his journey to Malinslee and beyond took him to the northern section of the town. It should be explained that in Dawley, there was an unspoken feeling that the two segments were in some way different to each other. Inhabitants either belonged to the south or north of 'the Street', as the case may have been. Whilst there was no discernible enmity or rivalry between them, the people tended to see those on the other side of the divide as not quite belonging to the same tribe as themselves. Their respective home locations seemed almost to belong to separate towns. It wasn't a question of living on the right or wrong 'side of the tracks', since the majority of the town's population lived in council-owned property, but straying over the border meant entering territory with which one was not quite as familiar. This was how it appeared to the boy anyway, even though he had friends living in the 'northern parts'.

To make the tour, the boy had to leave 'the Street' at the bottom end, near Captain Webb's memorial, and turn left, joining 'King Street'. At first blush, 'King Street' appeared to be as important as 'the Street' in that it looked like a main road going somewhere, even though it merely served to link Dawley with some of its suburbs. During the forties, a smithy still functioned

near the beginning of 'King Street' (opposite the current library), since many of the household milk and coal deliveries were by horse and cart. Amongst the immediate buildings to the right, was a little shop called 'Sports and Hobbies' where, in the 1950's, Eric Beard sold accessories for most of the better known sports. He also sold sweets, making it a convenient place to stop off and stock up with sugary delights on the way to 'The Royal' cinema, for the enterprising shop obligingly remained open into the evening. After the shop, came an open yard flanked on at least two sides by warehouses. Along the left-hand side of the road ran a fairly impressive row of mature, terraced houses the central portion of which housed the doctors' surgery. To get into the surgery, you had to walk intrepidly along an entry before turning left into a rather cramped waiting room. A dozen pairs of eyes watched as you carefully removed a numbered card from a metal spike, then found yourself a seat amid the sad-faced crowd, ready for the interminable wait to be seen by a doctor. In those days, it was not usual to book an appointment, patients simply turned up and took their chances on a first-come-first-served basis. The chief practitioner was Dr. Browne, a benevolent, middle aged gentleman with a soothing voice, and a reassuring manner. Dr. Browne had the habit of looking at you above his glasses when you re-counted your problem as if to say, *'I don't really need these spectacles, but they don't half help to concentrate the mind'*. He was a true member of that admirable breed of physicians known as 'family doctors'.

At the end of the row stood the 'Queen's Head' public house, on the junction with the quaintly named 'Meadow Road'. Quaint because of the close proximity of this little street of terraced cottages to the main 'High Street'. Then came 'The Royal' cinema, the slightly more up market of Dawley's two film emporia. Seats were a bit more expensive than at 'The Cosy'. 'The Royal' was built in the late 1930's and, during the early 1950's was the place to be seen on a Saturday night.When the lights came up for the interval between the first and second houses, heads would be turned and necks craned to see just who else was in town that night. Young people from outlying villages would mix with school friends or work-mates from within the town, for a good natter of the kind that did not seem possible at any other time of the week. Members of local amateur football teams would sit 'en-masse' in the middle rows, swopping news of the results of their respective matches of that day. Courting couples occupying the side rows would come up for air and, perhaps, cool-off with an ice cream from a lady who stood with a tray suspended from her neck, near the front rows. There was also considerable interest in the choice of music played through the amplifiers during this fertile interlude. The creamy strains of Mantovani's 'Charmaine' and the exhilarating tones of David Whitfield's - 'Cara Mia' were particular favourites, although it was all down to the whim of the projectionist on the night. Indeed the projectionist was also sometimes enlisted by the usherettes on busy nights, to turf out those members of the 'first house audience' who had brazenly remained in their seats for the 'second house' in order to watch a favourite portion of the 'little picture' for a further time. The 'little picture' was a supporting film shown before the main

feature, and lasted about an hour. The 'first house' would commence at about 5.00 p.m. and end around 7.45 p.m., when the first showing of the 'big picture' ended.

Beyond 'The Royal', 'King Street' largely consisted of rows of brown - brick cottages, backed in places by open fields and mounds. A group of cottages lying in a dip opposite the cinema was known for some reason as 'The Cunnery'. Amid a proliferation of cottages were such diverse buildings as the British Legion Social Club, and an impressive group of mature, detached houses. Some of the latter stood in their own attractive grounds, and seemed to constitute Dawley's 'professional quarter'. Apparently, in pre-N.H.S. days, you paid about 3/6d. to visit either Dr. Robinson at the big house on the right, or Dr. Davies at 'The Grove' on the left. What 'King Street' lacked in retail outlets, it made up for in the variety of its housing. Some of the tributary roads led to such pre-war council housing as 'Attwood Terrace', 'Johnston Road', and 'Ardern Avenue.' The Council Offices occupied a large red brick house that stood back from the road, commanding respectful attention. The boy remembered child-hood visits to this building during the early 1940's, when it also housed what were known as the

'King Street'
The former doctor's surgery is now a chinese
restaurant at the start of the second row.

'Welfare Offices'. There, the parents of 'war babies' would claim their allowances of a pungent liquid contained in a small bottle. The sticky and unappetising substance was described as 'orange juice', and reflected a government attempt at saving young children from being deprived of essential vitamins, as they coped with their formative years at a time of wartime austerity.

The tour continued past the 'Ring o' Bells' pub, and yet another terraced row, before turning right into 'Church Road'. Initially, there were yet more cottages, including one short row that stood at right - angles to the road. There was also one slightly superior row before the Malinslee institute building was reached. The boy assumed this was the church hall for St. Leonard's Church which dominated the scene at that point, standing amid a large graveyard containing some impressive chest tombs, and accompanied by an old vicarage. The boy wondered why the church was of such an unusual shape. Its main part was somewhat circular and very different from most churches of his acquaintance, although it did possess a small tower with a clock face on it. The boy passed by a side road leading to a strange - looking row of cottages on the right, commonly called 'Skylight Row'. Then he turned left at the end of the church wall, and cycled along a row of pre-war council houses called 'Alma Avenue'. Was it thus named to commemorate Britain's success at the Battle of Alma River in the Crimea, he wondered, recalling some fragment of information from school history lessons? The naming of nearby 'Rhodes Avenue' convinced him (wrongly) that the council had at some time decided to dedicate Malinslee's housing to the golden age of British History, and that Dawley would continue to commemorate it, at least until the houses fell down.

On the way out of Malinslee, the road took the boy past a garage that housed one or two motor coaches the colour of cold tea, belonging to 'Darrall and Company'. The council housing was then left behind, as the road simply became a narrow lane travelling past the occasional bungalow, but chiefly slicing between tracts of featureless open ground. There were unappealing tufts of grass, and low, man-made mounds giving the impression that something active used to happen there in the past. Now the land appeared abandoned and available to anybody who might happen to want it. Soon, the lane arrived at a T junction with a slightly wider road.

The road led from Dawley to the town of Oakengates, via the smaller settlements of Hollinswood and Old Park.The boy knew that those places also had their share of similar grass covered mounds, occasional woodland copses and open waste ground.

He turned left in the direction of Dawley Bank, and passed some cottages, detached houses and a social club in 'Park Road' before the strange shape of the tall, blue brick, Baptist Chapel came starkly into view. The road ran along the rear of the church, then arrived at a junction with another road emerging from Lawley Bank to the right, before descending towards Dawley. The boy turned right, so as to have a look at the small settlements of Dawley Bank and Lawley Bank. Bryce's little shop stood at the beginning of this road, but it became impossible to tell where Dawley Bank ended and Lawley Bank began.

First, the overpowering flanks, and somewhat ornamental frontage of the Baptist Chapel was encountered on the right-hand side. The sides of the building had three horizontal rows of windows, one above the other, and a short flight of steps led up to the main entrance door. The sheer size of the building was such that it completely overshadowed its surroundings, and bore no resemblance to the rest of the village. Perhaps it had to be so big and imposing because it was the only Baptist Church in the district, and, therefore, had to compensate for the profusion of Methodist chapels scattered around the Dawley area. The rest of the winding street consisted of one or two more shops, a short row of cottages on either side of the road, and Lawley Bank Methodist Chapel and schoolroom, keeping the spiritual balance at the far end. Opposite the chapel, the 'Bulls Head' public house was perched on a sharp bend and road junction. The pub also had the privilege of looking down on a triangular piece of grass resembling a small village green, a vast, downward sweep of open land including Lawley Common, and more distant wooded scenery overlooked by the brooding presence of the Wrekin hill, near Wellington.

A lane descended from beside the green triangle passing the occasional private house, a small crescent of pre-war council houses, and a haphazard sprinkling of old cottages. The boy knew that this lane continued to a level crossing where the Wellington-Much Wenlock branch railway crossed it, near Lawley Bank station. The lane also passed a small iron-foundry, then wormed its way towards a farm and ultimately, Lawley village. The road immediately in front of the 'Bulls Head' veered acutely to the right, then passed the aptly - named 'Wrekin View' pub, yet more cottages some of which had formed themselves into a little huddle known as 'Prince's End', before disappearing over the brow of the hill in search of the former mining community known as 'The Rock'.

From the 'Bulls Head' area, the boy retraced his route past the two chapels and the shops and cottages, before bearing right into 'Bank Road'. Ben. Breeze's humble undertaker's workshop virtually faced the junction between 'Park Road' and 'Bank

Road'. 'Bank Road' gently descended past the 'Queens Head' pub., rows of old terraced housing, the Co-operative store, Bank Road Methodist Chapel, and more cottages until the junction with 'Church Road' was once again encountered, near Hollis's shop. From the shop, the boy turned right, leaving the road so as to cycle across the 'Rough Grounds'. It was rough too, the uneven lane eventually ran through a bit of a wilderness of open land, quiet and undisturbed, as if it had been told to simply wait there until somebody could think of what to do with it! The neglected piece of land seemed to have been left to its own devices. After a few hundred yards, the track passed some cottages and then a long warehouse of a brick building with a pointed roof, and standing at right angles to the track-way. These unprepossessing premises at 'Blews Hill' were the place where Mr. Moruzzi later manufactured his celebrated ice cream. From there, the track developed into a narrow, metalled road, and in no time at all, ran along the side of the 'Royal Exchange' pub. The boy turned left onto the main thoroughfare at 'Burton Street' and into 'High Street' once again.

A tomb in St. Leonard's church yard with Alma Avenue in the background.

14

Chapter Four

THE FASCINATION OF HORSEHAY :
THE THIRD TOUR

STATION ROAD, HORSEHAY STATION AND WORKS, HORSEHAY VILLAGE, *FRAME LANE*, POOL HILL

During the boy's youth and for several years afterwards, Dawley's main employer was the 'Horsehay Company Ltd'. Through various amalgamations with other firms in the heavy engineering business, it became variously known as 'Adamson-Alliance (Horsehay) Ltd.', and ultimately, 'Adamson Butterley Ltd.' Around three-hundred people worked there in the 1950's, many of them engaged in the manufacture of huge overhead cranes for steel companies, amongst others. Every now and then, an orange girder of ridiculous proportions would completely block the local and other road systems, as an overworked tractor unit tried to negotiate its elephantine cargo towards a distant destination at a speed of about four miles per hour. At least it gave the public plenty of time to read the 'Horsehay Company' sticker on the flanks of the steel beam, as it inched its way along unsuspecting roads and around right-angle bends, sometimes knocking road-signs over in the process. It was truly one of the sights of Dawley. Workers watched the girder leaving the works with the same sort of pride as a group of shipbuilders would experience, when the hull of an ocean-going liner slipped decisively down the ramp and into the water for the first time. On the other hand, motorists with the misfortune to be on the same stretch of road as a Horsehay girder, would very quickly run out of expletives as the giant successfully prevented them from fulfilling their carefully planned schedules.

A cycle-ride to Horsehay and district was,

in view of the above, a must. The works were a bit out of town, which was bad news for those Dawley citizens who had to rely on either their bikes or 'shanks's pony' in order to get there, since the journey home would inevitably include a bit of uphill work in places. From his own home, the boy rode past Walter Hart's coach garage, along a short stretch of 'Chapel Street', which contained some interesting early twentieth century houses, alongside the council sports ground and the Victorian 'National School'. He then turned left onto a narrow track leading to the rather strange assortment of cottages at Brandlee. The small community lay oddly detached from the nearby centre of Dawley. It seemed to be hiding itself away, a huddled group of old dwellings perched on a slight rise in the ground, and fringed in places by small trees and gorse bushes. Soon, the boy turned right, along a track which ran close to the front doors of a row of lurking cottages, then turned sharp left and up a hill which led to 'Station Road', the main route to Horsehay. The road passed one or two smart detached houses and a row of cottages before descending into rather different territory. Billy Tarr's garage and its assorted haulage lorries lay below, to the immediate left. Then, the slightly hilly vantage- point revealed a motley pageant. The gorse-covered heathland at Brandlee overlooked cottage rooftops, the green slope at the top of which Pool Hill School stood, then a remarkably attractive background of undulating countryside and distant hills including Benthall Edge above the Severn Gorge, and the rounded summit of Brown Clee Hill lying on the horizon. In short, the wide view was both varied and inspirational, and made you wish you had the energy to cycle through the entire length and breadth of it in order to visit all the diverse elements it encompassed. As it was, the boy continued his gradual descent towards Horsehay. There were more gorsey hillocks to the right, then a drive way leading upwards between tall trees to a half-hidden and imposing mature residence called 'Prospect House'. It was said to belong to Mr. Frank Clayton, 'auctioneer and valuer'. It was surely one of the most elegant houses around, and you didn't find too many piles of this nature to the square mile in the Dawley area.

As if to redress the architectural balance, a small group of old cottages nestled round a bend in the road, which was almost opposite Noah Forgham's grocery store. These were the pre-supermarket days, and smallish general stores of this kind could be found in most of the outlying communities of the district. On summer Saturday afternoons, Mr.Forgham would dutifully load up the wicker carrier basket on the front of his delivery bicycle. He would pedal all the way to the council sports field in Dawley, to unload the ingredients required by the tea-ladies charged with the task of feeding and watering twenty-two hungry cricketers plus officials. Horsehay Cricket Club sported both a first and second eleven, so that there would be a match of some sort at the venue every Saturday through the season. The team's headquarters had previously been at a field in Coalmoor, near Horsehay on the lane to Little Wenlock, and then by the 'Woodlands Farm' on the opposite side of the village. Whether due to the unevenness of the latter pasture, or the minefield created by a proliferation of 'cow-pats' the boy wasn't sure. At some stage in the early fifties, the club moved lock, stock and

barrel to the council field in Doseley Road, Dawley, and thus ceased to remain a part of village life. To return to Mr. Forgham and his deliveries, the final leg of his one mile journey to the pavilion saw him triumphantly entering the main gateway of the field, then following a good fifty-percent of the boundary line before alighting to hand over the precious cargo. Mr. Forgham was fairly short in stature, and wore glasses with thick lenses. As he began his return journey, he again clung to the white-painted boundary with enormous determination, not to say courage, since the match would be in full progress, and the cricket ball would frequently hurtle over the line at varying heights and velocities. Miraculously, throughout his entire career Mr. Forgham always made it back to the gates without a hit ever being recorded on either his bike or his person. Onlookers, including some of the players, would breathe a sigh of relief as Noah's rear wheel finally disappeared through the gate exactly the same shape as when it had first appeared.

Next, on the journey to Horsehay, came the 'Station Inn' and some pleasant, twentieth century detached houses, followed by an elongated hut where cub scouts found amusement each week. From there on, the

A line up of staff on the single platform of Horsehay and Dawley station.

scene changed dramatically. A rough track to the right led to some isolated cottages near Horsehay Common. The main road continued over a brick railway bridge, below which lay 'Horsehay and Dawley' Station on the Wellington-Much Wenlock line. The boy had fond memories of this little station, since it was the point of departure for his family's annual summer holidays at a farm near Buildwas, during the latter years of World War Two. They would tramp like refugees across the rough, Brandlee track-way towards the station with suitcases that got heavier by the minute, then join the pavement near the 'Station Inn'. Finally, the intrepid travellers descended the steep, gravel path down to the railway station with obvious relief. The branch railway was single-track for most of its length, so Horsehay had only one platform from which you looked out on quite an attractive shrubbery on the bank opposite. A tiny signal-box stood next to the Wellington end of the platform, and the inevitable booking- office and waiting room occupied the central part. The building always had a particular smell about it, not repellent, but in fact rather reassuring. It was as if some important official attended about once a month, and sprayed a substance known simply as 'Great Western' all over the inside of the room. This was somehow, the way booking offices should smell, it seemed. When the train from Wellington arrived, you would hear its hissing sound before it rounded the bend to enter the station. The booking-office clerk cum-signalman would stand at the end of the platform holding a large token the shape of a tennis racket. He would deftly swap it for a similar one from the engine fireman, as the matchbox shaped tank engine and its attendant two coaches of chocolate and cream colour, rushed into the station with an air of considerable importance. How embarrassing, thought the boy, if one or other of the two players in this strange

ritual should fail to grab hold of the receiving token. He never saw such a thing happen. Apparently, the receiving token allowed the train to be safely signalled to enter the next section of single-track without meeting another train trying to travel in the opposite direction.

Beyond the station, and alongside the main road, were some sidings and a large, brick building which housed small locomotives belonging to nearby Horsehay works. A vast, open cast coal site lay to the left, then came the enormous, white buildings of the 'Horsehay Company Ltd.' themselves. This was the place where the giant cranes were manufactured and assembled, and the plant totally dominated the surrounding domain. Opposite the works, stood a deep and rather forbidding pool, with an ash

All is peaceful now at Horsehay Pool, looking towards Spring Village.

hill running down to the waters at one point. The company railway track ran alongside the road causing it to narrow at that point, whilst a long, low brick wall was all that separated road and rail from the steep drop into the pool. At the end of the wall, the railway traversed the road and ran into the open bridge-yard at the works. Along one side of the pool ran two lengthy bands of cottages which somehow didn't seem to belong to the present age, and at the far end, stood a conglomeration of cottages and a Methodist chapel at Spring Village, near the common.

The main road passed by a smaller group of cottages on the right which were accompanied by two retail outlets, the larger one sporting the title 'Ironbridge and District Co-operative Society', and the smaller one 'Bessy Ball, Grocer and Sugar Boiler' 'What on earth was a sugar boiler?' thought the boy. Whatever it was, it enabled Bessy's business to survive the obvious competition from her 'big brother' neighbour.

On its way towards the village proper, the road passed a row of old, brick stables, the company offices, a cottage lying in a dip beside a stream, and the works canteen (a brick building where amateur dramatics also took place twice a year), and an attractive bowling green. At a sharp left-hand bend, a pleasant row of cottages stood back from the road, then the route passed one or two mature houses before arriving at a busy road junction. This seemed to be the real centre of Horsehay, despite the still-beckoning presence of the works. On one side of the confluence of roads, the long, part timber-framed edifice of the 'Forester Arms' public house demanded attention, while a cream-coloured detached house doubling as Horsehay Post Office stood back from the road as if too modest to advertise itself. The road in question was the 'back road' from Lawley and Wellington, which had just passed yet another Methodist Chapel at Moreton Coppice, a few hundred yards away, and seemed to be a great favourite of thundering, heavy lorries. Behind this scene were fields separating the chapel and the scattering of cottages and mellow farmhouses constituting the small settlement of Coalmoor.

The boy knew that part of Coalmoor was also given over to open cast coal mining, basalt quarrying and other messy activities, since some of the more overgrown areas had proved to be particularly rewarding blackberry patches, which he visited with a group of friends each late summer. On those occasions, they took the bus to Horsehay. There then followed a three-quarter mile hike along the lane to the massive tangle of brambles where the dusky harvest awaited gathering. Each picker brandished a jam-jar as he foraged among the limitless vegetation. Every time the jar was full, its contents would be emptied into a wicker basket which had newspaper wedged into the inner bottom and sides. The task of actually filling the basket was totally daunting, as jar full after jar full seemed to make absolutely no difference. Miraculously, after a full afternoon's picking and filling, the various baskets would be filled almost to the brim, and then would follow the long, tiring haul back to the bus stop at Horsehay, and the final leg of the journey home. The result of this exhausting yet strangely enjoyable annual activity, was a proliferation of home-made fruit pies, crumbles and jams, the gradual consumption of which gave abundant pleasure to all, and enormous satisfaction to the pickers.

The boy's journey continued ahead from the 'Forester Arms,' along Wellington Road, as if making for Coalbrookdale. A long row of mostly terraced cottages looked out over quiet fields and distant woodland, lending a pleasing, rural flavour to what had hitherto been a predominantly urban scene. Beyond the cottages, stood a small estate of twentieth century houses built for employees of the Horsehay Company, which had some traditional houses and further on, the impressive 'Myford House' as neighbours. The boy ventured several hundred yards along the main road, and witnessed a curious kaleidoscope of scenery. There was the unspoilt countryside near 'Woodlands Farm', then a long, red, corrugated steel fence (hiding some kind of grimy manufacturing activity), and a grey 'moonscape' of clay mining mounds. Then came more terraced cottages, and some amazingly sublime distant views of the kind of South Shropshire hill country which always seemed to be grinning at you and saying, *'we have not been messed about by industrialists like you have, and we never will be'*.

On arriving at the summit of the steep and twisting Jiggers Bank on the way to Coalbrookdale, and near the strange little cottage-settlement of Stoney Hill, the boy turned around to cycle back to the 'Forester Arms' road junction. Here he turned right into 'Woodhouse Lane' another collection of terraced houses, a shop belonging to 'H.B. Williams', and one or two small cottages. The lane descended towards the 'back end' of Horsehay works whose brick buildings looked down on to the road from a commanding height. Near the 'Traveller's Joy' pub which lay in a dip to the left, 'Woodhouse Lane' gave way to 'Frame Lane' and immediately, the landscape changed. To the right, lay an undulating wasteland of scrub-covered hillocks, dominated by a grassy volcano-shaped hill locally referred to as 'Chilly's Pimple'. It was clearly man-made, and had been left there for posterity by some forgotten industrialist a long time ago. Once clear of the Horsehay works wall, the opposite side of 'Frame Lane' became altogether more attractive. It was studded with attractive old houses, some with teeming gardens, then there was the inevitable row of old terraced cottages, and finally, one or two twentieth century council houses. The back drop to this part of 'Frame Lane' was a portion of the Great Western Railway line, as it ran down from Horsehay station towards Doseley Halt. The terrace and council houses had the misfortune to face a

group of active kilns commonly known as 'the brickle'.

In a short distance, the high, brick railway bridge encountered on the Little Dawley ride was reached, and this time the boy had to turn left in order to pass beneath this well known 'echo chamber'. He turned left again, towards a short line of quite smart-looking semi-detached houses which people referred to as the 'Fletcher Estates' houses, presumably private housing built by a firm with the afore-mentioned name. Behind the houses lay a huge, flat field stretching from Sandy Bank Row at the one end to the cluster of cottages at Pool Hill on the other. The 'Fletcher' houses looked out on to a fairly typical Doseley scene. It was a combination of semi-rural charm personified by a field called 'the Poplars' (because an impressive line of those lovely trees ran along its roadside border), and of industrial intrusion represented by the railway embankment on the far side, and a glimpse of the Horsehay works complex. The boy resisted the challenge of climbing the alarmingly steep Doseley Bank up to Dawley, and instead diverted to the left, along an uneven road leading to a rather strange place called 'the Potteries'. At first, the road ran along the bottom of the Brandlee hill, at that point quite a pleasant, gorse sprinkled, green slope. On the other side of the road the view was rather different. A high wall half concealed a large, impressive dwelling named 'Hartfield House' that stood in its own, considerable grounds. The boy remembered attending a garden fete there years earlier, organised by Little Dawley Methodist Chapel. He recalled that it had a large, well-kept lawn and flower gardens to the rear, and mature trees gave it surprising privacy. It was said that the stately property was once a school run by a Mrs. Gough, and had been built by the brother of the man who constructed 'Prospect House' in 'Station Road'.

Soon, the lane presented a view of a world far removed from the likes of 'Hartfield House'. Further along the road lay, to the right, a peculiar conglomeration of buildings that seemed to be distancing themselves from the rest of society. This was the place everyone called 'the Potteries'. It really did seem to be a little town within a little town. Dull brick homesteads of all shapes, heights and sizes lay in disorderly fashion, one facing this way, another that way. Some leaned on others for support, and all of them were crowded together within a confined area. The scene was dominated by an enormous, cone-shaped building that people described as a kiln, but quite plainly, there were windows set within its curious flanks, and a doorway indicating that to some brave person, this was home. It was rumoured that it had once been the home of William Ball, the forty-stone 'Dawley Giant' of the nineteenth century, and you were apt to believe it, as it certainly looked capable of housing such a colossus, even though it never had. One man who had lived at the Potteries, was the well known character 'Man'. Wem. He had become part of Dawley folklore, uttering such phrases as *'I was in our buzzer when the closet rang six.'*

The boy then returned along the lane back to the bottom of Doseley Bank, near 'Hartfield House'. He crossed the Doseley-Dawley road and explored the quaint settlement of Pool Hill. This entailed a climb up a somewhat rocky incline with sloping, green fields initially to the left and long gardens behind a rock wall on the right. The gardens belonged to a row of cottages running towards the 'Fletcher' houses. About half way up the hill was a gateway on the left, leading to a detached house among some trees. Each day, a lorry would deliver a number of milk churns to the yard of the house, and the occupant subsequently supplied the local area with

the white liquid by means of a horse and cart. A turn to the right, led to another of Dawley's half-hidden places. The bumpy little lane turned sharp left again to climb past some old, detached cottages of differing styles, then left again to rejoin the original hill. The remainder of the climb went past more cottages, some set at right-angles to the road and thus looking down the slope towards 'the Poplars'. The upward journey then crossed the track-way leading to Pool Hill School, and continued steeply alongside a brick wall to the right, belonging to quite an impressive, detached house.

The final leg of the journey took the boy along a short stretch of the rocky lane that had by then, levelled out to run between fields flanked with hedges. It was particularly rocky at that point, and the boy knew it ran on towards 'Old Vicarage Road', near the Parish Church. The lane had long ago been a tramway, carrying coal from nearby pits to Horsehay ironworks. He always felt sorry for those of his schoolmates who had to pick their way along a pathway so strewn with sharp and lumpy rocks. The boy soon turned left, and quickly found his way home.

The 'Forester Arms' pub at Horsehay.

Chapter Five

FROM THE STRANGE ROAD TO THE PEACEFUL VILLAGE : THE FOURTH TOUR

THE FINGER AND STIRCHLEY

This time, the boy's journey took him in a south easterly direction to explore a peaceful village which clung to a time-warp at the fringe of the town, inextricably linked with Dawley yet somehow possessing a tranquil heartbeat of its own. That village was Stirchley, and the way to it initially was along a stretch of the main 'A442' road, before entering a quiet lane which ran for about a mile to the small community in question.

The quarter mile section of the 'A442' in the direction of Bridgnorth was quite interesting. Having rounded the precarious Portley Corner, and passed some cottages on the right, the road descended alongside a portion of the pine-covered Paddock Mound, then curved past a bungalow and another group of cottages, and a pub called the 'White Horse'. The boy noticed that in the front window of the pub, they had one of those infuriating, oscillating, plastic ducks that were a bit of a craze in such places at that time. Basically, the 'bird' was placed facing a small tumbler of water, and was so designed as to swing back and forth on its own axis about two dozen times, so that on each forward stroke, its beak was lowered tantalisingly closer to the water, without actually entering it. Just when the watcher had given up all hope of seeing something mildly exciting happening, or more likely, when he had taken his eye off it to watch a bus go by, the stupid creature would drop its head straight into the liquid as if enjoying a crafty drink. Whether or not the display was designed to create a suitable thirst for the popular beverages

served within, he did not know, but the boy considered the exercise frustrating to watch.

The 'White Horse' marked the beginning of the community popularly referred to as 'The Finger'. Officially, it was 'Finger Road', yet the boy remembered stopping at Dorothy Fellows's nearby little shop one day to buy sweets, when one of his friends exclaimed 'Ooh! Look!' as he placed his index finger on the nameplate of a post box set in a wall near the shop. The nameplate read 'Peter's Finger', and since the index finger in question belonged to a boy named Peter, the incident was a source of amusement to the entire group of youngsters. The boy was intrigued as to the identity of the actual Peter immortalised on the post-box, and why his finger was particularly important to this part of Dawley. Opposite, the little brick Finger Road Chapel stood on the corner of Harp Lane. Dawley seemed to have a chapel or church to nearly every square mile. The boy remembered attending a harvest festival service there once and being amazed to find a coal-fired stove stuck right in the middle of the room, and an outlet pipe taking the resultant smoke up to a chimney in the roof. Hell-fire was clearly close at hand to any worshipper who may have fallen short of expectations! From Peter's Finger post-box, ran a line of those now-familiar dull brick cottages, culminating in Jervis's petrol station and lorry depot. By contrast, on the other side of the road, one or two mature, detached houses luxuriated with big gardens to the rear. 'Finger Road' then took a dogs-leg right turn towards a suburb called Southall, which was reached through passing a succession of detached cottages facing tree-covered mounds. The boy's maternal grandfather lived near Southall, and therefore he knew that the small tight-knit outpost consisted of, you've guessed it, groups of old cottages looking out over tree-covered mounds.

'Finger Road' - looking towards the Paddock Mound.

Instead of travelling to Southall, the boy turned left at the 'Queen's Arms' pub and into Stirchley Lane. Soon, the scattering of cottages and red brick houses was left behind, and the lane escaped into pastoral countryside, with teeming hedgerows running beside the peaceful roadway. Joe Brown's farm, not to mention his cows, stood across the field to the left. After a blissful quarter-mile cruise, the boy approached Stirchley. First, came the inevitable little Methodist Chapel and its attendant cottage. Every Good Friday evening, the chapel choir sang one of the seasonal cantatas. It was well known for this, just as Dawley and in fact, the entire Wrekin area was distinguished for its prowess at choral music. The road then crossed the L.M.S. railway line at Stirchley and Dawley station, by means of a stone

bridge. Here was the branch line that ran from Wellington via Hadley, Oakengates, and Malinslee to Madeley and Coalport. It was a single-track branch line whose passenger trains consisted of two maroon coaches with small windows that spoke of an earlier decade, perhaps the 1920's. Occasional, short goods trains trundled trucks of coal to a wharf opposite the station platform from which the Watkiss family, coal merchants, loaded the 'black diamonds' into sacks and on to their motor wagon for distribution to many of the district's firesides. This rather dusty site was accompanied by open fields leading to an impressive house called 'The Elms' that stood near the junction with a road to Tunnel Cottages and Aqueduct. The boy turned left at the junction, passing a large and elegant farmhouse that seemed to have stepped straight out of the pages of a history book. It was Stirchley Hall Farm, and its incumbents, the Wards, farmed much of the softly undulating countryside nearby. The Hall undoubtedly was historic, parts of it dating back some three to four hundred years.

Lower down the road, a small school building stood to the left. Some of the boy's high-school friends had received their junior education there. A rocky track to the right, led to a cluster of ancient properties including St. James's Church and the Rectory. Together with Stirchley Hall, they presented a tangible bond with centuries that had long since melted into oblivion. Yet this was no musty museum piece. People still lived and worshipped here as people had surely done for generations, and this timeworn little vignette snuggled along the lane as if determined to preserve its graceful antiquity, amid a world that had long since passed it by.

The main roadway began a fairly steep descent, affording appealing views of rolling, green countryside beyond. An unmade road to the left, led to a public house and a row of good-looking old houses known as 'Northwood Terrace,' apparently in the middle of nowhere.

Descending the hill, the boy noticed another historic, red brick house called 'Stirchley Grange', standing among meadows and close to a pool. It seemed strange that a small village such as Stirchley should possess so many properties of distinction, within an area not generally noted for its affluence. The more humble 'Brookside' cottages stood opposite along the roadway, and from there on, the main route wormed its way through pleasing countryside towards Shifnal while a smaller lane branched off and climbed a steep, green hillside at Lower Brands Farm (the Randlay housing now occupies the site). Oakes's ran the farm, and treated their cattle to some of the lushest pasture in the district. The farm also provided a quite extensive milk delivery service in the Dawley area, at least up to the late 1940's. The boy remembered a small, dark green van bearing the words 'Oakes's Lower Brands Farm', and driven by a nice lady called Ada, daily gliding down 'Portley Road' dropping off bottles of milk of varying sizes. There were standard pint bottles, but also 'kiddy-sized' ones, and 'big Berthas' presumably for those who wanted to bath in milk! Oakes's bottles had aluminium foil tops, unlike the more familiar cardboard ones with a perforated hole in the top that caused your thumb to sink into the layer of cream on opening. On a good day, the kindly Ada would let you have a ride down the road in the van - a novel experience in the days when private motor transport was the exception rather than the norm.

From the pastoral scene at the edge of Stirchley, the boy turned his machine around, and pedalled all the way back to Dawley.

Stirchley Lane Methodist chapel

Chapter Six

TO FAR-FLUNG PLACES :
THE FIFTH TOUR

CROWN STREET, LANGLEY, HINKSHAY, DARK LANE

The greater frequency of public transport together with the ability to purchase a reliable, new bicycle on the 'never-never' in the early fifties opened up new and absorbing pastimes to the youth of the day. One such hobby was the noble art of 'train-spotting'. In those days, train-spotters were less likely to be wearing nerd-like anoraks, but black, gabardine mackintoshes and school caps. Sometimes, the boy and a group of friends would travel by means of a combination of bus and train to such gripping railway locations as Shrewsbury, Wolverhampton, Crewe or Chester. Their 'home base' however, was a bridge over the main Shrewsbury to Wolverhampton line just beyond the old, industrial village of Dark Lane, some three miles to the east of Dawley. The regular cycle ride to that location entailed a journey through some of the town's easterly outposts, and a wander through a semi-rural landscape along a narrow lane containing one or two challenging inclines.

First, it was necessary to descend 'Finger Road' again, but then turn left immediately after Jervis's garage and into 'Crown Street'. That street provided a gradual climb between cottages, and past a small grocery shop owned by one Jack Tinmouth, and the 'Crown Inn' run by Mrs. Edith Walton. Mrs. Walton's other claim to fame was that she tutored a generation of talented Dawley youngsters in the playing of the accordion. Her accordion band was an extremely popular attraction at local concerts and dances for several of the post war years. A narrow roadway ran alongside the pub and into another 'tucked away'

community known as Langley Fold. From the top of the hill, the road descended between sloping fields, the left hand one being the sports field belonging to Langley School. The boy remembered playing for Pool Hill School football team at the venue and experiencing for the first time, the extreme partisan emotions of the numerically superior home supporters. Their chants, not to mention insults often proved a greater distraction than the on-field ministrations of the opposing players. It was always like that when teams from Dawley schools faced each other. Beyond the field, lay the row of red brick council houses called 'Bush Avenue'. Langley School, an elderly-looking building, also lay to the left, overlooking the sports field and backed by mounds now re-colonised with grass. In the distance, the brooding presence of the pine-covered Paddock Mound, complete with humble Scout hut at its summit, separated Langley from the centre of Dawley.

The road, and its frequent potholes, continued past cottages and bushy waste ground to a mound near the 'White Hart' pub. The pub, a tall old building was itself painted white and stood at right angles to the road. It was always referred to as 'The Jerry'. Amongst other things, it was the home of Hinkshay United Football Club, an amateur team more lowly placed than Dawley Athletic in the soccer hierarchy, yet having a very successful side throughout the fifties. The team played on the big field next to the pub. From the left-hand side of the road, some quite nice old detached houses looked out over the field.

A tiny Mission Church was also a nearby spectator. All along the far side of the football pitch ran a long, terraced row of cottages in similar dark brown brick to that encountered in other parts of the Dawley area. The difference here was the sheer length of the many - chimneyed row. It was as if the builders had deliberately set out to gain immortality in the 'Guinness Book of Records' for creating the longest row of cottages without a breathing space! To the left of the field, yet more rows of cottages stood grouped together to form a distinct community of their own. In some places, part of a row would stand on slightly higher ground than its next-door neighbour, so that there would be two or three drops in levels within a particular row. There would be quite lengthy gardens between the rows, littered with an assortment of ramshackle garden sheds and improvised greenhouses. The whole place seemed stuck in a time warp, a separate, forgotten society belonging to Dawley yet somehow distanced from it.

Hinkshay Row, 'Single Row'

The boy's journey continued past the roadside Mission Church and round a bend where the road then became a narrow lane running through open countryside. A bungalow nestled at the roadside, then for a while, the lane threaded its meandering way between hedgerows with fields to either side, and tree-covered mounds lay in the distance. The boy knew that a rough track on the right descended towards 'Boulton's Randlay Brickworks', and the 'Stirchley Dodger' line. He also recollected a certain Saturday morning (so he thought) in the early 1950's. From his bedroom in 'Portley Road', he heard the incessant mournful wailing of an L.M.S. tank engine's whistle as it pulled the last ever passenger train from Coalport to Wellington, between Stirchley station and this stretch of its route.

Soon, a small cluster of stone cottages known inexplicably as 'The Lodge' stood in peaceful isolation on the left. Exactly why such a tiny locality should have stationed itself so distantly was not readily apparent. The road passed the unseen 'Withy Pool', then turned sharp right, and began its approach to the far flung village of Dark Lane which lay at the bottom of a fairly steep valley. At the beginning of the descent, stood a farmhouse and accompanying buildings. One or two more houses dotted the initial slope that led to a bridge over the railway line at Dark Lane's railway station, curiously bearing the name 'Malinslee'. The choice of name seemed an idiosyncrasy to the boy. Of more immediate concern, was the fact that there were a few holes in the road as it passed over the apex of the bridge - and it was possible to see portions of the railway track below.

Once the bridge had been safely negotiated, there remained the final plunge down a further incline to the bottom of the valley. What a sight confronted the traveller at that point! Although there were undulating fields on the right, the scene on the left - hand side came as something of a shock. Keeping company with the gradient was a continuous row of about a dozen old, terraced cottages, each segment joined to but standing a little higher than the next. Every cottage also sported its own tall brick chimney, and the roadside walls were covered in a rather faded rendering and had only a few small windows. The gardens at the back were lengthy, and contained the usual jumble of sheds and other outbuildings. The row seemed to be saying *'if you didn't get a close enough view of Hinkshay, well take a look at us!'* Admittedly, there weren't as many cottages as at the other village, but the effect was much the same - that of a community continuing to live in conditions created during a much earlier era, and making the best of it. At the bottom of the hill, a small, detached house stood to the right, and a rather untypical Methodist chapel was on the left. Untypical, because it was

particularly small and narrow, and of plain brick with a pointed roof, and only single storey. Just before the chapel, a single-track railway ran across the road, and was used to link local industries with the main sidings near Hollinswood. Beyond the church, the lane soon turned sharp left to climb a steep hill between crop-fields, and onwards towards the main railway line, and ultimately, the village of Priorslee.

Having become aquainted with the Dawley area in its different guises, we must now have a look at its history through the ages. We'll get an idea of how it gradually developed into the sort of thriving town it became in the nineteenth century, and how it managed to still live and breathe through the twentieth.

Dark Lane, Long Row - looking up at the slope towards the 'Stirchley Dodger' Line Railway Station.

EARLY DAYS

Chapter Seven

How Dawley got here :

A trip down the ages

If we go back far enough, we'll find that Dawley, like much of England for that matter, was once smothered in dense forest until those beaver-like Saxons started spreading their tentacles across the landscape, clearing spaces among the trees in which they could live and work. It is said that the Wrekin forest (or Forest of Mount Gilbert) stretched from near Newport to the Severn Valley, including Ironbridge Gorge. During the tenth and early eleventh centuries, these Teutonic conquerors got extremely busy chopping down trees here and there, creating *leahs* (clearings) in which small townships were established. They tended to add the word *leah* to the end of the name of the 'boss man' who had supervised the work and established his home in a particular territory. Thus, present-day local place names such as Dawley, Doseley, Langley, Portley, Malinslee and Brandlee probably derived from this process.

The important, though admittedly small, townships dating from Saxon times were Great Dawley (situated next to where Dawley Parish Church stands), Little Dawley and Malinslee. It's comforting to know that before 1086, the Manor of Great Dawley was, according to the record books, in the name of someone called *GRIM*. Grim couldn't possibly have known how aptly his name might have described the area, following the actions of the 18th and 19th century industrialists, but that's another story to be told later in the book.

Saxon Dawley found itself part of the huge

parish of Idsall (Shifnal, as we would know it). This may help explain why people used to receive even in the early 1950's, regular copies of the 'Shifnal Rural Deanery Magazine' from Holy Trinity Church - perhaps the ecclesiastical boundaries had their origins in much earlier times. It is known that the Normans tended to apportion their newly acquired land with at least some regard to ancient borders, so perhaps there is a connection here.

When the Normans arrived they too, demanded a slice of the action, so that from 1086, Earl Roger de Montgomery became the new Lord and Master of the Manor, and promptly leased it to a 'gent' named William Pantulf. He liked it so much, that he styled it Dawley Pantulf. People can take vanity a bit too far sometimes!

It seems that gradually, the Normans and their successors continued hacking away at the trees to provide yet more clearings, until at least the 14th century. In fact, some small enclosures were established out of woodland waste at Great Dawley in the mid-16th century. Could this process explain at least partly, the large number of scattered communities abounding in the Dawley area, right up to modern times? There was still plenty of woodland about during the medieval period, and the largest tract of it was at Little Dawley. The trouble was, the little manors kept on changing hands through the next few centuries (one of the owners was no less a noble than the Earl of Arundel, around 1345). The local serfs must have awaited news of the arrival of a new landlord just as today we await the results of the General Election, though with much more excitement. After one hell of a roundabout of buying and selling, one record book then calmly states that *'in 1623, Sir John Hayward sold most of Dawley to Fulke Crompton'*. The statement has all the charm of a newspaper article telling us that 'today Hartlepool United sold Ernie Knobblyknees to Bridgnorth Town'. Despite all these transactions, the Manors of Great Dawley, Little Dawley and Malinslee managed to be tied to the main Manor of Leegomery for quite a while.

What was very different about Dawley during those earlier centuries, was that the scenery was almost entirely pastoral (chiefly woodland), and the economy agricultural. Although mining was recorded from the 1500's, it was carried out only on a small scale until the real blow fell during the middle 1750's. Instead, medieval Dawley people busied themselves rearing horses, goats and pigs, in fact to such an extent that some of the blighters (the animals, that is) were frequently damaging crops in the mid-14th century-especially in the Malinslee area, for some reason. Around the edges of the town were various large enclosures, chiefly for keeping stock-especially horses. Such spaces were called 'hays', and as a result, the names Horse Hay, Dawley Hay, Smeeth Hay and Charles Hay (somewhere near Heath Hill), and also Hinks Hay came on the scene. Citizens of Dawley will know that both Horsehay and Hinkshay still survive.

Keeping a watchful eye on all this activity would be the Lord of the Manor, who in the case of Great Dawley lived, not surprisingly, in a Manor House which was situated on a hill just to the south of Dawley Church. In fact, in 1315, a patent granted at York, no less, allowed William de Morton to surround his Mansion at 'Daliley' with a stone wall as a fortification. Exactly who was posing a threat to him at that particular time is not certain. It wouldn't have been his 'subjects' since they would have been only too grateful for the opportunity to continue eking out an existence on the land in relative peace. However, peace was a commodity hard to come by in the mid-17th century, while the respective armies of King Charles I and the English Parliament insisted on bashing seven bells out of each other at every opportunity. Perhaps the Manor House was even further fortified at that time, because some of the King's troops occupied it for a while, until elbowed out by Cromwell's squaddies in 1645. The Royalists unsuccessfully tried to grab it back again in 1648, so that a garrison could be established there. In due course, the place outlived its usefulness as a military base, and an order was made for its demolition. It wasn't going to give up that easily, and served as a farmstead during the 18th century and, in fact, the various buildings surrounded by bits of the old moat were still there until 1817. The once mighty property then came to an ignominious end by being knocked down and smothered in slag from the nearby Castle Furnaces. People persisted in referring to it as 'Dawley Castle' although, as we have seen, it was nothing more than a fortified manor house, as also was Stokesay in South Shropshire.

The tag nevertheless outlived the building, so that we subsequently had Castle Mound and Castle Pool - they both still exist, and bear the same names even today. There were also Castle Colliery and, as mentioned earlier, Castle Furnaces dating from the Industrial Revolution. To keep the link going, one of the nearby post-second world war housing developments is named 'Castle Road'. It just goes to show how fame can mushroom from one little rumour. To help balance the equation, it should be said that a farm in 'Old Vicarage Road' was known as 'Manor Farm' until its demise in the early 1950's. The farmland grew houses instead of crops from then onwards on what was referred to as the 'Manor Farm Estate'.

'Castle Pool',
near Little Dawley. Castle Mound provides the backdrop.

Chapter Eight

ALL CHANGE IN THE
EIGHTEENTH CENTURY

When the seventeen hundreds arrived, they didn't make an awful lot of difference to life in Dawley to begin with. The few people living in the district continued amusing themselves with agricultural tasks, especially dairy farming and cattle rearing. On a smaller scale, there was a little crop growing, including hemp, peas, corn and orchard fruits. Some places still managed to survive the woodcutter's axe, with Little Dawley in particular, having a large tract of woodland just to the north of the village itself. The lifestyle sounds idyllic, if not very prosperous for the working man and his family, but changes of seismic proportions were already lurking around the corner.

While local farmers were pre-occupied watching the landscape gradually changing, a veritable 'time bomb' was ticking away in the minds of certain persons with more than a passing knowledge of Dawley's geology.

What the farmers were concerned about was the ongoing transformation from the medieval 'open field' system of agriculture, to the more logical 'enclosure system'. With the former, each landowner or tenant was allocated a series of unconnected, narrow strips of land on which to grow his produce. With the latter, the previous open tract of land became divided up into more convenient, manageable units or fields, as we would know them today. Hedges surrounded each separate piece of land.

Records show that, for example, there were still at least two areas of open field in Great Dawley (near the Parish Church) during the seventeenth century. In the eighteenth the enclosure process brought into existence 'Pool Hill Fields' to the north west of the church, 'Rednal Fields' (a small community is still known by that name today) to the south east near Little Dawley, 'Castle Field' (again the name lives on) and 'Coppy Greave Field' near Portley.

Apart from the obvious purpose of feeding both himself and the local populace with fresh, unadulterated produce, the farmer's business of growing crops locally, whether in open fields or enclosed land, had a rather important spin-off. He was, by ancient custom, obliged to hand over one tenth of the annual product of his land to the Vicar of the Parish as a form of tax known as a tithe. Thus, depending on circumstances, the Vicar might receive this payment in the form of a load of corn, a few cows, a cart-full of apples, or even several barrels of beer! Presumably, the clergyman would sell off at least some of his vast horde of goodies in order to pay himself a living wage. Eventually, some men of the cloth got a bit fed up with the business of gathering all this paraphernalia into large and probably smelly tithe barns near to the church. Instead, they made arrangements for payments in cash. At least it would make the giving of change a lot easier! The 'Tithe Commutation Act' of 1836, finally made it obligatory to pay in cash, and the process of compulsory support of the church in this way, surprisingly continued until as recently as 1936. In the old days, the money or money's worth went simply to keep the Vicar suitably fed and watered. From the 1836 act onwards, the tax had to be used to upkeep the fabric of the church buildings. Presumably, they didn't need to pass the plate around the congregation with quite the same degree of resolution in those days.

It seems pretty obvious that had it not been for the discovery of a vast treasure-trove of virgin coal, ironstone and clay lying in wait beneath the farmers' very feet, Dawley's story would have been very different. The undulating district would have gently cruised through to the twentieth century as an acknowledged Shropshire beauty spot, on a par with the likes of Church Stretton or Ellesmere. People might have paused for tea and scones at say, a half-timbered, converted cottage tea room in 'Old Vicarage Road' after a stroll around the Castle Pools. Charabanc loads of summer trippers might have enjoyed picnics on Brandlee Hill, while rejoicing in the views towards the Severn Gorge and the distant Brown Clee. There might even have been an 'East Shropshire Way' enticing ramblers to hoof it from the ancient woodland of Oakengates's Cockshutt Piece, over the lumpy hills and pleasant fields of Old Park, and down the tree-clad valley from Dawley Green to the delights of the Bath Spout at Doseley. Ultimately, there would have been the spectacular descent into Coalbrookdale and Ironbridge Gorge. Well, it's a thought, anyway!

In a nutshell, almost the entire Dawley area sat on precious seams of workable coal. Along the north west edge of Dawley parish, from Old Park to Heath Hill, the productive Middle Coal Measures lay near the surface, as did those in the southern extremity, near Lightmoor. In Great Dawley and Malinslee, however, on the eastern side of the Lightmoor Fault, the little devils lay some 120 metres below the ground under a 'crust' of silt stones and sand stones of the Upper Coal Measures. It wasn't until a posse of ironworks began springing up in the area in the 1750's, that serious mining of the 'black diamonds' began in earnest. To begin with, well-informed landowners such as the Eytons at Malinslee, began to exploit the riches beneath their territories.

The eighteenth century then saw the initiative pass to industrialists, who presumably wanted to ensure a plentiful supply of materials for their hungry furnaces, scattered throughout the East Shropshire Coalfield. The Darby family was prominent among the entrepreneurs, and its Coalbrookdale Company lost no time in bagging some of the best sites in the Dawley, Little Dawley and Lightmoor areas. Even before the eighteenth century, industrial workers' cottages had begun to appear in the district, and the process gathered pace right through to the late - Victorian era. Thus, the landscape started to lose much of its rural appearance. It gradually fell prey to the voracious whims of woodcutters, coal-miners, ironstone-miners, clay-miners, iron-makers, brick and tile makers, and who- knows-what makers. All of those were happy to jump on the industrial bandwagon for as long as it was capable of earning them (that is, the owners) a lot of money.

As a consequence of the above activity, another major upheaval took place, in that the centre of Dawley had moved to Dawley Green where the High Street now stands. The Dawley Green and Dawley Bank areas were becoming increasingly industrialised. The impressive, gabled houses and half-timbered cottages at Dawley Green were demolished to make way for mines, and mineworkers' cottages. Even worse, as one historian put it, '*where birds once reared their young, beneath some blackthorn spray, not a twig or blade of grass is seen, whilst the once green surface is hid by mounds of earth raised one thousand feet from beneath it*'*. He may have been exaggerating a little bit, but there is no doubting the basic truth of his message. A kind of Armageddon had arrived on Dawley's unsuspecting doorstep. No longer would rustic cottagers trip daintily around the Maypole on the village green. In fact, in much of the Dawley area a fair amount of agricultural land was commandeered for industrial use from the late eighteenth century. The dwindling numbers of people employed on the land found themselves working to fill the mouths of a growing industrial population.

INDUSTRY GETS CRACKING

In some cases, farm-owners themselves dabbled in a bit of mining 'on the side' you might say, in order to cash-in on the new boom industry and, of course, to supplement their incomes. It was, however, the big boys of the trade, the 'professionals' who really went into it in a big way. Personalities such as Richard Hartshorne of Ketley (the leading East Shropshire Coal Master of his day), Isaac Hawkins-Browne and Thomas Botfield both at Malinslee, Abraham Darby the II and others became the 'star names' in the mining and iron working businesses, when the Industrial Revolution knocked heavily on Dawley's door during this frenetic period.

To start with, most of the mining was confined to places where the coal was easier to get at, where it lay just below the surface. A hole, or adit, would simply be dug into a hillside and the much-prized mineral extracted and transported to wherever it was needed. Where good quality coal lay deeper, it became

necessary to sink fairly shallow, vertical shafts towards the bowels of the earth. It's thought that some of the earliest in the area were to be found near Dawley Bank, Heath Hill and Brandlee (quite close to Dawley Green), Great Dawley and at Old Park in the north and near Lightmoor in the south.

When Darby's Coalbrookdale Company built its important iron-furnaces at Horsehay in 1754, and at Lightmoor in 1758, the race for even more coal was on. Abraham the II obtained Hartshorne's expiring lease on the Slaney estate at Great Dawley, and in the fullness of time, the Coalbrookdale Company gained control of most of the coal and iron stone resources in the Great Dawley area.

Thomas Barker, William Ferriday and others, had leases for mining at Little Dawley. A group of Dawley and Madeley men started the Lightmoor Company, leasing land from Beriah Botfield in 1753. This seemed to give the fledging ironworks the lift-off it needed, because the business soon became very prosperous, later attracting the attention of Thomas Botfield, son of Beriah. Thomas was an interesting character. Originally, he manufactured breeches, but couldn't go with the flow when fashion decreed pantaloons should replace the former garments. He then joined the Lightmoor Company as a humble clerk. The story goes that he used to remove a brick from his office wall, so that he could overhear the private discussions of his employers. This inglorious piece of espionage seems to have paid off for Tommy Bot., since he eventually managed to rise to the status of partner in the business. He later founded the Old Park Ironworks, lived at Little Dawley Manor House, and subsequently retired to the idyllic pastures of Hopton Wafers. He had become one of the richest men in the county. A real breeches to riches story, if ever there was one.

It doesn't take too much imagination then, to see that both the character and appearance of the area became drastically altered as the century wore on, and the rustic charm wore off. To use a hackneyed phrase, the course of Dawley's history was 'changed for ever', and the legacy of the eighteenth century lives on in one form or another to this very day.

Perhaps we should get off the subject of industry for a while at least, lest we get too despondent about the eighteenth century. Many praiseworthy things happened in Dawley at that time. It is not that industry wasn't in its way praiseworthy, it's just that it left such a hell of a mess in its wake - that's the hard bit to swallow.

Several honourable characters also made their mark, and we need to take a closer look at a cross-section of Dawley society to get an impression of the town's essential ethos as the calendar moved onward towards the following century. 'Dawley Wake' - an annual fair on All Saints Day (1st November) was taking place even in the early 1700's, and was last recorded in 1873, so at least people were able to have some good, clean fun once a year.

LOOKING AFTER THE WORKERS

Now that serious industry had arrived, those responsible for it began to feel a few twinges of conscience towards their over-stretched workforces. One result was the setting up of a number of Friendly and Provident Societies in Dawley, to give workers the prospect of at least some measure of financial support in the event of a catastrophe. Their respective committee members held meetings either in one of the various alehouses springing up in the district, or in the non-conformist chapels which were also establishing themselves on the scene. Whilst members would have to

pay a subscription, it has to be said that the likes of Browne and the Botfields also made contributions to the funds to help keep them viable. The Coalbrookdale Company is to be commended on the creation of a medical and educational fund to which employees subsequently contributed in the early nineteenth century.

On the question of housing, some of the earliest 'miners' cottages' were simply 'squatter cottages', whilst the late eighteenth century saw employers beginning to take responsibility for housing provision. A 'squatter cottage' was often a pretty rough and ready dwelling, hastily thrown up by its inhabitants on land close to the mines. In some parts of East Shropshire, the builder was set an 'Anneka Rice challenge' of getting the building substantially up and running, and at least having smoke coming out of its chimney by sunset on the first day, in order to be legally entitled to live there.

Incredibly, one of the cruder forms of such cottages, a rather primitive stone affair, survives to this day on the rural fringes of Blists Hill Museum, near Madeley. It was originally built at Burroughs Bank (near Lightmoor). In fact, the small mining settlements of Burroughs Bank, Gravel Leasowes (Little Dawley) and Stoney Hill (near Horsehay) chiefly consisted of squatter cottages of one sort or another. Most of this cottage-building happened in rather haphazard fashion, although the development at Holywell Lane (Little Dawley) was an exception. Here, the cottages were strung out in a rather uneven row on land belonging to the Earl of Craven. Since Craven (of Craven Arms fame) was an absentee landlord, he raised no objection to the squatters' activity, especially when he realised that the income from his land would be somewhat swelled, thanks to the industrial goings-on nearby. It is thought that at least one of those cottages was built about 1740, and there were five of them by 1772. More were soon to follow. A few were built of local rubble sandstone, though most were of brick with rough timber framing. At least one had been built on agricultural land used in medieval times under the 'ridge and furrow' method of crop-cultivation. This might help explain why some of the cottages seemed to stand at different levels to those of their neighbours. The cottages at Holywell Lane were not demolished until the late 1970's. Thus, families occupied them through a period of some two hundred years, and we shall meet these dwellings again when we talk about Dawley life in the nineteenth and twentieth centuries.

It's good to report that church attendance was also flourishing in the late 1700's, so much so that not all those who wanted to could find room in the old Parish Church at Great Dawley. Instead, some went either to Madeley, or even Wellington for public worship. At about the same time, John Fletcher, who had become Vicar of Madeley in 1760, and was a friend of both John and Charles Wesley, began preaching out of doors after evening prayers on Sundays in order to 'get through' to the ordinary working man. This didn't go down too well with either the church authorities or the farming classes. Undaunted, Fletcher also encouraged John Wesley to preach to the workers, and set up Non-Conformist Methodist Churches throughout the coalfield, including several parts of Dawley. The process was to continue and consolidate through the nineteenth century.

Darby's Coalbrookdale Company set about constructing an ironworks on the site of a water mill at Horsehay. The first furnace began to function in 1754, a second one in 1757 - which was then rebuilt in 1799, and a third in 1781. Coal from the Darby mines in the Dawley area kept the furnaces fuelled at an increasing rate, and the main product was wrought-iron, chiefly for use by Black Country forge-owners and merchants. These furnaces were roughly on the site of the subsequent Horsehay Works, which became such an important part of Dawley society until its eventual demise in the 1980's. Soon after the first furnaces were built, the Coalbrookdale Company constructed a terraced row of brick cottages on its own land, opposite the works at Horsehay. This was the 'Old Row' comprising twenty-five, one and a half storey properties which were for the company's local work force. They are still inhabited today, and are known as 'Pool View' and gaze onto the tastefully landscaped former furnace pool.

At the other end of the Dawley empire, Isaac Hawkins-Browne built fifty eight cottages for the workforce of the Old Park ironworks and mines in the 1790's. Twenty-four further cottages were built at 'Forge Row' on the site of the demolished 'Park Farm' also to accommodate ironworkers' families.

William Ball

During the past couple of centuries, some

Dawley citizens have gone on to make their mark on society in one way or another. As well as those already mentioned, the eighteenth century also witnessed the elevation of Samuel Peploe, a Little Dawley farmer's son, to the office of Bishop of Chester in 1726, and the birth of William Ball the so-called 'Shropshire Giant' at Horsehay, in 1795. When Ball became a big boy (and what a big boy he was to become!) he managed to push his weight up to 40 stones, as he worked first as a puddler, then a shingler at Horsehay ironworks. For the benefit of the uninitiated - a puddler stirred the molten iron in the furnace, while a shingler fed solid iron into the rolling machine. To Ball, either job would have been a 'doddle' and we shall talk about his eventful working life in the next chapter.

On the downside, it has to be said that sanitary conditions in many of Dawley's cottages of the period were, to put it mildly, not of the best. Water-courses often became polluted, and what was euphemistically referred to as 'street soil' was carted away by a Contractor who then used it as a cheap source of manure on his land. It gave a whole new dimension to the term 'growing your own produce!'

Alehouses in the district were nothing new

in the seventeen hundreds. In fact, there had been a hostelry or two since at least the fifteen forties, and they eventually became places where illegal gaming and card playing took place. The rising population, and the thirsty work of its labouring members, led to ten or more licensed alehouses by the turn of the nineteenth century. These included 'The Wicket' near the Parish Church, the good old 'Dun Cow' at Dawley Green, and 'The Finger'. The latter two lay on the Wellington to Worcester turnpike road (established in 1764) which at the time, was the main route through Dawley. It entered the parish in the north west at Dawley Bank, passed along Dawley Green Lane (nowadays, 'Bank Road' and 'King Street') descended Dun Cow Bank (now 'New Street') and eventually, the sloping 'Finger Lane' to Southall in the south east.

This then, was the Dawley that spilled over into the nineteenth century. The seeds of industrial expansion were already beginning to sprout into something frighteningly larger, making the nineteenth century one of the most momentous in the history of both Dawley and Great Britain as a whole. In the following few chapters, we will find out exactly what happened.

FROM BOOM TO BUST - BIG THINGS HAPPEN TO DAWLEY IN THE NINETEENTH CENTURY

Chapter Nine

MINES AND FURNACES, SHOPS AND ROADS, PEOPLE AND PLACES

You only have to look at some of the things that happened in Dawley during the 19th century, to begin to appreciate how the place appeared at the time the boy grew up one hundred or so years later. What had gone on before had played its part, but the Victorian era in particular witnessed changes of Gargantuan proportions. The effect was to leave an indelible mark on the whole area for generations to come, and indirectly influence the creation of Telford New Town in the late 20th century - another momentous revolution!

What were those changes, then? Why and where did they happen, and how did they so monumentally affect the way Dawley looked, and the way its people lived for such a long time to come? Piece by piece, we'll try and explain these things in this section of the book. We'll also look at some of Dawley's personalities whose fame has lived on, way beyond the 19th century era in which they lived.

Iron was undoubtedly 'King' at that time, and Britain led the world not only in its manufacture, but also the essential craftsmanship to convert it into goods of both domestic and industrial importance. Iron-works and forges spawned wherever there were significant reserves of iron stone and coal beneath the ground. The Dawley area was one such place. Not only were major furnaces developed by the Darbys at Horsehay and the Botfields at Old Park and Stirchley, but smaller ones also sprang up at Lightmoor, Dawley Castle, Hinkshay, Lawley (where a contemporary 'bus stop' is still known as 'Lawley Furnaces'), Dark Lane and Hollinswood among others. The furnaces couldn't function without coal and iron stone, so the ground was ripped open with all the enthusiasm of a child opening a Christmas present, and with just as much residual mess! There were mines of one sort or another, virtually everywhere. With all that going on, who could wonder at the total transformation brought about in a district that had for centuries been predominantly rural?

The inhabitants of Great Dawley, close to the Parish Church, had to put up with the fact that with so many mines being sunk at Dawley Green, and with hordes of people desperate to come and live by them, the centre of Dawley transferred from the former to the latter. This happened during the late 18th and early 19th centuries. Whether the Great Dawleyites were relieved or aggrieved at the loss of their township's status as hub of the area's life, we may never know. What is certain is that by the mid-19th century, Dawley Green had taken on the appearance of a small town. Several buildings strung out along the roadway were rebuilt and then carried shop-fronts. By 1851, a thriving commercial centre had developed there, and the name was changed from 'Dawley Green' to 'High Street' for that is what it had truly become. It was now an avenue of some several hundred yards in length, with a row of shops on either side. In other words, Dawley Green had become a typical small town shopping centre catering for an increasing number of nearby cottages and houses, not to mention the smaller village communities scattered around the district.

This was how 'the Street' came into being, the same 'Street' that serves its neighbourhood today, as far as it is able. Incidentally, the name Dawley Green lived on as far as 'officialdom' was concerned, until well into the 20th century. For instance, if you had got married at Dawley Methodist Chapel in 'High Street' in the 1960's, your marriage certificate would state that the event was solemnised at 'Dawley Wesleyan Chapel, Dawley Green'. Registrars, it seems, did not let go of ancient designations easily.

At about the same time as Dawley 'High Street' was finding its feet, its two main side roads 'Chapel Street' (referring to the Wesleyan Chapel) and 'Meadow Road' (starting practically opposite the chapel) first saw the light of day. Sufficient of the original buildings survive to give a good impression of what these two places were about. 'Meadow Road' (also known as Meadow Well) consisted of rows of terraced, brick cottages gradually sloping down towards a field, whilst 'Chapel Street' contained a mix of cottages and one or two imposing detached houses. It was joined in the 1860's by a Wesleyan Sunday School building at the 'Street' end.

The road that ran through the High Street was subsequently promoted in importance. For some time, it had been a fairly narrow road eventually administered by the Madeley/Bridgnorth Turnpike Trust. It originally entered Dawley near Old Office Road at a place called Ball's Hill. It then passed close by what was to become the 'White Horse' Inn at 'Heath Hill', before descending to Dawley Green. The High Street may have been wide enough in the 'horse and cart era' but was later to prove sadly inadequate in coping with the escalating demands of 20th century motorised traffic. The reason for this narrowness was simply that the newly created shops were fashioned out of existing buildings along either side of the old road. It saved knocking them down and starting afresh, and there seemed no need to bother about the width of the street. Thus, it was left to the 20th century 'age of the motor' to worry about how the heck a 'Midland Red' bus and a lorry laden with building bricks could pass each other without squashing some poor pedestrian against the front of a grocery store.

Nevertheless, in 1827 or thereabouts, a new section of roadway was built on the track of an older route from Ball's Hill to Lawley, the village where the Wellington-Worcester road turned off towards Dawley Bank. The upshot was that a continuous road now ran from Wellington, through Lawley to Heath Hill, then Dawley 'High Street'. The Wellington-Worcester turnpike was diverted to follow this new route from Lawley. This was later to become part of the A442, which continued down 'Dun Cow Bank', ('New Street') and 'Finger Road' then wandered onwards to Bridgnorth and Kidderminster. The original main road through Dawley Bank to Dawley Green was effectively made redundant by the new Wellington to Dawley road, so far as through traffic was concerned. Whilst we're talking about roads, it's also worth mentioning that another major highway ran from Wellington to Coalbrookdale via Lawley and Horsehay, and the turnpike opened around 1817. Dawley was connected to this by means of 'Brandlee Lane' (later to become 'Station Road') and the 'Coalbrookdale Company' originally made it a private toll road, with a turnpike at Horsehay. I hope readers will not be too confused by all this 'roady talk', but instead get an idea of how the contemporary road system in and around the town, came into being.

The other big 'High Street' development in the 19th century was the arrival of Dawley market. Both population and money were pouring quite happily into the town during the first half of the century (hence the need for the shops), and some sort of market building was built as early as 1836. The idea caught on pretty quickly, but there was still competition from the market at 'big brother' Wellington. Dawley hit back, and built a new Market Hall just opposite the original, in 1867. It was a typical Victorian affair, with a fancy arcaded brick facade and a clock tower whose clanky bell was still announcing the hours to shoppers nearly a hundred years later. The Saturday market's fortunes mirrored those of the town itself, and it began to fall into decline as the 20th century approached. It was still breathing during the early part of the new century only to 'peter out' and then stand silent and deserted thereafter. The building was sold to 'Lloyds Bank' in 1958, and a new, rounded clock tower was imposed, presumably to fit in with the image of a modern, money dealing enterprise. The clock, however, remained taciturn, with no longer a bell to reverberate around the street reminding folk that the next 'bus to Wellington was due. So, Dawley had a Market Hall but no market for a good deal of the 20th century.

'High Street' and the Victorian Market Hall Frontage

The local authority took things in hand in 1977, and established a Friday outdoor market, with stalls running most of the length of 'High Street' on a good day. The street market still functions, but it only became possible at all after a by-pass road was built in 1976, to stop traffic passing through the main street.

Other venerable institutions first saw the light of day during the mid-19th century. Dawley's first post office was opened in 1840. The event was no doubt accompanied by a 'gun salute' of furious banging on the desk with those rubber stamps we heard about earlier, leaving no one in any doubt that this new emporium was open for business! Having an official post office where postage stamps could be bought, letters and parcels despatched, and money saved and transferred (and documents pummeled by rubber stamps) proved immensely popular with the local populace and businesses alike. So much so, that it wasn't too long before some of the outlying villages were clammering for a slice of the action. Both Little Dawley and Horsehay established sub-offices in 1856, Dark Lane in the 1890's, whilst Old Park had to wait until the early 1900's for the privilege.

To accommodate the felons of the area, there was a lock-up at Dawley Green by 1843, and it is said that Dawley boasted one constable in 1840. Either the crime-rate was unbelievably low, or the crooks of this world had a field day. By 1856, there was a full-blown Police Station, resulting in the sale of the original lock up, presumably minus any surplus stock!

The cause of all this social and commercial activity was, of course, the boom in the iron-making and mining industries. As we've already heard, the 'Coalbrookdale Company' built a major ironworks at Horsehay in the 1750's, and it was soon knocking up pig-iron at a phenomenal rate. Things continued apace, and the works also gained a considerable feather in its cap by rolling the iron plates for Brunel's massive steamship, 'S.S. Great Britain' launched in 1843 and still surviving at Bristol Docks. The impressive 'Albert Edward' bridge, taking the Great Western Railway over the river Severn near Ironbridge was also a product of Horsehay.

Not only did Horsehay's products help make history but some of the firm's employees left a considerable mark, also. Perhaps the best known was William Ball, whose birth we have earlier said was in 1795. By the time he was eight years old, he was working at the Horsehay Works, eventually graduating from puddler to shingler, before an eye injury during his adult life caused him to stop working altogether. The intriguing question is, how on earth could a man weighing forty stones, with thighs four feet in circumference, a chest nearly six feet round, and the calfs of his legs measuring twenty-five inches, manage to move at all? Yet move he did, and one of his most impressive feats at the work place was to lift a half-ton piece of iron and place it under the forge hammer, ready for it to be beaten into shape. If every heavy manufacturing firm had had a 'Billy Ball' on its books, it could have saved itself a fortune in lifting-gear! What a pity he was born too soon for T.V's. 'The World's Strongest Man' competition, or Dawley would surely have had a world champion on its hands.

We know quite a bit about his vital statistics, but what sort of person was Billy Ball? By all accounts, he was a nice bloke. He was the kind of fellow that you would still expect to meet in Dawley to this day, affable and always ready to enjoy a joke. He had a great memory for detail, and was full of tales. In fact, it seems that despite his overpowering physical presence, he was the sort of chap you knew you could go up to and have a friendly chat with, and

not be in danger of being put down, in any sense of that expression.

William Ball 'The Dawley Giant'

He was a very active man and one of the star attractions when Dawley celebrated the birth of Alfred Darby in 1850. A procession was organised to tour the district, as was the custom on such big occasions in those days. At its head, were the company's largest and smallest employees - 'Big Billy Ball' and 'Little Benny Poole', respectively. The men were lifted by a pulley block, with Billy then being lowered on to a powerful horse and Benny on to a pony. As they lowered Billy onto the unfortunate horse, he was heard to yell *'dunna yo drop me'* (don't let me fall), which at least shows that the Dawley vernacular was already in full swing at that time. Quite how far the procession trudged is not certain, but the sad conclusion was that Billy's steed, having transported the giant to the delight of the onlookers, had subsequently to be destroyed due to a broken back.

The Coalbrookdale Company showed off some of its products at the Great Exhibition of 185l, at London's Crystal Palace. Billy was taken along too. A man with a 70-inch chest and 80-inch stomach would naturally find it a bit challenging to fit comfortably into a standard railway carriage. Thus, Ball travelled in the guard's van. When some businessmen boarded the train at Birmingham, they tried to take the 'mickey' out of him. *'How much material would it take, and how much money to make you a proper suit?'* one of them jibed. *'Thee tek me to a tailor, 'ave me measured, and pay for the suit, and I'll tell thee!'* the Horsehay mon retorted - end of conversation. Needless to say, in London he was the target of Cockney pickpockets.

William Ball died the very next year at Sandy Bank Row, Doseley, at the age of fifty-seven. Now it was the turn of the crowds to turn out just for him. Countless pairs of eyes watched about twenty men bearing Billy's coffin to Doseley churchyard, using straps and poles. His grave is near the chancel of the now redundant church.

In 195l, members of the Coalbrookdale Institute exhibited some of Billy Ball's artefacts at the Festival of Britain. Amongst other relics, his watch, stick and chair were put on display, and they have since been donated to the 'Ironbridge Gorge Museum.'

How did the works at Horsehay manage to survive Billy Ball's demise? Not awfully well it seems, for the furnaces were 'blown out' during the 1860's, and pig-iron for the forges and rolling mills were then supplied by the company's Lightmoor and Dawley Castle furnaces. Horsehay's forges and rolling mills were themselves closed down in 1886, following a continued decline in the demand for iron. That was the end of the Coalbrookdale Company's involvement with Horsehay. The Simpson family (originally of Rotherham, Yorkshire) acquired the premises, and subsequently

developed the heavy engineering side of the business. The firm became known as the 'Horsehay Company' (a partnership of two brothers) and it was trading under the name 'The Horsehay Company Limited' right up until re-organisation during the 1960's.

Lest we should think that Horsehay was the only 'big noise' in Dawley iron-making circles, we need to record that the second biggest ironworks in the country was once situated at Old Park. It was Thomas Botfield (senior) who had the works constructed as early as 1790. For those who remember the world as in pre-Telford New Town days, let me say that it was roughly situated between Hill Top Methodist Chapel, Old Park and the original Hollinswood. If you were travelling from Dawley to Oakengates via Old Park by bus, you would approach the village along a narrow lane that ran from the 'Coal Wharf' bus stop to 'Forge Row.' On your right, the lumpy landscape fell away in a series of ugly hillocks and craters, gradually plunging steeply towards Hollinswood and the Wellington-Wolverhampton railway line. This was where the Botfields began amassing their considerable fortune, courtesy of a lease from the landowner, Isaac-Hawkins Browne, who also agreed to supply coal and ironstone from his mines in the area. Today such commercial enterprises as 'Holiday Hypermarket' 'J. Sainsbury' and 'P.C. World' are eagerly trying to swell their own company profits where Shropshire's biggest iron-works once toiled.

Initially, the Old Park Works was quite a success story. During a meteoric rise to stardom, forges, mills and further blast furnaces were added. Pig iron was produced in large quantities and sold mainly to forges in the Black Country, Lancashire, and the Severn Valley. It seems that one person (besides Thomas Botfield) deserving a pat on the back for this success was manager, Gilbert Gilpin. Not only was he a wizard at running the works, but he also found time to fathom out how to make better chains for industrial use. What peculiar hobbies some people have! It was a 'hobby' that paid off for Gilpin, however, because later he packed in the job at Old Park to start his own chain-making works at Coalport. It's amazing the inspiration that can come to a person whilst lying in the bath! Certainly, the industrial world had cause to be grateful for Gilpin's inventiveness.

The modern 'Forge Retail Park' - standing approximately on the site of the Old Park Iron Works.

Sadly, as the century wore on, the Old Park Works went the way of all flesh and eventually disappeared from the scene. The Wellington Iron and Coal Company had successfully negotiated a sub-lease for the works (and also for Stirchley Furnaces, Randlay Brickworks, and all the associated mines). The company spent a lot of money on improvements to its newly acquired possessions. Unfortunately, there was an irreversible decline in the market for its products, and the business 'went to the wall' in 1877. The Old Park ironworks were no more. The public legacy of the works and that of the nearby redundant

mines, was the 'moonscape' of waste-land formed from the 'leftovers' and scrub-covered contours that greeted travellers for the best part of a century afterwards.

The names 'Botfield' and 'Isaac Hawkins-Browne' have flitted vaguely through these pages intermittently for some while. Now it's time to have a closer look at these folk who once were so active in various parts of Dawley and district, including Old Park, Malinslee and Stirchley.

Let's look at Hawkins-Browne first. To understand how he came on the scene, we'll have to know a little of the earlier history of land-ownership in the Malinslee area. From the earliest times, the Lords of the Manor of Leegomery owned the settlement of Malinslee. The Eyton family, of Eyton-on-the-Weald Moors, leased the land from at least 1334. Much later, one Soudley Eyton sold his rights to Isaac Hawkins who came from Burton on Trent, in 1701. Up to that point then, it was just a question of buying and selling land, presumably as a safe investment of funds as well as an opportunity to reap profits from the produce of the soil. It's nice to think that the name 'Eyton' lives on in the Malinslee district, with such street names as 'Eyton Road', 'Eyton Fold' and so on. Meanwhile, the land was passed down the line through Isaac's daughter, Rebecca Walthall, in 1736 to his grandson Isaac Hawkins-Browne (senior), a poet, and thence to Isaac Hawkins-Browne (junior) in 1760. This was the I. H-Browne so far as we are concerned, and he happened to be both an M.P. and an essayist. For good measure, he also bought the manor of Stirchley in 1777. He seems to be the one who cottoned-on to the fact that there were minerals under *'them thar acres'* and set about scooping them out.

When Thomas Botfield's Old Park ironworks really got going near the end of the 18th century, Botfield took a twenty one year renewable lease of the Malinslee goodies to ensure continuity of supplies. The Botfields were already an old mining family in the Dawley area, and the lease of Malinslee was subsequently passed down the family line by means of another Thomas, a William, and then two Beriahs. In 1856, the second Beriah was unable to agree terms with the lord of the manor for a new lease, so the Old Park Iron Company stepped in. Thereafter, the lease turned into something of a 'poisoned chalice', since the company was wound-up in 1871. It then passed to Wellington Iron and Coal Company and that folded only three years later. To complete the merry-go-round, the Haybridge Iron Company actually bought the manor in 1886, then promptly leased the mines to Alfred Seymour Jones of Wrexham, in 1893. Jones really bought

into a falling market, since the late nineteenth century saw a continuation in the decline of Dawley's main industries.

Incidentally, the Botfields also found the time, and the money, to buy land at both Stirchley and Hinkshay in the 1820's, where they promptly set about producing yet more iron. The Shropshire Canal, from Donnington Wood to Blists Hill and Coalbrookdale, flowed nearby. Remnants of both canal and blast furnaces can still be seen within Telford Town Park today.

Now that we've mentioned the mines (as well as other things), we'll have a good look in the next chapter at the dramatic impact the extraction of Dawley's underground resources had on the entire fabric of the area, over a very long period of time.

The route of the original narrow Turnpike Road from Wellington to Dawley as it passed near to the 'White Horse' at Heath Hill.

Chapter Ten

THIS REALLY IS THE PITS

We talked in an earlier chapter, of how the entire Dawley area had sat, unsuspectingly, on a huge cache of mineral resources for untold ages. The eighteenth century ironmakers and others had then set about getting them out of the ground, and putting them to better use. If mining got under way in earnest at that time, then what happened at Dawley in the nineteenth century was little short of stupendous.

By the middle of the century, you would have been hard pressed to find a segment of the district which had not got a pit of one sort or another.

Hollinswood, Dark Lane, Malinslee, Old Park, The Rock, Lawley Bank, Randlay, Stirchley, Langley, Portley, Heath Hill, Brandlee, Southall, Deepfield, Dawley Church, Little Dawley, and Lightmoor to mention but quite a lot, were among the places where people suddenly had coal or iron-stone or clay pits for neighbours. Decimation of the landscape was almost total, and it was all in the name of industrial progress, not to mention employment of the proletariat and enrichment of the investors.

Some of the pits bore names or possessed a notoriety which still strike a chord with today's population. For example, 'Waggoner's Fold' coal pit, a Botfield small colliery, with other pits on adjoining mounds, was situated not far from the modern Malinslee housing, one street of which is named 'Waggoner's Fold'. Thus the street name is not so pretentious as it may sound! 'Spout Colliery' was on Spout Mound in the same neck of the woods, and the mound is now landscaped and available

for public enjoyment. The pit ceased to exist during the early twentieth century, and the head-stocks were given to Dark Lane Methodist Chapel which had a pulpit skilfully made from them. Langleyfield Colliery (behind the present Langley junior school) had at least ten shafts during the course of its history so not surprisingly, a very large, landscaped, mound remains.

Both coal and iron-stone were mined at Langleyfield up to the late nineteenth century. Several pits were connected by tramways, whose track beds were often used as pathways well into the twentieth century. Langleyfield Colliery was thus connected to Spout, Wood, and Little Eyton Collieries.

Portley Colliery (where the fir trees now tower over Portley Corner) was similarly connected with pits in the Little Dawley area, as well as the nearby Paddock Colliery (behind the 'Lord Hill' public house).

The large, tree-covered mound alongside 'New Road', belonged to the coal and iron stone pits known as Parish Colliery, due to its proximity to Dawley Parish Church.

At Dawley Parva Colliery (Little Dawley), the canal ran into the pit, which would have made loading easier. The mounds on either side of the canal (which itself tootled on to Coalbrookdale with a branch to Horsehay) were joined by an impressive, brick bridge. This historic structure was sympathetically renovated in 1994, so that future generations could appreciate something tangible from Little Dawley's industrial past. The bridge can easily be seen on the left, near the road descending from Little Dawley to Lightmoor.

Spout Mound

In one or two instances, small, nineteenth century pits continued to earn private owners something of a living until the late twentieth century. Billy Tarr at Brandlee, and Isaiah Jones at the Rock made a go of things with their coal and clay pits right up to the 'swinging 60's'. Otherwise, the vast majority of Dawley's infinite mines that, together with the ironworks, had once employed ninety per cent of the area's working population had given up the ghost by the early 1900's. As the ironworks declined, so, of course, did the demand for coal. Mining techniques had become more sophisticated, with deeper shafts being sunk in other places, and pumps developed to siphon-off excess water. Since fewer people wanted the coal, so there was little point in getting more of it out of the ground locally. An entire way of life was drawing to a close, as the end of the nineteenth century loomed.

Labourers, whose ancestors had been weaned off the land during the seventeen hundreds, and settled into the dark and dangerous existence of mining, iron-making and so on in the eighteen hundreds, were now turning into unemployed paupers, with little hope for the future.

Even when they had been earning, their working lives had been a constant flirtation with injury, illness (including tuberculosis) and death. It is recorded that a Funeral Club was started at Little Dawley Wesleyan Chapel in the 1840's. Every scholar contributed one penny per month. If the youngster died as a result of work activity, twelve-shillings would be paid to the parents 'to defray the funeral expenses'. When you consider that the 1841 census shows that two eight year old boys from Holywell Lane were working in the mines, and there was a nine year old thus employed in 1851, you realise that the monthly investment was no luxury. The fact that employment of boys under ten in the mines was unlawful, didn't seem to worry the mine-owners too much.

Women and girls were in on the act as well. They were employed on the pit banks, skilfully separating iron-ore nodules from the clays and shales brought from underground by their male colleagues. A horse-drawn truck on rails would convey the rubble from the pit-head to the top of the stone banks. A man would tip the truck's contents down the bank at the bottom of which, the ladies would be waiting with small hammers for the

The restored mineral tramway Bridge at Little Dawley. The Canal once flowed beneath it.

purpose of knocking the clay off the stone. These hardy lasses would then have to scramble up the bank, carrying the priceless lumps of iron stone in metal boxes balanced on their heads.

The worst mining disaster to hit the Dawley area occurred in 1872, at the Springwell Colliery, near Little Dawley. The pit mound, now naturally and amply tree-covered, gazes over the track-bed of the former Wellington-Much Wenlock railway line, close to the site of the level-crossing at Doseley Halt. Today's peaceful scene masks the fact that at the end of the Friday shift on 6th December in the year in question, eight young, local miners fell to their deaths when a chain snapped whilst they were being hauled up the 150 foot shaft. There was no pit cage, and it was the practice at Springwell, as at many other local pits, to haul cargoes, both human and otherwise, using a triple-link chain. There had been problems with the condition of the chain just two days earlier, and some of the miners were known to have been worried about its safety. Repairs had been carried out, and on that fateful Friday, many heavy loads of iron stone had been lifted out of the pit, apparently without a problem. At 4.30p.m., the first group of miners were due to be raised to the surface. Eight of them attached themselves to the lifting chains and were hoisted about 50 ft. up the shaft. Suddenly, three links on the major chain became broken, resulting in a fall by the men and the chains to the pit bottom. Seven were killed outright, and the eighth breathed his last soon after being brought to the surface. The eldest victim was 22 years old, and there were also three aged 21, one 20, one 19, one 18, and the youngest,15 years old Isaiah Skelton was reportedly carried out of the pit in his father's arms.

An inquest was held at the half-timbered

Grave of Springwell Mine disaster victims, Holy Trinity Churchyard.

'Crown Inn' in the centre of Little Dawley, at which the management of the Coalbrookdale Company - owned mine were 'severely admonished' for their failure to supervise safety repairs. Nevertheless, no criminal charges of any kind were brought. The badly mutilated bodies of the miners had been laid out along the floor of the 'Crown Inn' (now the 'Estate Office' at Blists Hill museum), 'by the ghostly light of tallow tapers'. To this day, they lie in a communal grave, surrounded by cast-iron railings, on the eastern slope of Dawley Parish churchyard, overlooking Castle Mound. The Vicar of Dawley, Rev. E. Cotterill Wanstall, initiated a public appeal in support of the bereaved families. Ironically, on the day of the disaster, Wanstall was in Pelsall, Staffordshire, delivering money raised by the people of Dawley to help families of the victims of a similar disaster there. In his absence, his curate, Rev. Drury did a sterling job in comforting and helping the distraught people at Little Dawley.

Dawley man, W.R. Morgan, wrote a poem in tribute to the fallen men, and the proceeds of its sale went to the bereaved.

One of its nine verses went:

' *The band had started, eight ascending,*
Cheerful as the noonday sun,
When little thinking, for a moment,
Ev'ry man his race had run.
When lo, a whirl that colliers call it,
Took its awful course, we are told,
And dashed the eight men to the bottom,
Smashed to atoms, but their souls were,
Wafted, quick as lightning, to their Master,
up on high....'

Before ending this episode on the mines, it's interesting to observe that the day-to-day running of the pits was in the hands of fellows known as 'chartermasters', or 'butties' as they were locally known. To obtain a charter from the pit owner or tenant, a 'butty' had to part company with anything up to £500 - an awful lot of money in those days. He then acquired the dubious privilege of hiring and firing workers, as well as obtaining horses, skips, tools and timber for the running of the mine. Needless to say, his pay packet was somewhat fatter than that of a miner, but he had to take the flak from both sides whenever anything went wrong. A look at some of the surnames of Dawley 'butties' reads like a 'Who's Who' of family names that have lived on in the area ever since those momentous days - *BAILEY, EVANS, PITCHFORD, OWEN, GARBETT, GOUGH, MACHIN, ONIONS, PHILLIPS, VAUGHAN, CALLEAR, POOLE, POWELL, BAUGH, JONES, TART, WATKISS, ARCHER, MARTIN, MORGAN, SHEPHERD*, etc. If you stopped everybody with a local accent in Dawley High Street on a busy Friday morning today and asked their surname, you would probably be able to tick off most of the names on the illustrious list above. Times may change, but some things will always be the same in Dawley.

A capped mine-shaft at Horsehay Common.

Chapter Eleven

WHAT ABOUT THE WORKERS?

We've talked about the hazards of discharging ones daily toil in those far off days, but sadly we have to report that getting paid for your work (or at least, getting paid fairly) could be equally perilous for the industrial worker. Even in the early nineteenth century, entrepreneurs who had risked their capital on setting up mines and ironworks, were looking for ways of speeding the returns on their investments. One solution was to actually reduce the wages of the workforce. After all, workers were individuals who knew nothing of collective bargaining, and were surely grateful for whatever pittance the employer awarded them for the provision of their families. A 'thunderbolt' was to disturb this approach in 1821, forever remembered as the 'Cinderhill Riots.'

Discontent had been bubbling amongst the workforce for some time, and the catalyst for extreme action was the decision on 10th January, 1821, for wage reductions to be imposed on employees of most Shropshire ironworks and mines. 'Bush telegraph' of the highest order must have galvanised the bulk of the east Shropshire coalfield into retaliatory action. A few days after the wage reductions were announced, large number of miners stayed off work and also demanded that those still down the pits should be brought to the surface. The big showdown was to take place next day, when the men were organised into groups who visited ironworks around a wide area, including Ketley, Hadley, Wombridge, and Donnington Wood. Miners they may have been, but they knew how to put a good ironworks out of action, damaging equipment to such an extent that it simply couldn't function properly.

Next, this tide of restlessness surged towards the Dawley area. On a dour February day, the relentless 'army' equipped itself with sticks and staves for protection, and marched from Donnington Wood to the Old Park furnaces, gathering new members on the way. At Old Park, they managed to remove the plugs out of the boilers at the furnace, thus striking a decisive blow to production. On they went, encouraged by their successes to teach the 'Coalbrookdale Company' a thing or two, at their premises at Dawley Castle, Lightmoor and Horsehay. Their ultimate goal was the Coalbrookdale ironworks itself. However, opposition at last asserted itself in the shape of an official-looking group of Yeomanry and special constables. They must have looked pretty awesome since their appearance persuaded the protesters to change course.

By 3.00 p.m., a flock of between two and three thousand men and women converged on the slag heaps above and around the Old Park ironworks, determined to make a symbolic outcry. Local people referred to slag heaps as the cinder hills, and they have unwittingly left the name to rest ingloriously within the history book of the Dawley area. In accordance with legal procedure, whenever a clamorous situation involving twelve persons or more seemed likely to result in a disturbance of the peace, a magistrate was brought in to read out the statutory warning from the Riot Act (1714). Where the crowd chose to ignore the magistrate's orders, or opposed by force the King's proclamation, or began to demolish any machinery in any factory, or failed to disperse within one hour of its reading, they were guilty of a serious felony. Exactly how much of the letter of the law was appreciated by the mob is not known, but their response was predictable. Far from dispersing at the sound of the legal niceties, the demonstrators became yet more aggressive. They also broke into football-style communal chants, such as *'if we are to fight for it, lets all get together'* and *'we will have our wages'*.

Convinced that they now had a statutory riot on their hands, the authorities grabbed two token protestors as prisoners, whereupon the miners pelted the constables with lumps of slag and cinder. The Yeomen tried to clamber up the rocky slopes in pursuance, but without success. Instead, they were ordered to open fire. They killed two miners, and wounded some more. One of the protest leaders, Thomas Palin, of Lilleshall, was subsequently arrested and executed for felonious riot.

The gulf between workers and their employers would have been significantly widened as a consequence of all these goings on. One result was that from April of that year, a surprising number of working people and their families turned to the Church for support and comfort. Thus began an astounding religious revival, and we will look at the impact of churches and chapels on the people of Dawley in a later chapter.

It seems that when it came to drowning your sorrows, you turned either to the Church, or the ale-house. As we have already seen, the number of taverns in Dawley increased during the eighteenth century, roughly apace with industrialisation. It follows then, that the creation of yet more mines and furnaces etc. during the nineteenth, meant even more people were driven to drink. A relaxation of the licensing laws led to a mini-explosion in the supply of places wherein to whet your whistle. By 1851,

Dawley was able to boast twenty- two taverns, and fifteen beer houses, most of them in or near Dawley Green. Another thirteen beer retailers had jumped on the bandwagon by 1879.

Whether they could afford it or not, some fellows simply did not know when to stop drinking. They would either make the ale-house their first port of call on their way home with the week's wages, or finance their over-indulgence by having the cost put 'on the slate'. Either way, there would often be empty stomachs remaining inadequately fuelled at home, or bodies unsatisfactorily clothed. Official concern at this state of affairs, and the generally disagreeable effects of alcoholism in the area led to the parish committee circulating handbills, stating the laws against drunkenness. The committee was even moved to appoint some worthy denizen to supervise the conduct of both innkeepers and punters. Later in the century, after the topers of the parish had had their boozy way for a bit too long, the churches (both Anglican and Methodist) led the way in promoting the temperance movement. They say it's an ill-wind that does nobody any good, and the churches were hard pressed to find enough seats, as the twin curses of insobriety and industrial exploitation sent sufferers into their pews in droves.

At least some lucky devils within the area were still able to earn a living from the outdoor life, although their activities were often linked to industry. In the mid-nineteenth century, the tenant of Horsehay Farm looked after between thirty and forty draught horses for Horsehay ironworks. Horses were used for hauling iron and other commodities between and within industrial sites. It is said that the bones of some of those gallant work horses lay buried for years beneath the turf, virtually opposite Horsehay Methodist Chapel, on 'Wellington Road'. If it was so, they would surely have been unceremoniously exhumed during the creation of 'Abrahams Walk', a smart new housing development constructed on the site in the late 1990's. Pit horses at Malinslee were supplied with grazing and fodder at the Botfield Works farm. It's also amazing to realise that between 1867 and 1965, the proportion of agricultural fields made over to grassland increased from under one half to over four fifths. Until well into the twentieth century, cattle were raised, and corn (chiefly wheat) and hay were grown in many parts of Dawley. That was to change by 1980, when only Little Dawley could claim to have retained something of Dawley's agricultural past.

Since the late eighteenth century, housing and the workplace had become inextricably linked. It's not surprising then, that as Dawley's industries gathered pace during the nineteenth century, so did the provision of housing for the workers. By the early part of the century, some sixty additional cottages had been strung out along Dawley Green Lane. A few survive, and some of those that don't, were still inhabited in the late twentieth century.

In most cases, the employers must take the credit for housing supply and that is how the curious little township of terraces at Hinkshay (described in Chapter 6) came into being. Somewhere between 1815 and 1833, Botfield freehold land was used to create a double row of back-to-back cottages, and a single row of twenty-one homes. Later, came the building of 'Ladies Row', ten more spacious cottages. During roughly the same era, over sixty cottages in three long rows appeared at Dark Lane, and six cottages built of sandstone blocks (appropriately dubbed - 'Stone Row') were erected along a quiet lane between Dark Lane and Malinslee. In 1838, the Coalbrookdale Company built 'Sandy Bank Row' (for some reason, the locals persisted

in calling it 'Dill Doll Row'). The company then erected the 'New Row' at Horsehay Pool in 1840.

On the bike ride to Horsehay and district (in Chapter 4), we briefly visited an area between Horsehay and Pool Hill known as 'the Potteries', with its peculiar round house and strange assortment of old dwellings, wondering about their origins. Well, a pottery was established there in the 1790's, but it didn't make fancy china teapots or anything so luxurious as that. It produced industrial ceramics, notably clay pots for making wrought iron in the local ironworks. To this day, the name 'the Potteries' still lives on there. When the pot making ceased, some of the Pottery buildings, including the main kiln (the round house) were converted into houses which, supplemented by some cottages, combined to create a half-hidden

The 'Potteries' kiln house.

community which again, existed into the late twentieth century. The 1851 census showed that there were forty-five dwellings, and the majority of men and boys worked in the iron trade, although there were also nineteen miners, two blacksmiths, and for good measure, (pardon the pun!) one tailor with two apprentices. One woman was described as a 'leechwoman', whatever that was. Evidently, she 'clung' on to her job into her old age! Incidentally, boys usually started work at the age of ten, whilst girls tended to stay on at school for a few more years, when they were then allowed the privilege of being pit girls working on the pit banks. The extra schooling must have been a great boon to them. Perhaps they were given additional tuition in balancing a meagre family budget, as well as iron boxes of stones on their heads.

'Frame Lane', Doseley

We also visited Frame Lane, at Horsehay, and Sandy Bank, at Doseley, on our travels in Chapter 4. Now it can be revealed that both sets of cottages (built by the Coalbrookdale Company) were constructed in 1838. They were joined with each other until the Wellington and Severn Junction Railway Company sliced the community in two, to enable the 'Doseley Dodger' branch

line trains to snort their pioneering way along the newly created track.

Accommodation was not quite on a par with that at 'New Row' Horsehay. There was but one downstairs room, with a small storage area at the rear. Despite the somewhat cramped conditions, several families had relatives living with them, and the average population per house was between five and nine persons. One such dwelling had no fewer than twelve people under its roof at one time! This must have been the place that invented the word 'claustrophobia!' Let's face it, all of those people couldn't have got on with each other all of the time. No wonder people were frequently in the habit of taking long strolls in the surrounding countryside, or losing themselves in the nearby 'Cheshire Cheese' pub! What it must have been like during hard winters is unimaginable. Most of the men and boys of the area were employed in iron making, whilst girls worked either as stone-pickers, or servants. The nearby rocky, tree-covered 'tunnel' at Sandy Bank discovered in Chapter 2, was part of an early tramway from Deepfield mine to Horsehay iron works. It is still used as a pathway today.

Chapter 6's journey finished at Pool Hill, where yet more of Dawley's rash of dark brown cottages lay huddled together. It's not certain when Pool Hill's old cottages were built, but the educated guess is that it must have been sometime between 1825 and 1850. When the 1851 census man came around, he would have found some twenty-one houses there, and one hundred and five people forming another of Dawley's communities.

The survey reveals an intriguing glimpse of life in such a place at that time. Firstly, they didn't *'pack-em-in'* as tightly as at Sandy Bank, so that only three families had relatives living with them, and a further one had a lodger. Breeding was obviously a popular pastime, since sixty-two of the inhabitants were aged under twenty. What on earth the youngsters found to do in their spare time in such a small, enclosed enclave, goodness only knows. Perhaps, when we look at how youngsters spent their time during the early part of the twentieth century, we may get some idea of the legacy of pastimes handed down to them by the children in question. In 1851, of the fifty-seven children living at Pool Hill, a mere eight were attending school despite the fact that the 'Coalbrookdale Company's' Pool Hill School was right on the doorstep! Maybe, the teacher shouted so loudly at the brave pupils who did attend the school on the hill above the cottages, that Pool Hill's own youngsters could take their lessons whilst remaining in bed! Certainly, for one reason or another, some forty-one children stayed at home, and eight were at work. Of the latter, one girl was a dressmaker, one a servant, while

the boys were, like their fathers, generally employed at the ironworks at Horsehay. Completing the picture, the document also reveals that a warehouse clerk, a miller, a house painter, and a Methodist Minister were also living at Pool Hill at that time.

The intriguing thing about Dawley's scattered communities as described in this chapter, is that during the bike riding boy's early years of the late 1940's and early 1950's, people were still living in those little hideaway localities. The mines and iron-works had long ceased their activities, yet new generations of school children, industrial workers, and housewives continued to occupy the properties which had been created to cater for a much earlier population. The dwellings remained relatively unaltered, yet the lifestyles of their successive inhabitants had to grapple with the burgeoning changes of the unfolding twentieth century.

''Meadow Road', just off the High Street

Chapter Twelve

A CLASS OF THEIR OWN

EDUCATION COMES TO DAWLEY

It's little short of amazing that in a nation which enjoyed its 'golden age' during the nineteenth century, the bulk of the younger generation received no compulsory education until the latter decades of that momentous epoch. In other words, while Britain was leading the world in industrial and scientific development, and casting the cloak of Empire over vast chunks of the globe, most of its children didn't have to go to school! Whether there's a moral to this story one can only speculate, but what is certain is that the way in which formal education developed in Dawley makes for an interesting story. Once again, the way things evolved during the nineteenth century, had a profound bearing on the picture that became so familiar to those who went to school in the town in the twentieth.

It wasn't as though no-body had ever tried to teach the youngsters a thing or two in earlier days. Somewhat surprisingly, records show that Richard Wilding, Curate of Dawley in 1605, and later William Banks, Rector of Stirchley, from 1715 to 1758, probably held classes in Dawley, although what was taught, and the length of the lessons is not known. One Richard Poyner appears also to have been a 'schoolmaster' between 1718 and 1722.

Good old Isaac Hawkins-Browne was by 1772, paying for the schooling of fifteen children, presumably in a Sunday school at Malinslee. Browne's tenants, the Botfields were also dipping into their pockets to support the same cause by 1799. Thus, we

can see that it was the church, ever the guardian of people's moral welfare, which took a leading role in trying to instil at least a modicum of knowledge into the minds of generations of youngsters, who probably would otherwise have simply missed out. We can see how the term 'Sunday School' came about, but just why the junior sections of many of our churches still insisted on being so called right up to the twenty-first century, remains a puzzle.

Thus it was then that during the first half of the nineteenth century, some of Dawley's working-class children were receiving some sort of instruction on one day a week, and on a purely voluntary basis. In 1833, the various Dawley churches were between them providing no fewer than eight Sunday Schools. The Church of England ran two of them, and the non-conformists six. The Weslyan churches had Sunday Schools at Lawley Bank from 1806, Little Dawley from 1813, Horsehay from 1819, and Brandlee from 1822. All of those places had, of course, seen a fair influx of population because of the developing mines and so on. By 1833, one of the schools even had a lending library attached.

Let's have a brief look at how the day schools which survived into the twentieth century, and were well-known to generations of Dawley folk, came into being. If we start this peep at Dawley's several seats of learning by looking at the most northerly outpost we shall encounter the school at Dawley Bank, in the building which was occupied during the 1950's and 1960's by the 'pyjama factory'. By the way, it was known as the 'pyjama factory' because that was where rows of ladies, including school-leavers, toiled incessantly each working day in order to produce pyjamas (not surprisingly), outdoor trousers and other garments which we won't describe. As far as the school was concerned, it began life as Malinslee Church of England school in 1832, as a day school for the increasingly populated Malinslee area. The education didn't come entirely free of charge. The pupils contributed two pence per week for the privilege, and the balance of the cost was borne by the Botfields. It was as early as 1844 when the school re-located to 'Park Road' in Dawley Bank. Some cottages were converted for the purpose, and by 1855, the 'new' premises were able to accommodate eighty boys and fifty girls under the management of R.H. Cheney and Beriah Botfield, and eventually acquired the name of Malinslee National School. It all came to an end in 1950, and thereafter, the primary school pupils faced a one-mile walk either to Langley County School or the school at Lawley. For their sins, any children over thirteen years of age, had to trek to Pool Hill School.

'Langley School'

An interesting offshoot developed in 1898, when a second infants department was set up to cater for Old Park children. Unfortunately, those poor souls had to find their way to Malinslee, since their new school was located at the former Mechanics Institute building near Malinslee Church. Built in 1859, the building was still referred to as 'the Institute' well into the twentieth century. The school's founder was Rev. Edward Parry, a larger than life Anglican clergyman who we shall talk about more fully in later chapters. Parry upset the Non-Conformist churches over this issue, but he had his way and actually bought the building himself, in 1897. He took a wise step in 1913, by vesting the property in the Lichfield Diocesan Trust. By 1920, following the creation of a further classroom, the school housed one hundred and thirteen children. However, the construction of the brand new St. Leonard's County Infants School in 1956, saw the closure of the school that Parry founded, and the subsequent transfer of pupils to St. Leonard's.

In the late 1800's, a School Board was compulsorily formed to oversee public day school provision throughout the parish, and the chairman was W.G. Norris, Manager of the 'Coalbrookdale Company'. Norris was a Quaker, and let it not be said that the industrialists of the day were only occupied in lining their own pockets. The Board opened a new school in 1878 on the edge of a spoil mound at Langley, close to Langley Field Colliery. The school still functions but, thank heaven, the spoil heap is long gone, or at least reposes camouflaged beneath a landscaped twentieth century veneer of lush grass. At the start, the school accommodated eighty-one older boys, seventy-six older girls, and some eighty infants. The building wasn't that big, so when they all turned up, it must have been like a practical lesson on the

'Black Hole of Calcutta!' For good measure, the 1873 infants' school at Hinkshay Church of England Mission Chapel closed through lack of sufficient funding after about five years, and the children helped swell the ranks at Langley.

The 'National School'

Next, in the geographical scale, comes the 'National School'. Pupils who went to that school were called 'the nats'- by pupils who didn't go there. Dawley Church of England (Aided) School was the grand name given when it was re-christened in 1952. The building was strategically erected in 1841 near the 'new' Vicarage at Brandlee. The school and house still stand, and the school functions mainly within its Victorian walls as a primary educator, just as it ever did. R.A. Slaney, the landowner/industrialist of Hatton Grange, near Shifnal, generously gave the land for the school. As often was the case with early C.of E. schools, this one became united with the National Society. Hence, it joined the ranks of 'national' schools, and that tag has stuck with it ever since. By 1863, fifty-nine boys and fifty-six girls were paying between one penny and four pence a week, depending on their parents' means. The industrial

decline in the late-nineteenth century didn't stop the people from breeding. The school had to be enlarged both in 1892 and 1898, and by 1903/4, its combined population was an amazing 292.

The school at Pool Hill was the largest and most southerly. It is now known as 'The Captain Webb School'. Its history is fascinating. In 1843, the Coalbrookdale Company opened a British Boys School. To be more exact, Abraham and Alfred Darby set up a temporary schoolroom for children of the workers at Horsehay forge, in the large lofts above the stables at Horsehay Farm. It was a brilliant exercise in 'worker participation' as surplus money from a voluntary sick fund at the works was, by agreement of the fund committee, hived-off to help support the children's education.

Delighted with the school's success in widening the horizons of previously un-tutored youngsters, the Darbys decided to go for 'the big one'. In 1846, Alfred Darby had a large building constructed for seven hundred children at Pool Hill, where it looked down over the roof tops of the settlement, and out towards the works at Horsehay. This was the sturdy, fortress-like building described in an earlier chapter. It saw the passage of numerous generations of Dawley families through its unchanging precincts, until a mysterious fire put paid to it in 1977. In one night of pyrotechnical mayhem, the childhood memories, not to say initials carved on the wooden desks, of hordes of Dawley people, had disappeared in a pall of smoke and flames. Poor Alfred Darby must have turned in his grave, and not only once, either. If ever a Dawley building deserved to live on, albeit as an educational museum piece, into the third millenium, it was that one. We shall talk about it again later in the book. Incidentally, Charles Crookes designed the school building, and the long warehouse beside the River Severn at Ironbridge (now the Museum of the Gorge) was another of his creations. Crookes dabbled with a similar Gothic style for the school, which explains why it had such an elaborate, yet sturdy appearance until the end.

For the moment let us record that originally, the premises were heated by under-floor hot water pipes, rather more luxurious than the cast-iron stoves endured by pupils at other schools. Funds contributed for medical and educational purposes by company employees, were used to help finance the venture, and the school charged between three pence and six pence a week to children of non-company employees. Employees' children went free of charge. A girl's department was added in 1849. Some 270 pupils were in attendance in 1855, and any child with ambitions to follow Dad into Horsehay Works, had to complete a satisfactory grounding at the school first, and certainly

couldn't leave school until reaching the age of twelve. By the mid-1880's, the company had ceased to support the school due to the downturn in the iron trade, and the good old School Board took over its management.

One former Dawley area school which is lovingly preserved for the benefit of visitors from near and far, is the little Victorian building which used to stand near the top of the hill at Stirchley village. Its catchment area also included nearby Aqueduct, but by the middle of the twentieth century it had closed. It was dismantled brick by brick and re-assembled at the Blists Hill site of the Ironbridge Gorge Museum, near Madeley. Schoolchildren from other parts of the country sometimes visit the preserved school, in which both staff and pupils dress up in late Victorian costume. It's nice to think that a little bit of the old way of doing things lingers on.

Pool Hill School – sadly, no longer with us.

Chapter Thirteen

TAKE A PEW

THE CHURCH EXPANDS WITH THE POPULATION

Given that the bulk of modern British society seems to have turned its back on its Christian heritage, it becomes increasingly fascinating to enquire into the enormous popularity of the Church during the heyday of Dawley's industrial history. Eventually, there were five main Anglican Churches in the area, whilst Non-Conformist chapels broke out like a rash just about wherever there was a coal mine. What is more, the buildings were generally full on Sundays, and some even had to be modified in order to get everybody in! There were often three Sunday Services at some places. Why were people so eager to find themselves in church on their one full day off? Were there lives so much of a living hell the rest of the week, that they needed a taste of heaven on a Sunday? The answers to these questions can only be deduced after taking a look at how those places of worship evolved over the years.

Holy Trinity Parish Church, Dawley

Most Dawley people will be familiar with Dawley Parish Church of the Holy Trinity, which stands on a bit of a rise above the houses of Manor Farm Estate, and opposite Castle Mound, on the way to Little Dawley. The impressive, sandstone building we see today was built as recently as 1845. Experts tell us there was a 'chapel' at Great Dawley in the twelfth century, and there has been a place of worship roughly on the same site ever since. For most of the time, it would have catered for a small and not very well-off agricultural population. Thus, the living was not an attractive proposition for the incumbents.

At some stage, a larger church was built, which eventually had to be heavily buttressed on one side, because the nearby mines were determined to show the Almighty that they too, were capable of moving mountains. A tithe barn stood close by, on the south side of the churchyard. The original Vicarage, a timber-framed building stood, and still stands though altered in appearance, opposite the church in what has been appropriately dubbed 'Old Vicarage Road'.

The old, stone church was fairly small, and the increased population during the late eighteenth century, meant that the building simply wasn't big enough to cope with all the people bursting to get through its doors. Rather than be squashed to death, many worshippers decided to troop off to church at Wellington or Madeley. The answer, it seemed, was to build a brand new edifice closer to the scene of the action. That meant Malinslee, and the new church, called St. Leonard's, was opened there in

1805 with room for 795 bottoms. It was deliberately built on the border of the two townships of Great Dawley and Malinslee. This meant that the increasing populations of Old Park, Dawley Bank and Dawley Green could conveniently pour into the new building in great numbers, and be pretty certain of getting a seat. The old Dawley church became redundant, except for burials, and everybody expected St. Leonard's to become the parish church of Dawley.

However, there were some folk who didn't like that idea and pressure grew on the powers that be, or rather that were, to re-open the old building. The pressure group also managed to drum-up support from other residents, so that by 1818, Services resumed. In 1851, it was recorded that 160 adults attended worship at the Dawley church on a particular Sunday morning, 80 in the afternoon (perhaps others were sleeping-off their roast beef), and a magnificent 370 in the evening. Business was clearly booming, and somehow the money was found to erect a new church fairly close to the site of the original, but without risk of danger from mining subsidence. The church was opened following demolition of its predecessor, and given the name 'Holy Trinity'. Happily, the new and the old were linked by the inclusion of an intricately carved Norman font, a set of ancient bells, a medieval communion plate, and an eighteenth century chalice, within the new place of worship. All those items had played their due part in the history of the Dawley church, even though some of them had been temporarily transferred to Malinslee.

What of events at Malinslee? Well, we do know that there was a small 'chapel' thereabouts from the twelfth century, because the little sandstone beauty is still with us. Before Telford New Town descended upon the scene, the chapel's crumbling remains stood almost unnoticed,

just above the lane from Dawley to Dark Lane as it approached the latter village. In medieval times, it would have been secreted within the vast Wrekin Forest. Weary travellers trying to puzzle out which track to take in getting from say, Stirchley to the market at Wellington, could put up there for the night, and sleep on the problem before setting out again next morning. The redoubtable Rev. Parry wanted it re-opened, back in 1909. He bought the ruins himself (so he wasn't short of a penny or two!) and went so far as to have a design professionally produced, so that it could be opened again for worship. Quite where he thought his congregation was coming from, (since Dark Lane was only a small village with an already existing Methodist chapel) goodness knows. Reality seems to have got the better of sentimentality, however, and Parry abandoned the idea.

St, Leonard's Church, Malinslee

St. Leonard's was built under the direction of Isaac Hawkins-Browne and Thomas Gisbourne, with money left by Browne's great-grandfather, Isaac Hawkins. His will had insisted the cash be used for charitable purposes within the district. It's interesting to observe that in the 1830's, an assistant curate's salary of about £105 per year was paid by a roughly equal contribution of pew rents, and subscriptions from the

major landowners and industrialists. In
return, the assistant curate, who initially
lived at Dawley Green, had to conduct two
Services each Sunday, with sermons. The
number of Services had doubled because
the new parish's population had rapidly
increased, and as we know, lots of folk
were 'clammering' to get into church on a
Sunday. By the 1840's, Malinslee had its
own vicarage, on the north side of the
church, and business became so brisk, that
from the late nineteenth century through to
the early twentieth, a vicar and a curate
were needed in order to cope. Sadly, the
Victorian vicarage went 'the way of all
flesh' in 1975.

In 1883, a mission room was built on the
south side of the churchyard because the
church felt the need to do something
positive to deal with the increasing
problem of drunkenness in the Dawley
Bank area. Ironically, a clergyman from
Burton-on-Trent, a place which owed its
prosperity to the supplying of beer to the
populace, led a determined mission to
those members of the local working
community who couldn't get enough of the
commodity! It should be noted that it was
adults who were being anti-social in those
days, since teenagers weren't invented until
the 1950's. Its initial work done, the
mission hall later became a conventional
church hall, occupying a familiar corner
spot along 'Church Road' until demolition
in 1974.

The main church building itself is
deserving of comment, because it was so
unusual. It was built of local sandstone,
but created in a very distinctive, octagonal
shape, with a square west tower. Where did
such an idea come from? Well, Madeley's
St Michael's church, built in 1794 by one
Thomas Telford, is roughly the same shape.
John Simpson who often did work for
Thomas Telford, constructed St. Leonard's,
but it's a matter of debate between

historians as to whether or not T.T. himself
was responsible for scaling down his
Madeley design at Malinslee. The church
gallery had to be extended in the 1830's to
make room for a further two hundred
enthusiastic worshippers.

The church in the Dawley district which
can really claim not only to stretch its
hands back towards the mists of the ages,
but also to have clearly held on to much of
its original Norman stonework up to the
present day, is St. James's at Stirchley. In
fact, it's the only one in Telford which can
boast a substantial quantity of Norman
masonry within its walls (except, of course,
for the defunct little Norman chapel
mentioned earlier).
Though itself redundant today, St. James's
stands grouped with the old Rectory and
other buildings as an island of antiquity
amid a sea of modern housing. Standing in
the leafy churchyard still gives a feeling of
tradition and timelessness, a village heart
yet without a village community seeking its
ministrations any longer. Even the Rectory
can claim to have seen the more tranquil
days of the early 1700's, having been built
in 1738 to replace a much earlier one.
Although enlarged in the 1830's, and
'modernised' in 1894, it retains an aura
belonging to a bygone period.

At first blush, the church has a slightly
more modern appearance, since its nave
and west tower are dressed in red brick,
though of the eighteenth century. The
chancel, however, is its pride and joy,
being of twelfth century stone, and there is
a Norman chancel arch inside. We already
know that a nineteenth century influx of
population resulted in a heavy demand for
seats in church on a Sunday. The Botfields,
who had also donated plate and bells to
Malinslee church, created space for more
worshippers at Stirchley by building a
north aisle containing a gallery (for the
workers of course). The nave had

distinctive box pews of the eighteenth century, whilst the church also possessed a seventeenth century communion table, a sixteenth century wooden chest, and tower bells spanning the fifteenth and seventeenth centuries.

There are memorials to both the Botfield and Clowes families inside the church, and there is one to the Botfields, in the churchyard. One can only say they probably deserved it. After all, in 1813, Stirchley boasted only about twenty houses, and some of those were nothing more than converted cattle-stalls from which the cattle had been unceremoniously turned out, and the prevailing smell hadn't! It was also said that if a man of little more than average height and wearing a tall hat, ventured into such a property, he would probably have got wedged against the ceiling. The answer would surely have been to be good mannered and take your hat off before going inside! Also *'no man could stand upright in the bedroom, excepting in the centre*'*. The problems that might have caused must be endless.

St. James's Church, Stirchley.

Along came the Botfield's who not only found work for the 'head bangers' to do, but greatly improved the quality of living accommodation in the village. New

cottages were built, and the impressive, surviving 'Northwood Terrace' just down the lane which faces the church, was apparently built for clerical workers at the Botfields' 'Old Park Company'. They must have felt extremely spoiled.

To complete the picture of Dawley's Anglican churches, we must record that in 1845 (a busy year for church building in the Dawley area), St. Luke's Church was built at Doseley. It stands on a little hill near the pipe works, where it can also keep an eye on the track-bed of the former 'Doseley Dodger' railway line. It is therefore quite close to that large, brick bridge with the wonderful echo effect. There appears to be no early tradition of churches in Doseley, but St. Luke's was designed by R. Griffiths of Broseley, who decided to go for a somewhat Norman style in a red and pale brick with sandstone dressings.

St. Luke's was built when the townships of Little Dawley and Horsehay were merged into one parish, known as Dawley Parva. The use of the Latin probably confused some of the local folk, but it was done to distinguish the new parish from the larger one based on Holy Trinity and known of course, as Dawley Magna. Simple, really!

As ever, demand for the new church seems to have been fuelled by the desire of an expanding industrial population to have a convenient, if rather small in this case, place to worship, chiefly on Sundays. Some people think there may have been a medieval stone chapel at Little Dawley (perhaps, the 'Old Manor House' demolished in 1911), but the jury is still out on that. St. Luke's ceased to be St. Luke's in 1974, when it was sold, and eventually became a private house.

In 1865, another smallish Anglican Church was built at Lawley, alongside the main road to Wellington. St. John's was designed by John Ladds, and is clad generally in brick, with a tower having a pointed roof. Lawley seems to have begun life as a Saxon clearing in the Wrekin Forest, and was named after Leah's lee. There was much coal and iron stone mining around Lawley during the industrial revolution, so once again, a place of worship was needed by the many new workers in the area.

Whilst each parish had an Anglican Church of its own, every little group of pits seemed to have an obligatory chapel. No self-respecting neighbourhood would be without one. It was as necessary as a washing-line, or a down-the-garden loo. The Non-Conformist Churches appear to have decided that in order to cope with the competition for souls provided by the Church of England, they would have to take their chapels to the heart of the community which they intended to serve.

John Wesley, the founder of the Methodist Church, had been a clergyman in the Church of England. He wholeheartedly fell out with the Anglican hierarchy, and was no longer allowed to preach in the churches. He spent the latter half of the eighteenth century riding around Britain on horseback, and preaching the gospel to 'the common folk', mostly in the open air. That says a lot for the weather in the British Isles in those days! The main thrust of his mission was to the newly industrialised areas and indeed, he visited the East Shropshire coalfield. Wesley found a soul mate in John Fletcher, Vicar of Madeley. Fletcher, a Swiss National (actually called Jean Guillaume de la Flechere) carried Wesley's torch of evangelism into the coalfield. After conducting evening worship at his church of St. Michael, he would go off and talk informally to groups of miners and foundry workers outdoors, feeling that he could in this way, reach the hearts of men who would never have

darkened the doors of the church. They, in turn, responded to him, and he was convinced that the industrial population needed a form of 'religion' better suited to them, and with which they would feel 'at home'. They had extremely hard lives, and needed convincing that the Lord was as interested in helping them as He was in looking after the more wealthy members of society.

The energetic and gifted Fletcher pursued his philosophy throughout the nearby coalfield, thus embracing the Dawley area as well. The general feeling of helplessness, further fuelled by the failure of the Cinderhill Riots, led the workers and their families to seek solace in the Christian religion. By 1824, at least half the population of Dawley was said to be 'dissenting', that is, worshipping other than in the Church of England. Sometimes, worship was taking place in cottages and houses. A strong revival of religion quickly spread through the area as Fletcher's theories proved to be unerringly accurate. While most people 'followed the Methodists' there was a well-supported Baptist church at Dawley Bank, and also a Congregationalist mission station at Dawley High Street, and, of course, attendances were similarly high at the Anglican churches.

In 1821, a mission of Revivalist Methodists arrived at Dawley. Benjamin Tranter, Manager of the 'Coalbrookdale Company's', Horsehay Works, and a staunch Wesleyan, actively supported the work of the mission, and the next year a large chapel was built at Brandlee. The Brandlee chapel pretty well mirrored Dawley's economic history of the nineteenth and early twentieth centuries. In 1851, it had two hundred members, as industry boomed in Dawley. A fine choral society was formed there, under the initiative of William Tranter, son of

Benjamin. As the pits suddenly stopped breathing, so the numbers of worshippers declined, and by 1937 it was no longer possible to carry on. The chapel was duly closed and demolished. A century or more of fervent worship and tradition was ended, and disappeared practically without trace. Some of the few surviving members transferred to the Methodist chapel in Dawley 'High Street'. The Brandlee chapel had stood beside the road from Dawley to Horsehay, just a few hundred yards down 'Station Road' on the left-hand side. A red brick house now stands in its place, and incorporates the reversed roundel from the former place of worship in its front wall.

The middle portion of the nineteenth century saw the move from house meetings to new chapel buildings gather pace. Such was the demand for places. Several of the church buildings are still standing, and Services held in them. In 'High Street' (or Dawley Green, as some still liked to call it), a plain, octagonal chapel was built in 1819, to be replaced in 1860 by the more striking, blue brick version, with the Italianate tower. That one was designed by a Bridgnorth man named Griffiths, who surely designed Bridgnorth's old market building, which looked as though it was the Dawley chapel's mother! The chapel was demolished in 1976, and replaced on a nearby site by Dawley Christian Centre, in 1978.

Just out of town, the little chapel at 'Finger Road' was built in 1863, but is, alas, no more. A bit further down, at Stirchley Lane, the Wesleyans were unable to buy land in Stirchley village, so the small, brick chapel was built in 1840 in the lane leading to it, but just inside the parish of Dawley. Worship continues there today, and so does the tradition of good choral music that once was a feature throughout the Dawley churches. Some sort of chapel existed at Little Dawley as far back as 1805

(somewhat close to the half-timbered 'Ivy Farm'), but in 1837, a much bigger building replaced it on land kindly donated by the Earl of Craven. It was to cater for the hordes of industrial workers then populating the area. It became nick named 'The Big Penny' probably because, as a Dawley person might put it 'It'd cost a tidy penny to build it'. Worship is still conducted in the building, which dominates the village centre as it ever did. In those early days at least, thirteen of the church's trustees were miners. In 1838, 'The Big Penny' was attracting one-hundred and forty six adults to afternoon worship, but by 1869, the number of regulars had dropped to sixty four. Strangely, those statistics clashed completely with the situation at Dawley Green, where some seventy-nine souls were attending in 1838, whilst one-hundred and twenty one were crammed in by 1869. Was there a transfer of allegiance between the two, or did Little Dawley run out of coal and ironstone quicker than did the centre of Dawley?

The 'Big Penny', Little Dawley Methodist Church

The Little Dawley area was once blessed

with no fewer than three Methodist chapels and Little Dawley's citizens had a mania for nick naming, it seems. Apart from 'The Big Penny', there was 'The Pop Bottle' chapel half a mile down the road at Gravel Leasowes. Officially, it was known as 'Lightmoor Primitive Methodist Jubilee Chapel', but some local wags, allegedly men from the 'Big Penny', quipped that *it's that small in theer, it's no bigger than a pop bottle!'* At least, 'pop bottle' was easier to say than 'Lightmoor Primitive Methodist Jubilee Chapel'. As ever, it was built to satisfy the spiritual needs of a local mining community, consisting chiefly of 'Holywell Lane', Burroughs Bank, and 'Frame Lane'. Its principal function was short-lived, however, since it closed in 1903 after only about forty years service. In the mid-1990's, its interior was greatly modified in order to create a modern dwelling place, so at least this evocative remnant of Little Dawley's past is still with us.

Near Lightmoor village itself, once stood another little chapel dubbed 'Fat Bacon'. This was the place where a pig was fattened annually, and donated as a money-raiser for the chapel anniversary.

The story goes on. Spring Village at Horsehay, near the northern shores of Horsehay pool, decided that it needed a chapel as early as 1816. Also at Horsehay, Moreton Coppice Chapel was built in 1858 alongside the road from Lawley and Wellington as it approaches Horsehay village. Nowadays, the two societies live together at the Moreton Coppice building under the name, 'Horsehay Methodist Church', the 'Pool Chapel' having been demolished in the late twentieth century.

The lonely little outpost at Stoney Hill, near the summit of Jiggers Bank between Horsehay and Coalbrookdale, acquired its chapel around 1838 when there were twenty-two members, yet the numbers fell to nine in 1869, and the chapel had expired by 1880.

The Lawley Bank area was in the thick of the coalfield hurly-burly almost from the start. There can be no surprise then that it took a few chapels as well as the 'New Church' of St. Leonard's at Malinslee, to cope with the bludgeoning demand for pews. Lawley Bank itself had a chapel of sorts as early as 1818. This was replaced by a large, brick chapel in 1840, the one which stood opposite the 'Bull's Head' pub. The 1851 census shows that 235 people attended morning worship, and an incredible 375 were there in the afternoon. Here again, the numbers took a nosedive to 83 in 1869.

Before we leave Lawley Bank, or perhaps more accurately, Dawley Bank, (where on earth does the one end and the other begin?) we need to state that the Baptists were also eager to get in on the seemingly unstoppable juggernaut of regular worship. Small groups had gathered in cottages at such diverse locations as Horsehay, and Little Eyton Fold, and a farmhouse at Lawley Bank. Baptists believe in total immersion in water at a baptism (thus, the person involved needs to have obtained a certain double-figure age), and the first such occurrence in Dawley took place in Morgan's Pool, Rough Grounds. By 1846, a church building was erected on land used previously for bull baiting. There were thirteen members to begin with, yet the church could accommodate two hundred. As elsewhere, people couldn't stop themselves from going to church. In 1851, galleries had to be added to get everyone in. By 1860, the building was creaking at the seams-such was the demand for seats. The church and its attendant schoolroom and minister's house were demolished so that they could be replaced. So, in 1860, the striking building with the blue brick, and ornamental frontage came into existence. It served the area until the end of the twentieth century. An impressive, multi-purpose building designed for a new millenium, opened its doors on Christmas Eve, 2000. Now you can't get more symbolic than that!

A short hop down the road towards Dawley stood Bank Road Methodist Chapel built around 1859, and originally referred to as Dawley Green Lane Chapel. Certainly during the 1940's and 50's its speciality was religious drama. There are black and white photographs in many a Dawley chest of drawers showing church members, attired in 'biblical clothing', acting some scriptural scene having previously plundered their wardrobes in a commendable attempt at authenticity. The church trustees built a 'preacher's house' in 1890, lower down the road in 'King Street', and called it 'Rock Villa'. It still had a resident minister there during the 1950's, but alas, by about 1958, the church was closed and 'Rock Villa' sold. The membership dispersed to various neighbouring churches.

The roll call continues. Old Park had two chapels within a few hundred yards of each other. Near the bottom of the hill, still stands a chapel building bearing a stone tablet engraved with the words 'Primitive Methodist - Bethesda' and dated 1857. The chapel was built very much with the local miners and iron workers in mind. Light Industry now occupies its interior. At the top of the cottage-strewn hill, 'Hill Top' chapel was built in 1856. Its brick features were relieved with distinctive lancet windows having cast-iron frames. Both chapels kept going until the 1960's, when the canker of closure finally caught up with them. The 'Hill Top' chapel buildings and adjoining schoolroom are also still with us, but have been tastefully converted into a private residence. A few of Old Park's cottages also survive, and have acquired a

number of more contemporary neighbours. The old road soon peters out near Hill Top and the vast units of the 'Forge Retail Park' megastores lurk nearby. It's interesting to observe that despite all the chapel building, cottage meetings were being held at Park Forge Row until about 1890, and within Old Park village until as late as 1913.

There's more. Dark Lane's Chapel opened in 1865, but like the rest of that village, was flattened in the 1970's to make room for Telford Town Centre. The Rock Primitive Methodist Chapel, not far from Lawley Bank, and on the road to Ketley, was built in two stages, a brown brick building in 1861, and an adjoining one of blue and yellow brick in 1877. They both stand at the top of Rock Hill, where once a host of mines would have kept them company. The church still functions and some of The Rock's early cottages also survive. It has also acquired new companions in the welter of modern housing built nearby.

Finally, in Dawley itself there was a group of religious edifices whose influence scarcely made it into the twentieth century. The Congregationalists had a mission near 'High Street', around 1866. They had a minister living in the town in the 1870's, but the chapel closed during the 1880's. The building still stands near the top of 'Dun Cow Bank', and was for several years the Dawley branch of Shropshire County Libraries, during the mid-twentieth century. The Gospel Army Mission Room was in 'King Street' from 1883 to 1896, and 'King Street' also hosted a 'Salvation Army' barracks from 1885 to about 1902. While we are in the centre of Dawley, we need to mention that at some stage during the nineteenth century Holy Trinity Church held services for Dawley Green Anglicans, just off the High Street. This was presumably to make sure that they were not tempted to pop into the High Street

Wesleyan chapel, to save their legs from walking all the way to the Parish Church! Visitors to the High Street today, can see the ecclesiastical windows of the upper part of the building, above some shop units, including 'Essence of Beauty', in a side alley not far from 'Tribe Unisex Hair Salon' and 'Supersavers'.

So, once again, why this universal passion for going to church all those years ago? It does seem to be the case that whenever the going gets really tough, people are prepared to acknowledge their need of a force beyond the merely human. The huge general increase in attendance at churches during the World Wars of the 20th century, were a later example of this phenomenon. Of course, Dawley's population suffered a huge decline towards the end of the nineteenth century. This, coupled with a

gradual improvement in working conditions and even more gradual development of 'rival attractions', left the churches suffering a serious fall in attendance by the end of Victoria's reign. The process continued through the twentieth century, as we shall see later.

What we have seen in this Chapter is that during Dawley's industrial boom, people made only too readily for their nearest place of worship, be it the established Anglican building or one of the many chapels which brought religion to where the workers actually lived. It should not be overlooked either, that at many of these places there were week-night meetings of one sort or another, which provided people with things to do, ranging from Bible study to choir practice, and so on. How times have changed!

The former Anglican place of worship, near 'High Street',
now has retail units on the ground floor

Chapter Fourteen

DAWLEY'S 'INTERNATIONALS'
TWO DAWLEY MEN WHOSE FAME TRAVELLED ACROSS THE GLOBE

Practically every little town has its home-made heroes, people who, for one reason or another, have achieved something, perhaps through exercising an exceptional talent, which has caught the attention of the nation at large. In the nineteenth century, Dawley had at least two phenomenally gifted men who were talked about thousands of miles from the shores of Britain - and they hadn't been transported to Botany Bay either!

DR PARKES CADMAN

First, let's have a look at Dr. Samuel Parkes Cadman. Who?- you may be thinking. He's not as well known as the other hero we shall be talking about, Captain Matthew Webb, but he was a remarkable character who discovered his real forte across the Atlantic.

As a youngster, Samuel attended Lawley Bank Wesleyan Church, and when he was sixteen years old, he went to an evangelical service in Dawley, conducted by Rev. J.M. Pascoe. The call to Christian commitment struck a deep chord within the young man. He was later to attend a Wesleyan Theological College at Richmond, Surrey, and became a Methodist Minister. He quickly became renowned for his eloquent preaching style, fulfilling the early promise noted by Sir John Bayley when Samuel had attended Wrekin College.

In the 1890's, Parkes Cadman, having by now married Lillian Wooding of Lawley Bank, went to the USA. His preaching went down a storm with the Americans, but he was to achieve even wider notoriety during the 1920's, when he began preaching on the radio. He could thus be described as a pioneer of the new medium, and he was able to communicate very effectively with a much more extensive audience.

His hobby was collecting china, antiques and rare books. He was especially fond of his copy of the 'Wicked Bible'. This was a seventeenth century Bible whose publishers (presumably accidentally) printed the seventh commandment to read 'THOU SHALT COMMIT ADULTERY'! Surely, this doesn't explain the church's popularity during the nineteenth century!

Parkes Cadman's end was both dramatic and appropriate. Whilst delivering a marathon sermon at the Central Congregationalist Church in New York, he was suddenly taken ill. Nevertheless, he continued preaching for a further hour before agreeing to go to hospital. Sadly, Samuel did not recover. Some 5000 mourners attended his funeral such was the esteem in which he was held. Cadman's wife kept in touch with her home locality, and especially with Rev. Gordon Cartlidge, Vicar of Holy Trinity Church, Oakengates. She was guest of honour at the opening of Ketley Playing Fields in the 1930's.

CAPTAIN MATTHEW WEBB

There's an awful lot more written about

Webb than there is of Parkes Cadman, so we can tell his story in fuller detail. It seems he really was a 'Boy's Own' hero, fearless and a bit of a 'superman' swimmer. He even looked the part of a male pin-up when at 27 years of age, he attracted the civilised world's media to cover his daring deed of swimming the English Channel. His lightish-coloured hair was cut short with a fringe, and he also sported a fashionable 'blond' moustache. If Webb had been born 150 years later, David Beckham would have been given a good run for his money in the beefcake stakes!

Webb seems to have been a larger than life character, as well as a remarkably strong and courageous swimmer. However, let's begin at the beginning. Matthew was born at Dawley in 1848, in a house behind the bottom end of the High Street. He could swim well when he was scarcely out of nappies. They must have had a huge bath at the house! Since his parents had twelve children, this could well have been the case!

Matthew's father was a very popular doctor in the town (as had been his Grandfather). It must have been heartbreaking for the people of Dawley when Dr. Webb decided to 'up sticks' and sample pastures new by moving first to Madeley, then to Coalbrookdale. In the 1850's, that was really entering foreign territory. For Matthew, the great thing about the transfer to Coalbrookdale was that the River Severn was readily to hand, so that he could develop his already impressive swimming skills. Besides this, he had by now outgrown the bath! He seemed destined to make a name for himself as a swimmer. As a young boy in short trousers, he fished one of his brothers out of the Severn when the latter had got into real difficulties. Although all eight brothers learned to enjoy the delights of the Severn, often swimming in a group, it was Matthew who was always the star of the show. He could do acrobatics with great aplomb, and one of his specialities was staying under water for an unbelievably long time.

Another of Webb's hobbies as he grew a little older, was avidly reading books of all sorts. The ones that lit him up the most were those containing stories of the sea. For a person born very much in a land-locked county, Webb developed a surprising fascination with the briny, even singing sea-shanties with some gusto. His imagination was truly ignited and, as a young teenager, he travelled to Liverpool to join the Merchant Navy. Again, he impressed with his strong swimming ability, and twice saved colleagues from drowning. He was the first person to be awarded the Stanhope Gold Medal for bravery (presented by the then Duke of Edinburgh).

Webb worked his way up the promotion ladder in the Merchant Navy, whilst also dedicating himself to increasing his ability to swim long distances. Once, he even won a bet that he could stay in the water longer than a Newfoundland dog! The dog eventually 'threw in the towel' - as a puppy, he must have been brought up in a smaller bath than the one used by Webb! Matthew, despite his promotion was obviously eyeing- up 'the big one'. At the back of his mind, he was planning something pretty spectacular, and it was to happen in a fateful year for him, 1875, the year he was appointed captain of a prestigious vessel called 'Emerald'.

His vision was to become the first person ever to swim the English Channel. At least two other people had attempted this preposterous feat, but couldn't crack it. Webb, the 'superman' from Shropshire, who had amazed people over the years with a variety of deeds of great skill and endurance, and not a little dose of

Captain Webb

but the resilient Webb knew differently. The media got wind of Webb's plans, and assembled at Dover on 12th August, 1875, to witness what they thought would probably be a 'damp squib' of an event. Nevertheless, they were there just in case the impossible happened, and they could give their editors a gigantic 'scoop' - such was the pressure on Webb to produce a show worthy of their attentions. Although the sea was mis-behaving, Webb expected it to calm down later and, at 6.00 p.m., suitably greased with porpoise oil, hurled himself off Admiralty Pier to commence his day-trip to the Continent. Floating out to sea with him was a small flotilla consisting of a lugger, carrying an experienced Channel pilot plus a posse of press men, a rowing boat containing a referee, and a small boat acting as a despatch vessel between the two others. By 7.30 p.m., the press men and others were busy puking into the sea while Webb, who'd been swimming contentedly at one and a half miles per hour, enjoyed a coffee and a chunk of under-done meat. By 11.00 p.m. the sea had got even rougher, and it was becoming difficult to take bearings. Webb, who felt fully fit to carry on, realised that the two occupants of the rowing boat were in some danger from the seriously billowing waves (and no doubt had also turned an enchanting shade of green), and decided that there was no point in carrying on. They had, in fact, just passed the half way mark, but sensibly the decision was made to abort the attempt, and everyone returned by boat to Dover.

eccentricity, had few doubts that he was the man who was born to be the first to do it. He must have amazed his employers and colleagues who had had so much faith in and admiration for him, by retiring from his job to concentrate on his real passion - being a swimmer 'extraordinaire'. He caught the attention of the press by swimming twenty miles down the Thames estuary, from London's Blackwall pier to Gravesend in four and three quarter hours. The man who had grown up bewitched by the sea in all its moods, was now ready to take it on in the most challenging way. Before man reached the South Pole, or climbed Everest, the perceived wisdom was that it probably could not be done. It was the same with the Channel swim in Webb's day. It surely was a swim too far,

Tuesday, 24th August, 1875, was to be the day when Webb achieved international stardom. At nearly 1.00 a.m he once again plunged off Admiralty Pier, and settled into a steady breast-stroke rhythm this time, the venerable deep was altogether more calm and friendly. Some five hours later, and with Webb untroubled, a French ferry passed close by on its way to Dunkerque.

The crew could hardly believe their eyes - an Englishman, supported by a group of hangers-on, was actually trying to swim all the way to France! *'Les Anglais'* they probably shrugged - *'anything to save the price of a ferry ticket'!* They didn't even bother to cheer the man on. It's not recorded whether they made any other kind of gesture.

On pressed Webb, assuring his followers that he was *'as right as a trivet'*. Frequently, shoals of frolicking porpoises swam close by, evidently showing more interest in the strange procession than did the crew of the ferry. Soon after drinking a hot coffee, Webb announced he was going to swim on his side for a change, but he soon wished that he hadn't, because he was stung on the shoulder by a star fish for his trouble. At least the weather was still kind, and he was given brandy to prevent him from being sick. Later, the British ferry, the 'Maid of Kent' glided by towards Calais, and this time some three hundred patriots repeatedly cheered their heroic countryman. That must have helped settle his stomach, to say the least of it.

As the French coast came into hazy view, Webb was still in good spirits. The sea began to remind him that it could bite as hard as the star fish, but our champion was equal to all it could muster against him. After a swig of brandy, he claimed he was *'as right as a bird, bar the sea'*. In fact, his mind as well as his body had been on good form throughout, and now he was bucked up at the thought of achieving his objective, and having a good feed at the end of it. The 'Maid of Kent' came out of Calais harbour as Webb approached, and the enthusiastic crew gave him an encore of cheers. In fact, they cheered even more loudly as they realised that Webb was going to make it.

The statistics show that at 10.04 and 15

seconds, after 21 hours and 40 minutes in the water, and having covered some thirty-nine miles, Captain Webb the Dawley man set foot on French soil, or sand, having fulfilled his dream in amazing fashion. What he had done was to make him known the whole world over.

Someone drove him to the 'Hotel de Paris' where he retired to bed, not surprisingly. He got up for a while later, and had the meal he had longed for. He eventually returned to bed at 10.00 p.m., whereupon a local band which had been hired to serenade him, only succeeded in stopping him from going to sleep! His immediate comments, whether in French, English or broad Dawley, are not recorded. His remarks on receiving a bill from the landlord are, however. Since the account included 50 francs for taking his pulse and examining his tongue, both ministrations unsolicited, Webb told the creditor that he had arrived in Calais without any money on him, and he would pay him the next time he swam over!

In the meantime, Britain was growing increasingly wild over the news that an Englishman had actually achieved the 'impossible'. Webb arrived back to be proclaimed a National hero. The Mayor of Dover thought he had done something that nobody else would ever do again. The 'New York Times' exclaimed that there would not be a person in the entire British Isles who would not by now, have heard of the great man.

After being duly bowled over in the South of England, Webb later made his way to Shropshire, by train. As a measure of the awe in which he was held, a band was playing 'See the conquering hero comes' as he boarded the train for home.This was mega-stardom, if ever there was such a thing! Needless to say, news of the successful channel swim had soon reached the Wrekin area, as indeed had news of

Captain Webb's train journey home. To be honest, Wellington and district went completely mad, but unashamedly so. The narrow approach to Wellington station was jam-packed with people, and there were banners and ribbons flying around as Webb emerged from the station building. He would have been flattered at the sight of the ladies crowding nearby balconies to get a good view of their new found pin-up, but equally exhilarated at the loud shouts of approval from the men folk. For good measure, a military band had been engaged to lead the triumphant procession, and groups of local men were urged to pull Webb's carriage, giving the horses a night off. Predictably, the cavalcade took about two hours to reach Webb's family home at Coalbrookdale. If Wellington had gone mad, Coalbrookdale had gone completely crackers with enthusiasm. A triumphal arch had been erected, bonfires were lit, Chinese lanterns blazed, and there were the ecstatic sounds of a fog signal, cannon, bells and a band combining to assault the ear drums of the returning champion. That French band at Calais would have sounded like a wood warbler by comparison! Someone gave a welcoming speech to which Webb suitably responded.Both Ironbridge and Madeley also feted Webb with vigorous acclaim.

What of Dawley's welcome? After all, Webb was undoubtedly a Dawley man - his home town would surely greet him as a hero! Well of course it did. Rather like the Queen toured her 'London Empire' immediately after her Coronation in 1953, Matthew Webb circumnavigated the district he was brought up in with equal devotion. Thus, there was a procession around the Dawley area and again, everyone turned out to give the man the riotous acclaim his achievement had deserved. In the early twentieth century, a spoof postcard was produced giving the impression that even a pig had reared itself onto a wall, to watch Webb's procession go by. As we shall later learn, that was simply down to a local photographer having fun!

Neither Coalbrookdale nor Ironbridge has any lasting memorial to the great man, despite the overwhelming welcome they gave to Webb at the time of his triumph. Dawley, it must be said does have one. It was a while getting there, but in 1909, following a successful public appeal, a concrete edifice (forever after referred to simply as 'the monument') was erected at the bottom of the High Street not far from the house where Webb was born. It wasn't just a lump of shaped concrete. It was also meant to be functional, having a 'chandelier' of gas lamps at the top, and a drinking bowl on each of the four sides of the main structure. The bowls, complete with cast-iron tap knobs, were still in place during the 1950's. They had long since ceased to purvey any water, except when rainwater collected in the bowls to be mixed with a dust-polluted cocktail of fag-ends and sweet wrappers. That was by no means the intention of the 'city fathers' when the stone tribute was originally installed! What is disappointing, is the 'monumental' understatement contained in the inscription engraved on one of the sides. It blandly informs us that - 'in addition to several feats of life saving, he (Webb) also swam the English Channel'. Admittedly, most Dawley people even today, are not very adept at 'blowing their own trumpets' but for goodness sake, here we are commemorating a man who had done something completely earth-shattering, and yet we had almost apologised for mentioning it on his memorial!

The Captain Webb story does not have a happy ending. He got frustrated because none of his subsequent career plans got off the ground. He wanted to be an inventor, such as the producer of a flying machine.That would have really put him on the map. He also fancied running some sort of swimming academy, but surprisingly, his efforts were to little avail. He wanted to prove both to himself and the general public, that he was still capable of achieving something truly spectacular. He scratched his head, and decided to attempt swimming the rapids at the base of Niagara Falls. Once again, no one had succeeded with this quest before, and Matthew was in no doubt that he was the one to do it. He had given many swimming exhibitions in Shropshire since the Channel swim, but never made enough money from his various activities to make him a wealthy man. If he swam the Niagara rapids, surely both his reputation and his bank balance would be truly magnified.

In 1883, the 35 year old Webb, his wife and two young children sailed to America for the attempted swim. Such was Webb's confidence in his ability, that he was prepared to take his family with him to witness what he expected would be his most outstanding achievement.

The press, as ever, were eager to follow his exploits, although they and others had warned him that this one was probably a no-win situation. Tragically, their predictions proved correct. On 24th July, 1883, Matthew Webb the man from Dawley, whose life had been punctuated by outrageous acts of skill and daring, stepped into the swirling waters beneath Niagara Falls. At first, all seemed to be going well, and he eventually got through the trickiest part of the rapids where others before him had come to grief. He must have thought he'd cracked it at that stage, but a skulking whirlpool took hold of him and dragged him under the water. He was never to emerge again, alive. In fact, the river ultimately carried him some seven miles downstream, and several days elapsed before the body was found. Sadly, the man who had always felt at home in the water had reluctantly yielded his life to its unforgiving powers. Apart from the monument at Dawley 'High Street', there stands a granite memorial to Captain Matthew Webb at Oakwood Cemetery, Niagara Falls, New York State.

Following the successful channel swim, Webb was immortalised by an enterprising matchstick-making company, who put 'Captain Webb Matches' on the market. The box would include a portrait of the man himself duly sporting that trendy moustache, and wearing some sort of stripy bathing suit. Remarkably, the brand survived to at least the mid-twentieth century. Dawley people, on seeing a box of the said matches, would look at the portrait with a feeling of pride and think, 'that's our boy', even though he had been dead for up to seventy years. Present-day Dawley calls one of its junior schools 'Matthew Webb School' and there has been a 'Webb Crescent' ever since a major council house building programme was begun in the early 1950's.

The new doctor's surgery complex in 'King Street' was named 'Webb House', when it opened in 2002. It stands virtually opposite where Doctor Browne and others practised decades ago. There is also a 'Captain Webb Way' nearby.

Incidentally, one of Matthew's brothers succeeded his father as family doctor in Dawley, and his son Henry was to marry Mary Meredith, later to become the celebrated Shropshire author, Mary Webb. Thus, the name Webb lives on in one way or another, to illustrate the achievements of gifted Salopians.

Chapter Fifteen

Meanwhile, back at the High Street

Dawley life towards the end of
the nineteenth century

We know that a colossal slump took place in the fortunes of Dawley's industries as the late eighteen hundreds wore on. This didn't mean that everyone just packed up and disappeared, far from it. New technology being used in the Black Country, coupled with the working-out of many of Dawley's mines, saw activity tumbling from its earlier heights, but the town and many of its inhabitants soldiered on. Amid all this, the foundations were being laid for many of the features that became so familiar to generations of Dawleyites during the momentous twentieth century.

By the time in question, the High Street was looking more and more like a High Street should, its long rows of shops on either side giving the place the air of a 'proper' small town. It was a fitting centre for Dawley's population, which peaked at 11,254 in 1871, and that of the outlying villages. It should be mentioned that by 1891, there were some 4,000 fewer people living in the area, due to industrial stagnation. People were getting out of Malinslee from about 1878, some deciding to emigrate. Australia seemed to be the favourite destination for various families who believed that a brighter future lay ahead of them on the other side of the world. Business was sufficiently brisk for an emigration agent to make a go of it at Dawley Bank in the late1880's.

Nevertheless, Dawley still believed in its own future and its amenities and social life

were developing apace. For many working people, their shrine was either the Church or the pub. Dawley had over twenty pubs and a further twenty-eight 'beer retailers,' with the 'High Street' area having the lion's share of them. Two of Dawley's best known (and still functioning) pubs are the 'Elephant and Castle' at the junction with 'Burton Street', and the 'Lord Hill' at the opposite end of 'High Street', both of which have existed since at least the early nineteenth century. The same could also be said about the 'Cheshire Cheese' at Doseley, except that at one time it offered stabling for one horse. In the same boat are also the 'Unicorn' at Little Dawley (three horses), the 'White Hart' at Hinkshay (no fewer than four horses), and the 'Rose and Crown' at Stirchley (just room for one horse, again).

Apart from downing pints, enjoying a sing song, and coping with the smell of one to four horses at the local, did Dawley people know how to have fun? Of course they did. The grime and drudgery of daily working life was such that amusement had to be sought wherever time and money permitted. 'Dawley Wake' had been an annual event since the early eighteenth century. It was originally held on All Saints Day and with the 'dark nights' upon them, Dawley's citizens would have had every excuse to let their hair down, get drunk, and generally enjoy the festivities before the winter set in. The last recorded Wake was in 1873, and was held at the end of

73

September. For some reason, the people couldn't wait until the clocks changed that year.

The fun didn't end there, because the 'big top', well, perhaps it wasn't all that big, but certainly a circus anyway, visited Dawley on a regular basis during the latter part of the nineteenth century. What an attraction that must have been to a people who had no television sets, and probably few picture books to warn them in advance of what an exotic animal looked like. In 1843, sport was represented by both horse and foot racing at Dawley Green, and in 1863, the annual June livestock fair began. The latter served to show that the Dawley area was still partly agricultural, and the event itself really took off with the local populace. It became a time for indulging in something very different from the daily grind, and soon had a social as well as an agricultural purpose. In time, it was referred to as the 'pleasure fair'. Yet more sports and games followed on after the animals had been put to bed. Sadly, the entire event seems to have petered out by about 1895.
On the down side, it has to be reported that bull bating had a following in the Dawley area, as in Oakengates also. There was certainly a bullring at Dawley Bank in the early eighteen hundreds. Cock fighting was another 'sport' popular with some, and there is a suggestion that it continued in Dawley until the early twentieth century.

While all this was going on, Dawley Green was becoming better known as 'High Street', Dawley. It had shops and offices, and the feel of a small town centre. Local farmers and others were producing foodstuffs in sufficient quantity to supply eager Dawley stomachs, and needed a suitable market place at which to peddle their wares. Dawley's Saturday market continued into the early 1900's, and like the Wakes and Pleasure Fair before it, became for a while, an indispensable social

meeting point for Dawley's inhabitants. The facade, slightly altered, still stands today, and there are shops enclosed within the arches. We will tell some tales of the market's latter days in a later chapter.

THE DEMONSTRATION

Mention 'The Demmon.' to anyone who had lived in the Dawley area at any time during the first seven decades of the twentieth century, and eyes would light up. An instant flicker of recognition would spring into the facial expression, just as if you had asked people to recall their favourite grandparent. 'The Demmon' (short for 'The Dawley Sunday Schools Demonstration') was for many years one of two truly big events in Dawley's calendar, the other being the annual carnival, which brought the people out on to the streets in great numbers during the twentieth century. Both events created a buzz of excitement akin to the welcome once given to Captain Webb.

Some of the Demonstration's earliest traditions were still being followed in the latter years.

So what was the Demonstration all about? This yearly pageant so much a part of

Dawley life until the 1970's, first saw the light of day as early as 1876. Before even that, scholars of the various Sunday Schools were given an annual treat, probably including sports followed by a tea-party, and also involving some sort of procession. Some forward-looking person, or persons, decided it would be a good idea to get the different Sunday Schools to join forces and have one whacking great procession through the town's streets. There would be an open-air religious service, then the enthusiastic youngsters would return whence they had come, so that the sports and tea parties could still be enjoyed on their individual patches, as before. A wonderful idea, it gave the children the best of both worlds, an exciting, marathon walk through the town in company with lots of others, and also the chance to pig into sandwiches and jelly on arriving back at their own Sunday School premises, or an adjoining field.

It was the Non-Conformists (mainly Methodists, Baptists and Congregationalists) who dreamed up the idea, though no one is completely sure why. We do know that in the 1840's, Primitive Methodism reached the Dawley area. It was inspired by revivalists such as Rev. John Moore, of Wrockwardine Wood, who could see the need for the Church to cater more meaningfully for the deep emotional needs of a bruised and battered working-class population. Cottage meetings and great open-air services were frequently held. The 'Prims.' would often process along the streets and roads to the meeting place, witnessing not only to their own faith, but no doubt hoping to attract more people to 'come and join us'. Maybe it was a logical progression from those humble origins to the grand parades that were to become such a familiar sight in Dawley for almost one hundred years. It is believed that in parts of Northern England, similar 'demonstrations' at one time also

took place. For many years, the Dawley version was held each August Bank Holiday Monday, when that day was celebrated on the first Monday in August.

The name 'Demonstration' actually meant a procession of Christian witness. Thus, the parade of countless Sunday Schools each one walking behind its own elaborate and distinctive banner, was meant to be a signal to the public. It was something to the effect of *'look at us, we go to Sunday School regularly, we are joining together with other Sunday Schools today, and we and many grown-ups as well are going to worship in the open-air. This is something worth making a fuss about.'* In the 1878 'Demmon.' (as people liked to call it), a staggering two thousand five hundred children plus about three hundred teachers and others, made up the procession (there were even more at the first one in 1876). There were so many that it must have been easier to march than stand in the High Street watching them all go by.

In the earlier years, the town itself contributed to the occasion's somewhat festive air by decorating the High Street to greet the marchers. Flowers and greenery, not to mention a multitude of flags, were on show so that nobody could be in the slightest doubt that this was considered a very exceptional occasion. Most of all, there were people, masses of them, filling the pavements with an eagerness which couldn't have been much less enthusiastic if the Queen was passing by.

In those days, and in fact until the start of World War II, the procession would converge on a field at the corner of 'King Street' and 'Meadow Road' (roughly where 'The Royal' cinema was eventually built). When the cavalcade reached Mr. William Rushton's field at 'King Street', the proceedings would take on a fairly standard format. There was hymn singing led on the first occasion by Silas Richard North, a Baptist, and on the next twelve occasions by the redoubtable Ephraim Worsey, a Wesleyan from Lawley Bank chapel (sometimes assisted by Thomas Jones). Worsey apparently hailed from Worcestershire, and he was to play a major part also in the development of Lawley Bank Wesleyan Church choir. Anybody who could get three thousand children and others singing reasonably in tune and to time in the open-air must have had a gift beyond the merely ordinary! Usually, there was also a rousing rendering of 'God Bless our Sabbath Schools' (to the tune of the National Anthem), and various votes of thanks were given before the marchers returned through the main streets and back to the individual chapels.

The practice of giving an address appealing to both children and adults seems to have appeared much later than the Victorian era. So did the use of the hymn 'Onward Christian Soldiers' which, although first sung at the 1895 event, didn't become a permanent fixture until sometime during the twentieth century, when it seemed to be the unofficial anthem of the annual Demonstration.

Sadly, the weather sometimes played a disappointing role in the proceedings. A sharp shower came during the hymn singing in 1889, and the Rev. G.G. Pinder said they were indebted to God for the showers that had refreshed the earth. However, in 1905, persistent rain in the days leading up to the Bank Holiday had the organising committee wondering whether to switch the muster from the field to some drier spot. It was decided to go ahead as usual, but as the Horsehay cohort was entering the field, down came the rain in buckets full, and people 'ran helter-skelter for refuge' - some even diving under the speaker's platform! Needless to say, on that occasion, the event was then called off.

Since the Demonstration figured prominently in Dawley life until 1974, it became very much a part of the town's twentieth century folklore, also. In a later chapter, we shall join a typical 1940's march from one of the outlying churches, to see what taking part was really like for a young child at that time.

Chapter Sixteen

THE DAWLEY WE KNEW BEGINS
TO TAKE SHAPE

People who lived in Dawley during the pre-Telford part of the twentieth century, would easily be able to tell you about its main features. It had a compact main street, (including a post office) a police station, a Town Hall, an attractive park, a gas works, library, and an assortment of public houses. These were familiar old friends which gave a sense of identity and seeming permanence to a mature, small town where little seemed to change from one year to the next, and that was exactly how the inhabitants liked it.

The strange thing is that while Dawley's industries were declining during the late Victorian era, the town itself was steadily developing its facilities in a way that suggested a dogged faith in a successful 'after life' during the next century. We already know that Dawley Green had been successfully transformed into Dawley 'High Street'. This had become the busy shopping and commercial centre where local people loved to meet and natter, as well as stock up with the necessities of life.

What of the large, dark and austere looking building shyly standing half way down 'Dun Cow Bank'? For long enough, it has been known as the Town Hall, but this was not the seat of local government administration usually associated with such a title. Its dreary appearance was chiefly explained by the fact that it was originally built as a Temperance Hall in 1873. After the Temperance Movement fizzled out (presumably due to a lack of intemperate clients) the town was left with a pretty hefty, but not very pretty 'white elephant' of a building. For a time, it was used as the

Royal Windsor Variety and Picture Palace, but even that had gone the way of all flesh by the time of World War I. In the 1920's, Dawley Urban District Council took it on, and received some sort of an income from lettings for public meetings, concerts and dances.

Dawley Town Hall, and Dun Cow Bank.

While we are talking about the Council, how and when did that important undertaking come into being? If we go back to 1807, we can see that there was some early public dabbling in people's affairs, when the parish began taxing every householder who owned a dog (talk about a tax on wealth!). This was known as the Poor Rate (could that have resulted in an increase in stray dogs about the place?), whereby those who coughed up were supporting the really poor of the locality. A 'poor house' was rented and enlarged by the parish in Dawley Green Lane. An unfortunate cholera epidemic that hit

Dawley in the early 1830's caused a board of health to be formed in the area. From this, Dawley became an urban sanitary district in 1876, with a board of some twelve members. By process of evolution, the board became an urban district council in 1894, with its office within the Market Hall. So there you have it. Out of genuine public deprivation, came the council. Dawley Urban District Council was to gain in influence through most of the twentieth century, so we will catch up with it, as with many other fledglings of the Victorian era, when we look more closely at that particular epoch, later.

The early Sunday Schools were the places at which many working-class children received their basic education, but the time came when steps were taken to encourage the adult population in their reading skills, as well as the general pursuit of knowledge. Thus, in about 1856, a building in the High Street was designated a Library and Reading room. By 1870, it had somehow acquired the rather grand title of Literary Institute, and had a committee to run it. By the turn of the century, it was said to have some three thousand volumes, and the committee secretary was the Headmaster of Langley Board School. Reading seems to have really caught on, so that a further building was occupied at 'Bank Road', and called Dawley Bank Institute, between 1910 and 1917.

One of the great pleasures of Dawley for many years, and for all generations, was that nicely kept arena just off the main shopping street, known as 'the park'. It's still there, but perhaps doesn't receive the overall patronage it once did. The Victorians had a passion for creating public parks giving working people a breath of fresh air, and somewhere pleasant to relax as they escaped the grime of their working existence. In Dawley's case, it was the death of Victoria in 1901 that led to the

creation of a public park in her memory. Before that, in 1886, Rev. R.C. Wanstall, vicar of Dawley Parish Church, had tried to initiate a recreation ground on the site of an old cricket field given to the parish in the mid-nineteenth century, and he even proposed that the site could be levelled and converted, using unemployed workers. The idea didn't get off the drawing board, yet in 1901 a two-acre site was given to the town by landowners W.S. Kenyon-Slaney, of Hatton Grange, Shifnal, and H.C. Simpson of Horsehay. Ironically, part of the chosen site had been the very cricket ground championed by Rev. Wanstall fifteen years earlier.

The 'Elephant and Castle', at the junction of 'High Street' with 'Burton Street'.

Another great innovation in Dawley in the eighteen hundreds, was the setting up of the gas company, so that at least the main streets of the town could be illuminated by the new marvel. To make sure all went swimmingly, the Dawley Gas Company was formed in 1848. They built a gas works in the rocky 'Chapel Lane', at the south end of 'Chapel Street' on the way to Pool Hill. Suitable street lighting was erected around the central part of the town, and it seems the bulk of the cost was raised from ratepayers.

In 1849, an impressive 'bun-fight' was staged at the 'Elephant and Castle', to commemorate such a colossal achievement. Presumably, most of the money for the gas lighting must have come from an exclusive coterie of rate payers, since each of the fifty or so diners seems to have been a 'somebody'. The 'Wellington Journal and Shrewsbury News' recorded that they were treated to *'a most sumptuous repast, consisting of every delicacy of the season'*. It doesn't get much better than that, does it? After the meal there were numerous speeches, as one might suppose, and also songs from local soloists. Toasts were both proposed and drunk, to - the Queen, Duke of Wellington, the Army, Lord Hill, (Lord Lieutenant of the County - as opposed to the rival pub down the road), and Mr. Slaney, Lord of the Manor of Dawley. A toast was also drunk to 'The Ladies', after an eloquent, not to say Pickwickian speech on the subject by Edmund Garbett Esquire, coupled with suitably poetic quotations from the bard Alexander Pope. The 'city fathers' certainly knew how to have a good time in those days, and all they were doing was celebrating the opening of a gas works!

An interesting side line to all this is the speculation in the same newspaper report as that quoted above, that the town of Dawley with its population of some 12,000 souls, and its recently acquired amenities, would rise to become 'a second Wolverhampton'. At first blush, this seems little more than mere journalistic hype, or was it an inspired piece of crystal-ball gazing, in view of the New Town development of a hundred or so years later? It's fair to say that had Dawley become 'a second Wolverhampton' from 1850 onwards, that unique semi-rural, small town ethos being celebrated in this

book, would have been snuffed out several generations before our boy and his bike rides came on the scene. Surely it was right that the town should have remained small and intimate, despite some times of real hardship through much of the twentieth century.

We mustn't forget that also during the second slice of the nineteenth century, another novelty known as the railways stretched its expanding tentacles into the Dawley area. In fact, it's quite accurate to say 'the Dawley area' in this case, rather than simply Dawley, because neither of the two lines actually entered the town at all. Presumably due to a combination of difficult terrain, and the welter of mine shafts encircling central Dawley, the building of the railways was shunted to the suburbs, where the lines could worm their way through the district with comparative ease.

The Shrewsbury and Birmingham Railway got in first, by building a branch from their main line north of Shifnal and through Lightmoor, in 1854. Today, this is the line that takes incessant, huge loads of coal to Ironbridge 'B' Power Station. Next, in 1857, came the Wellington and Severn Junction Railway (substantially owned by the Coalbrookdale Company) who ran their branch line from Ketley Junction (yet another spur of the main Birmingham line) to Horsehay. The one-platform station bore the name 'Horsehay and Dawley' although it was about three-quarters of a mile out of Dawley. The aim was to get a line down to Coalbrookdale and beyond. Thus, around 1858, the track was extended to Lightmoor, and by 1864 it reached that 'hot bed' of industry, Coalbrookdale. Surprisingly, given the size of the working population of that time, some of the intermediate stations did not see the light of day until well into the twentieth century. The line's original purpose must have been to facilitate the carriage of goods, and passenger mobility was clearly not a big issue at that time.

When the Wellington to Coalport line was opened in 1860, the cunning engineers 'borrowed' a lengthy stretch of the old track bed of the Donnington to Blists Hill canal. From Wombridge to Aqueduct, they simply plonked the railway onto the former canal track-bed, not only rubbing the canal-builders' noses in it, but also making life much easier for themselves. Since the canal had passed close to Stirchley, it made sense to build a railway station near the lane connecting the village with Dawley.

Presumably, to give it a bit of commercial pull, the station was named 'Stirchley and Dawley', even though it was at least a mile from the centre of the town. The station at Dark Lane was called 'Malinslee'. Admittedly, it was close to the original Malinslee, but a long walk from the community that was to develop around St. Leonard's Church.

As a momentous century drew to its close, Dawley was slipping further into economic gloom. The working population, when not at work, was attending church and chapel meetings, drinking at the pub, indulging in rabbit coursing, bird trapping, playing quoits and dabbing, and generally hoping a new century would somehow bring with it a renewed means of 'keeping going'.

THE CENTURY THAT GREETED OUR PARENTS

Chapter Seventeen

TURN OF THE CENTURY DAWLEY

WHO WAS WHO IN THE HIGH STREET

Whenever the calendar turns over the page to reveal a brand new century, it seems to trigger off a reaction in the Great Order of Things. The fledgling era seems determined to say to the world something like 'hey, I'm the twentieth century, this is the start of something big and new. Things are going to be different around here from now on.'

The parents of the boy whose bicycle rides around Dawley were described in the earlier chapters, were born during the first decade of the twentieth century. By the time of their birth, the new age had already got down to the serious business of changing the world order. Queen Victoria died (1901) after 64 years on the throne - change doesn't come much greater than that! The Labour Party was founded in 1900. 1901 also saw the Commonwealth of Australia being established, the first transatlantic radio transmission, the launch of Britain's first submarine, and the marketing in America of the first safety razor blades. In 1902, Britain, under Kitchener, finally managed to get the better of their Dutch rivals, the Boers, in South Africa. The Wright brothers got their aeroplane to stay in the air for a while in North Carolina, in 1903. In 1904, Henry Ford set a speed record for a car, of 91.37 miles per hour. Such events may seem far removed from the deteriorating pit-mounds of Dawley. Nevertheless, these and other happenings would have a profound impact on life in this country generally as the century progressed, and thus, of course, on every local community. Above all, this was to be a century of enormous, if gradual change, and generations of Dawley people would inevitably be caught up in what was going on in the wider world. Let's catch a glimpse of the way things were for Dawley children born in the early 1900's.

We'll start at the hub of the district, 'the Street'. Like any self-respecting High Street, its main business was to supply an expectant public with what it needed. In fact, in those days, the emphasis of the rows of little stores was on supplying what the customer wanted, rather than what the retailer wanted them to want!

Among those early-century traders were Clayton's the butchers, occupying a shop at the bottom of the street, which much later in the century became Yates's the butchers, and very much later, what was to become the Telford and Wrekin Council shop, then the Wrekin Housing Trust shop. Somewhat behind this property had once been the house where Captain Webb had been born. Clayton's speciality was pork, including its own pork sausages and that perennial favourite, the home-made pork pie. Further up the street, Dockley Lewis was also a butcher. The main newsagent was Thomas Weaver (who was also a printer), and his wife kept a millinery shop next door. Who on earth could make a living out of making and selling ladies hats in Dawley today? The well-known Greenhall family ran a wholesale grocery business from premises next to the High Street Methodist Chapel. For years, Greenhall's supplied many of the small grocery shops around the district. W.L. Woolley took on the business in later decades, and their large, green delivery van became a familiar site around the area, certainly in the 1950's.

Benjamin Moses Preece and his wife

Elizabeth, ran a shoe shop almost opposite the Market Hall. That bald statement hides the fact that Preece's is Dawley 'High Street's' longest surviving business. The Preeces are thought to have started up somewhere between 1851 and 1861, and dealt in both the selling and repairing of shoes. Their son, William, carried things on through the early decades of the twentieth century, and his son took over the reins in the latter part. He is still trading from the original premises, selling though no longer repairing shoes. His wife, Barbara, looks after the shop, and the name 'Preece' still adorns the front of the premises. To have kept going for such a long time is a wonderful achievement in 'bucking the trend'.

The oldest surviving retail business in Dawley 'High Street'.

Herbert Slaney-Jones ran his ironmonger's store, as he was to do for several decades to come. In the early days there was a large space between Slaney-Jones's shop and the one next door. For a time, Dockley Lewis's sisters traded from that open area, but subsequently, Mrs. Slaney-Jones had it covered in so that a quite impressive, glass-fronted shop was created from which she sold quality chinaware, including the

famous 'Coalport'.

Invariably, a local trader was more than just a person who bunged your required goods onto the counter. Many of the street's shopkeepers were among the town's well-known personalities. For instance, it seems that Dockley Lewis had a certain air of authority about him. The church going, Old Hall educated Dockley was clearly one to approach with respect.

Benjamin Moses Preece was described as a big man, who could often be seen standing outside his shoe shop. With arms folded, he would while away the intervals between customers by intently observing the traffic passing along the High Street.

Richard Somers dealt in leather, and some shoemakers from Wellington would make the journey to Dawley in order to purchase the raw material from him. Richard was also a churchman, and he often read the lesson using a very distinctive voice. Slaney-Jones was yet another 'big churchman'.

In fact, Dawley's turn of the century shopkeepers must have been a pretty up-right lot since many of them were regular worshippers, notably at Holy Trinity Parish Church. What on earth would they have made of our contemporary Sunday trading laws? It was quite usual in those days for a trader's family to occupy an entire row of pews on a Sunday. Several of the traders in the early nineteen hundreds were still going strong in later decades, and we shall renew our acquaintance with them later in the book.

One well-known Dawley enterprise was moving closer to its demise during the early nineteen hundreds. This was the once thriving Dawley Saturday market. For over thirty years, merchandisers and customers had mingled in the busy atmosphere of frantic buying and selling, chiefly at the Market Hall which fronted the High Street. By all accounts, things were still pretty lively at the turn of the century, and for a while thereafter. Sadly, the lack of spending power of Dawley's reduced population caused this well-loved institution gradually to fade away, leaving just the brick facade in the street as a ghostly tomb stone reminding passers-by of what used to be. Exactly what were those early nineteen hundreds Saturday market days like in Dawley? Fortunately, there are those whose memories have been passed down, so that some sort of picture still emerges.

At the market there were, as there must have been for years, numerous open stalls behind the Market Hall frontage and clock tower. In order to keep children amused, while parents zig-zagged around the stalls, there was a set of swingle-boats also behind the Market Hall. One elderly lady, who was a teenage girl during those days, has said she used to visit the market on Saturday nights for 'some fun with the boys'. On one occasion, after asking her brothers to take her on the swingle-boats, the boats swung so high that she reckoned she could see into the High Street, and could make out Pugh's shop. In the Dawley vernacular, the lady exclaimed that the exhilarating experience *'frittened me to jeth'* (frightened me to death)!

Such was the clamour to provide the Dawley public with the necessities of life, that there were over-spill stalls in parts of the street itself. One was on the corner of 'High Street' and 'Meadow Road'. There was one on the forecourt of the 'Crown Inn' in the middle of the street, and another on the 'Lord Hill' forecourt, right at the bottom of 'High Street'. Lo, and behold, the present - day, and relatively new, Friday street market also has stalls at the latter two locations, as well as a scattering of others

throughout the length of the thoroughfare.

As with the shops, the market stalls were manned by local characters who had become 'household names' around the district. There was farmer Joe Brown from Manor Farm, near Dawley Parish Church. He sold meat and other farm produce. Hubert Jaundrell, yet another butcher, was the one who had the stall at the corner of 'Meadow Road'. Later, he was to have a butcher's shop in 'Burton Street'. (The street was named after Robert Burton, a Dawley landowner in the early 19th Century, by the way.) Jack Timmis ran what was gleefully referred to as a 'variety stall'. Dickie Bird, who lived in a cottage in 'Finger Road' sold genuine home-made humbugs and toffee. People said his humbugs were unbeatable, yet he was also sometimes known as 'Toffee Bird', so the sticky stuff couldn't have been too bad either. His son, Tom, would have the job of pushing a three-wheel trolley up the hills to Dawley on market days, lugging a fresh batch of sweetmeats to Bird's Market Hall stand. So confident was Dickie of the quality of his fare, that he would put his hand out and offer a sample humbug exhorting in his distinctive nasal voice *'always taste before you buy'*. You can't say fairer than that can you? In fact, those words became Dickie Bird's eternal epitaph.

There seems to have been pretty stiff competition in the confectionery stakes, since Joe Ball, from Horsehay, also sold home-made sweets. He was the one whose little shop near Horsehay works had the words 'Grocer and Sugar Boiler' painted on the shop sign. During the week, Joe could be seen wheeling his three-wheel truck (three-wheel truck making must have been a boom industry, also) around various parts of Dawley, bringing his goodies to the attention of a wider public. His wife,

Bessie, continued the sweet making tradition, and the shop flourished into the 1950's. Sam Bould, from Ironbridge, was yet another toffee maker. He was 'bold' enough to cart his goods right into enemy territory, by selling at Dawley market. His toffee would be displayed on a tin tray, and he used a small hammer to break it up into little pieces to meet customers' requirements. Needless to say, there were many other stalls, several of them supplying less luxurious goods than humbugs and toffee, but it's strange how the novel always sticks (if you'll pardon the pun) in the mind, rather than the hum-drum bare necessities.

Perhaps more than anything else, people remember the heady atmosphere of those hectic Saturdays. Folk would start turning up in greater numbers after lunch. Many workers had to put in a half-day shift on a Saturday, and wouldn't get paid until going home time. This was an astute way of getting the workforce in on a Saturday. However, the real excitement started after tea, especially during the dark evenings. Money was relatively scarce and family fun not that much more plentiful during weekdays, so Saturday night was the night to go into town 'en-masse'. The entire town seemed to have turned out, so that people were virtually shoulder to shoulder, as they caroused along the High Street, or wandered around the market stalls. Gas lamps would light the way, and add their own hissing glow to the ambience. Even the shops did a better trade than at any other time of the week. The tradition of crowded Saturday nights stretched back to the earliest days of the market. There is a (probably true) story that in the days of the fledging market, a postman trying to get the mail coach through the throng,

threatened to draw his revolver if people didn't stop getting in his way!

For shoppers with the stamina to last the whole evening, there was a huge incentive in hanging around until the stall-holders were all but ready to pack up and go home. Perishable items such as meat had to be sold off there and then. Refrigeration as we know it, was not available in those times, and the meat simply had to go or be thrown away. Shrewd customers who didn't mind late nights, would patiently wait until the prices fell to give-away levels. They would then proudly march home with a joint to feed a large family, having paid a pittance for the privilege.

Dawley's industries continued to decline as the new century progressed. As money became yet more scarce, so the viability of the market fell under serious threat. During the second decade the main market was in its death throes, although a few traders carried on selling. To all intents and purposes, a much loved part of Dawley life had passed into history. Of the remaining stall-holders, Dickie Bird and his humbugs and toffee were the last to disappear. Mr. Bird had jealously guarded the recipes throughout his working life, and then passed them onto his son who apparently did not put them to any practical use. At least the Market Hall frontage still stands near the top of the High Street. It looks forlornly down at today's shoppers, wistfully remembering those evocative Saturdays, when the whole town came clamouring for the goods and the banter dispensed by so many well-loved characters.

Chapter Eighteen

THE ONLY WAY IS DOWN

DAWLEY ON THE SLIDE

Those of us who went to bed on 31st December, 1999, and got up again on 1st January, 2000, will know just how optimistic people can get the moment a new century begins. Life being the way it is, it's not long before we realise that the calendar has no power at all to wave a magic wand, and suddenly make all things new and better. It didn't take long for Dawley to realise that the twentieth century was going to see a continuance of the struggle to make a living, which had set in during the previous few decades.

In 1901, the large Stirchley Ironworks, situated about one-third of a mile north of Stirchley and Dawley railway station, was dramatically closed. The workers had become extremely disgruntled at the level of pay they were receiving for their efforts. They had, of course, no trade union to fight their corner, and all they could do was plead with the management to lend a sympathetic ear. This didn't pull up many trees, and eventually some of them decided to get a bit physical. It is reported that clods were thrown at owner, Mr. Kenyon-Slaney, who was none too impressed with this method of attracting his attention. *'You'll remember this. I'll close these works, and you'll regret having done this,'* was apparently his well-measured reply. He was true to his word, and soon afterwards the entire plant was shut down. Whether imminent closure was inevitable any way is open to speculation. However, close it did, throwing many Dawley families into poverty. Whatever the causes of the termination, the result so far as the workers

were concerned, was catastrophic. Those directly affected received a real taste of what poverty was all about. Boys would have to be content with patches sewn onto worn-out trousers - a new pair would have been out of the question. The children of unemployed fathers were given free bread and jam at school. One more fortunate woman, who was even more fortunate to have a butcher as her father, would once a week, put meat and vegetables into a boiler of water. She then allowed women whose families were suffering the deprivation, to fill their jugs with the resultant soup, and take it home to feed their families.

Some ex-Stirchley employees managed to find work at the nearby chemical factory (whose tall, brick chimney still towers over Telford Town Park). One gentleman went to work at the John Maddocks Foundry at Oakengates. As was the custom of the day, he walked to work (a good four miles) setting out at 5.25 a.m., so that he could clock-on at 6.00 a.m. He was so consistently punctual, that people at Hinkshay, and at Stone Row near Malinslee, would set their clocks by the sound of his clogs. How he managed to set his own clock so accurately remains a mystery!

For over one hundred years, pits - mostly producing coal and ironstone - had sprawled their disorderly way across the bulk of the Dawley landscape. There were so many that they found employment for a huge chunk of the working population. Most of these collieries had ground to a halt by the end of the eighteen hundreds, but at least twenty soldiered on into the new century. The mining tradition continued as a way of life for quite a lot of people for a few further years.

The surviving pits were fairly well spread around the district. At Dark Lane, Lawn Colliery was still producing coal during the second decade. It may well have been the last of the original Botfield pits to expire. Today, Telford Town Centre roughly occupies the former village of Dark Lane, and its ring road known as Lawn Central commemorates the colliery.

Park Forge Pits that lay near the Old Park furnaces and forge survived until about 1900. To lift the solitary cage up the main shaft, a counter-balance weight in an adjacent shaft was used. On occasions, twenty men had to be used in order to lift the balancing weight out of the shaft. Life was anything but easy for a miner in those days. Imagine one of those fellows from Park Forge arriving home after a long shift and saying - *'Missus, me and nineteen other blokes have spent the whole afternoon pulling the counter-balance weight right up the shaft, because the cage had got stuck. Me backs killing me!'* *'Oh yes'* replies his wife, *'well, your dinner's in the oven. It'll be a bit dry by now. When you've finished, the vegetable garden needs rough-digging, the garden gate's gotta be mended, the grate needs black-leading, and the kids' shoes have gotta be mended for morning, and by the way, we've run out of bread and cheese for supper!'* The poor man would probably be up at five the next morning, ready to walk to work and start yet another day of hard labour. Malinslee still had various working pits, including Hall pits in the first decade. Spout Colliery (where Spout Mound stands green and pleasant today) was eventually accompanied by a large mound of spoil, indicating a pit which had enjoyed a long

life. The pit began in the nineteenth century and continued producing coal until 1912. During the winter of 1963/1964, a precious remnant of Malinslee's long gone mining era, literally fell under the plough. Getting the ground ready for some early crop sowing, an eager farmer managed to plough-in some remaining embankments of a tram-way which had linked with the colliery years before. Little Eyton Colliery, a coal and ironstone pit since 1828, was recorded as having been sold to a Mr. Bache, of Ruabon, for £125 in 1904.

Lawley Colliery, on the north-western fringe of Dawley was still 'open for business' supplying coal and ironstone in the 1920's, after first seeing the light of day somewhat before 1881.

Clares Lane coalpit, between Mossey Green and Lawley Bank (roughly where Mossey Green Way runs today), was a shallow pit still working in 1945, and the coal was wound up the shaft by hand.

Farmer Bevan of Higgs's Hole (always known to locals as 'Eggsole') on Lawley Common, just off Station Road, Lawley Bank, decided that if you can't lick 'em, join 'em, and sank a shaft in his stack yard during the nineteen hundreds. His Farm Mine, or Higgs's Hole Mine, the last of Mr. Bevan's small pits, pushed coal to the surface from 1938 to 1954.

Moving south, we find that the Little Dawley area still had several pits working into the new century. Among these, Ashtree Pit and Gravel Pit near Lightmoor, produced clay at least up to the mid-nineteen thirties. Grimbers Pit at Lightmoor ceased yielding clay in the early nineteen hundreds, while the mound of Mill Pit at Botany Bay near Little Dawley's Castle Pools, was sold with a neighbouring cottage and garden in 1910, for £100.

The greatest survivors, however, were mostly at the extreme northern tip of Dawley. The Rock Colliery, originally producing both coal and clay, carried on spewing out coal until the late twentieth century. 'Jones's Pit' as it was commonly referred to in its latter days, really bucked the trend which saw the huge majority of Dawley's pits disappearing like melting snow, from the late eighteen hundreds. In the 1920's James Jones, of the Rock, took over the pit, and it was his son the well known Isaiah, who saw it through its latter years. Isaiah, also a local preacher, wit, raconteur, and fluent exponent of the Dawley dialect, eventually became a member of the Board of the Telford Development Corporation, adding his knowledge of local geology and living conditions to the deliberations of that body in its formative stage.

The other great survivor was Brandlee Colliery, just off the centre of Dawley. Created by the 'Coalbrookdale Company' in the nineteenth century, it was acquired by the Tarr Family during the twentieth, and like the one at the Rock, 'Tarr's Pit' lived on as a small, private concern until the late 1900's. They were local examples of non-nationalised mines, during the late twentieth century period of mass nationalisation of coal pits.

It would be easy to think of pit-work merely as a 'man's world' but that would be to ignore another phenomenon that spilled over into the early twentieth century - that singular tribe known as the 'pit girls'. These ladies really must have been a race apart. While others took jobs 'in service' with some wealthy household, and some stayed at home to help run a large family, the pit girls took on board one of the physically toughest jobs to come the way of womankind. Basically, their task was to sort out the good coal, or ironstone as the case may be, from the loads of stuff tipped onto the pit bank. It may sound a simple enough operation on the face of it, but the pit girl's life was one unbearably large slog.

The shift started at 6.00 a.m., so depending on the location of the pit, some girls would have to get up at an unearthly hour, and set off on foot for the workplace. When you consider that a fair number of Dawley girls worked at either Halesfield or Kemberton pits near Madeley, you realise that a lot of them had already done a day's work just getting there!

There were girls who walked from Lawley Bank to Kemberton pit. On the way, they would meet up with others from Rough Grounds, who would be waiting by the little shop at the junction with the road from Lawley Bank. In those days, Rough Grounds (now gone without trace, but where the likes of 'Chiltern Gardens' now stand), was a track between ugly mounds, and also harboured a group of miners' cottages.

Strangely, the Rough Grounds girls went from one rather desolate, mining enclave to another, in order to earn a living for themselves. Perhaps it's not surprising that this total gaggle of girls could be heard each early morning, singing to gee-up their spirits as they gradually advanced on the workplace. Their distinctive warbling became a familiar sound to the people living along the route, as did the sight of the print bonnets and the aprons, usually made for them by their mothers from material bought in Dawley. Thus, the good folk of 'Finger Road' and Aqueduct had no need of alarm clocks, so long as the trilling pit girls were going into work.

There would have been little opportunity to get their communal breath back when the girls arrived at the pit. Fresh from all that walking and singing, they would soon be confronted abruptly with the sight of a tub full of material from the bowels of the mine, being tipped down the pit mound which was their 'work station'. The girls would have to scramble down the bank of rubble and pick out the useful ironstone or coal, from the less useful clay and penistone. Then came the really tricky and demanding bit. Now wearing special head-gear, consisting of a working bonnet (not the nice print one) re-enforced with a roll of old stockings, each girl was required to fill an iron box with the selected substance. She then had to scale the precipitous slope, carrying the two- handled, loaded box on her head, then transport it in the same fashion to a set of racks into which the contents were emptied. Ironstone was required by local furnaces, including Blists Hill, and was conveyed by canal boat.

Novices had an especially hard time of it. Aside from the usual ragging from more experienced colleagues they simply had to get the hang of carting such an ungainly load on their heads while climbing the bank. All too often, a new girl would unbalance, the stones would fall out and roll back down the slope. With much inelegant slithering, the hapless youngster would retreat down the pile of rubble and

start all over again. Stiff necks were often par for the course, until the girl got used to the technique. What that job did for the long- term health of the ladies, can only be imagined. Did Dawley have an entire breed of short- necked adult females for instance? One can only assume that in later life, former pit girls would have suffered some painful legacy of those terribly hard-working days on the pit bank.

The job was especially harsh during the dead of winter. There was no shelter from the elements, and the lucky ones might occasionally have the luxury of a quick warm of their numb fingers on an 'ad hoc' fire. Even that was only available after the 'mountain' had been conquered, and the load of stones successfully carried to the racks.

One curious footnote to all of this was the sight of some older women returning from Dawley market on Saturdays, carrying their baskets of goods, African-style, on their heads. It would be a safe bet to assume such ladies had served time as pit girls, in their younger days.

In the early part of the century, workers were dabbling in other things apart from mining. Some were making bricks from local clay, for instance. The red clay of Randlay (if you'll pardon the rhyming) was a bit special. It was called 'Randlay Best' and it was the proud and true boast of Randlay Brickworks that a house built of 'Randlay Best Reds' never lost its colour. Many of the Randlay bricks, and some chimney pots, were hand-made. Today, the Red Pool in Telford Town Park, not far from 'Northwood Terrace', Stirchley, provides evidence of the distinctive material which used to be so profitably extracted from just below the ground.

Horsehay Works, by this time under the control of the Quaker Simpson family, was already making a considerable name for itself in the heavy engineering and structural steel world. As an indication of the sort of discipline in vogue at that time it is reported that the works hooter would go off at 5.30 a.m., reminding employees to get their skates on and be at the work stages by 6.00 a.m. sharp. Any straggler who didn't make it to the Time Office by three minutes to six would, on placing his brass check down on the open window ledge, find the friendly time-clerk would greet him by abruptly banging the window down, and blackening his finger nails. Not only would the unfortunate employee reach his workplace a few minutes late, but he would also be unable to do a tap of work until his finger-ends came alive again!

Horsehay's forte was the production of bridges, initially of iron, and later steel. It had other strings to its bow, however, and in the early part of the century, its busy foundry turned out castings for such diverse clients as the 'Liverpool Refrigeration Company', and the builders of the Aswan Dam. During the Great War, the foundry also produced a considerable amount of components for the war effort, including castings for gun trailers.

Dawley's working population certainly knew what hard work was. The reward in most cases, was just about enough money to provide for basic family necessities. Of course, where there was a particularly large family (not unusual in those pre-television days), or the breadwinner preferred to dive into the nearest pub as soon as his pay packet was opened, there would be an uphill struggle to keep body and soul together.

An early 20th century view of Horsehay Works, also showing the 'Old Row' cottages and the surrounding rural landscape overlooked by the distant Wrekin

Chapter Nineteen

'TIMES WUZ HARD'
A GLIMPSE OF EVERYDAY LIFE

So what was life like for ordinary families during the somewhat uncertain days of the early twentieth century? Where clothing was in short supply, it was not unknown for the mother of the family to get hold of an abandoned old (adult size) coat, and with skilful use of a well worn sewing machine, turn the garment into a jacket and trousers for a young lad. When that young lad ceased to be quite such a young one, the home-made suit would be passed down the line to the next youngest, and so on. Whether or not the suit, having completed its journey down the family line, was then cleverly re-cycled into a coat for an adult we can only speculate upon! Quite a lot of children's clothing was home-made or home-improved, and shoes would normally be mended either by father or mother, using materials purchased in Dawley 'High Street'. 'Sunday Best' clothing, however fashioned, could literally be worn only on a Sunday, and then had to be put carefully away until the next Sabbath day. Boys would be threatened with a swift cuff about the ears, if caught either whistling or with hands in pockets during that unique day of the week.

Improvisation was also sometimes needed for the essential task of feeding the family. Some families actually bred rabbits for the express purpose of supplementing the available meat supply, others baked their own bread. Fresh vegetables were grown in the spacious gardens that lay at the rear of many a cottage. Tap water was not the automatic utility we take for granted today. Whilst some lucky people might have a nearby water-pump, more often than not buckets of the ice-cold liquid had to be hauled from wells and natural springs scattered around the district. Cast-iron public water taps were eventually provided in most districts, but even in the early 1900's, spring water was the only source of clean water for most people. Such a spring could be found at the bottom of Single Row at Hinkshay. There was another one at Holywell Lane, near Little Dawley (its site can still be traced today), but it would sometimes dry up, necessitating a journey to the more distant and more reliable Bath Spout at Doseley, about half a mile away.

People collecting water from the Bath Spout spring, Doseley.

Water was never in greater demand than on Friday nights - family bath nights. The aqua was boiled over a kitchen fire, then poured into a tin bath on the hearth. Children would be given the treatment by the rapid action of a flannel duly laced with 'Sunlight' soap. Clean bodies would be wrapped in clean night clothes, awaiting supper and bed, in that order. In some households, the girls would be separated from their brothers by a curtain across an otherwise communal bedroom. Before the oil-lamp was blown out for the night, the eldest child would lead the others in a ritualistic bedtime prayer, along the lines of:

'God bless my father and mother, brothers,

sisters and all my friends.
Make me a good child, and when I die,
take me to thy happy home in Heaven.'

Children would have to amuse themselves
in their spare time, as best they could. With
no T.V., no radio, no comics - how on earth
did they manage to keep themselves from
absolute boredom? The answer is,
surprisingly well, thank you. The games
and pastimes they generally indulged in,
brought a welcome release from the
grinding 'three R's' at school, and the
drudgery of chores to help their parents at
home.

In summer, lads would play informal
cricket on nearby mounds. The more
ambitious would indulge in an extended
game of 'hare and hounds'. Two teams
would be selected, one of them armed with
numerous pieces of paper. The latter would
set off on a lengthy trek, dropping paper at
intervals for the other team to follow. It's
not recorded whether any children were
ever hauled before the courts for polluting
the environment! The idea was, of course,
for the chasing pack to find their quarries
by following (and hopefully, gathering up)
the discarded fragments of paper. One
elderly citizen has recalled such a game
terminating at Shifnal, some five or six
miles through the lanes from Dawley.

Somewhat less demanding, would be a
game of 'Tin-can murky'. Boys and girls
would play that together. Briefly, the
science behind the game was that one
person would be 'it'. He or she stood by
an empty tin-can at the game's base, while
allowing the rest of the players a set length
of time to disperse and hide. 'It' tried to
discover the whereabouts of the others. On
spotting one or more of the 'enemy', he or
she would race back to the can, put a foot
on it and shout 'murky, murky one, two or
three etc.', depending on how many of the
others had been spotted. It was also open to

any of the others to break cover, and kick
the can, signifying that 'it' would have to
remain 'it' for another session. Otherwise,
the first person to have been 'murkeyed' by
'it' would have to take over as pursuer.
Should any reader find the above rules a bit
complicated, it's a game that soon became
second nature, with practice. The problem
is, in the present-age, not many people
would be willing to give it a try! Tip-cat,
and marbles were other sporting pastimes.

During the darker evenings, there would be
much loafing about the streets, nattering
about this and that. When all conversation
was exhausted, youngsters might retire to
the rather dour precincts of the brew-house.
A brew-house (or *brew'us* in Dawley-
speak) was a fairly small brick building
detached from a row of cottages, and found
at the back of the properties. There might
be one brew-house to every three or four
cottages in the terrace, and it served as a
kind of shared laundry. A fire would be lit
beneath a large boiler full of water, and
families would take it in turns to do their
washing in the building. Home-brewed
beer would also be produced in some brew-
houses, but none of these activities would
have interested the youngsters. A few boys
would simply use the shelter and
comparative warmth of the *brew'us* for an
innocent game of cards, or perhaps ring
board which involved throwing rubber
rings at a board containing metal hooks,
each bearing a different numbered 'score'.
It seems that girls were more inclined to
visit the homes of school-friends, to talk
and, perhaps, swap reading books. Clearly
children were well able to survive on
merely simple pleasures.

'What about the adults', you may earnestly
be asking? *'What did they do for fun?'*
Some miners, and let's face it, there were
still quite a few of them around in the early
twentieth century, had the unfortunate habit
of amusing themselves by being cruel to

wild animals.

Whilst pigeon-racing might have been a reasonably civilised activity - at least the birds were well-fed and looked after, and they did get the chance to see a bit of the world - other pursuits were less constructive. Rabbit-coursing was popular in mining areas such as Lawley Bank and Little Dawley. The rules of the 'game' were: go out onto a nearby field frequently populated by rabbits. Strategically place a long net at one end of the field, drive a group of basking bunnies towards the net, grab one of the unfortunate captives, have a team of hostile lurchers (a cross between a whippet and a greyhound) lined up and straining at the leash, release the rabbit giving it a100 yards start, and finally loose the dogs in pursuit. The owner of the dog that got the rabbit would be the winner. Elementary really, but by today's standards, so cruel. Still, it's slightly comforting to be able to say that some things in the modern Western world, are less barbarous than they were years ago.

One popular venue for rabbit coursing was a field on the Lawley Bank side of the railway tunnel, on the way to Horsehay. At Little Dawley, such an event was the high spot of the week. On Saturday afternoons or summer evenings people young and old, would turn out to watch the goings-on. A miner with a whippet would be like a businessman with a brief case, they just belonged together. Whilst the miner would proudly walk his dog around the village during the week, there would be only one place to take it and unleash it on a Saturday afternoon. Competition was keen and colliers from Madeley, Ironbridge, Broseley and Lawley Bank would also parade their animals at Little Dawley, adding an additional competitive edge to the proceedings.

'Dabbing', that is trapping wild birds, was

another diversion enjoyed mostly by miners. The idea was to trap linnets (where have they all gone to, nowadays?) in a trap cage. Some 'players' would already have their own pet linnet in a cage, and the naive, feathered pet would obligingly call others down from the wild, and into the cage to meet a new-found friend. Others would simply be lured down by some enticing bait, rather than a fellow linnet. Perhaps the birds were put to some constructive use, such as sniffing out harmful gases down the pits, but it appears that for some reason, the local 'bobby' turned a blind eye to this, and other unsavoury pastimes.

For some good clean fun, the adult citizens of Dawley chose less harmful pursuits such as a game of quoits, to keep themselves entertained. In fact, quoits seems to have become something of an obsession, rather as hoola-hoops, or skateboarding did when they swept the nation in the latter half of the century. Every self-respecting part of Dawley had a quoits alley or pit. Everybody appeared to be playing. At the 'King's Head' pub near Dawley Baptist Church, Dawley Bank, a rough and ready quoits pit was dug in the ground, with a stake fixed firmly into a base of clay. Contestants had to throw from a set distance metal rings (quoits) to see who could get the closest to the 'pin'. Like all good crazes it was a simple idea. It caught on to such an extent that people were 'quoiting' at the drop of a hat. Little Dawley was another place to go for the sport in a big way. The 'Red Lion' pub (still thriving today), had a quoits alley set up on a patch of grass opposite ('Malvern Crescent' now occupies the sacred patch). About two hundred yards down the road, the 'Unicorn' pub had a skittle alley, but the 'in' place for serious 'quoiters' was the 'Crown Inn' at the heart of the village, near the Wesleyan chapel. Some of Shropshire's finest players converged on the 'Crown' so that quoits at the 'Crown' was the 'Premier League' of the local quoiting scene. Star players from such places as Ironbridge, Broseley, Wellington, Newport and beyond, would display their skills and show that even a simple game could be made into an art form, when taken seriously enough. Great entertainment would be enjoyed by the many spectators, and great, presumably, would be the sales of liquid refreshment. Informal games of quoits would also take place on surrounding mounds, including Springwell Mount, at Little Dawley. People whose enthusiasm had been fired by watching the experts at the pub alleys, would create their own excitement by having a go on their exclusive, improvised pitches. For good measure, both the 'Red Lion' and the 'Crown' also ran air-gun shooting clubs.

Those Spartan days were also blessed with 'professional' entertainment. Dawley Town Hall had been built, amid a certain amount of pomp, as well as of optimism for its future use. In the mid-twentieth century, it had seemed for the most part, an inglorious white elephant. A drab-looking old building, standing in perpetual shade about half way up Dun Cow Bank, the Town Hall seemed uncertain of what it was doing there at all. Its doors were always shut, nobody seemed to go into the building, and it simply stood there in a permanent sulk, a solitary goods wagon parked in a quiet siding and forgotten.

Things were very much different in 'grandfather's day'. Unbelievably, the building was alive with the hubbub of real entertainment. A Mr. Bannister ran the show, and drew the eager punters into the hall using a mixture of silent films interspersed with live entertainment, as bait. To help build up the excitement, Alf Teece would pace up and down the pavement outside (notwithstanding the slope of Dun Cow Bank), shouting *'this*

way to the 'Royal Windsor', 2,4 and 6 this way'. Although 'Royal Windsor' might perhaps have contravened the 'Trade Descriptions Act' in later years, '2, 4 and 6' referred to the prices of seats. In fact, if you paid an extra penny, you were given the privilege of choosing exactly where you sat. At least some of the 'seats' were little more than wooden benches, so that if someone got up at one end, the person sitting at the other would invariably end up on the floor. There was no additional charge for this impromptu piece of slapstick!

The Town Hall - once Dawley's top entertainment venue.

While a film was running, a local pianist had to fit suitable music to the on-screen action. This demanded considerable skill, and no small degree of concentration. Should the latter begin to lapse, the musician would soon receive an earnest nudge from someone nearby, so that sound and vision could be restored to some sort of harmony. A typical evening at the Town Hall would be billed as 'The Variety Show'. What you would get for your 2d, 4d or 6d, (plus, perhaps an extra 1d), would be some films sandwiched between which would be various live acts, and so on. One regular such entertainer was a fellow who walked around the stage, balancing on a huge ball.

So confident was he in his abilities, that for good measure, he also took the ball for an excursion up a wooden plank. Apparently, the rate of pay at the Town Hall was insufficient to keep body and soul together. The gentleman would put in a spot of overtime, by balling up and down the High Street three times, including a skilful circumnavigation of a lamp-post near the 'Elephant and Castle' pub, at the top of the street. Postman Jimmy Corfield would follow in support on foot, holding out a hat into which shoppers were invited to toss a coin or two.

Sometimes the gaps between the films would be filled with more conventional entertainment, such as a vocal soloist, or a troupe of dancers, and the entertainers often travelled to Dawley from some other part of the country. The evening would often be rounded off with dancing. 'Fight Nights' were held as an attraction for the blood thirsty. Acknowledged wrestlers such as 'Ackon Smith', would challenge muscle-men to a public two-round bout in the ring. Imagine the roar of approval the night little Bobby Jarvis of Dawley not only survived the two rounds, but also got the celebrated 'Ackon' down, and held him on the canvas. That would really be something to go home and tell the missus about!

Not all the live entertainment took place in the Town Hall, however. Free entertainment was provided by some of the more extrovert street-market traders, who travelled from town to town. 'Buffalo Bill' stood outside the 'Lord Hill' pub at the bottom of the street, providing serious, and possibly cheaper, competition for the local G.P. He sold cure-all medicines, and attracted the crowds with his extravagant claims. One evening, he caused a minor sensation by apparently licking the cataracts off the eyes of old Mr. Harper, of Horsehay. The old man yelled to the nearest onlooker, '*I can see lad, I can see*

lad, I can see you!' It seemed a miracle of New Testament proportions, and it is hoped that Mr.Harper's 'cure' was long lasting.

Fairs used to visit Dawley, even in the far off days. The yard at the back of the 'Dun Cow' inn was one favoured venue, and the attractions included hobby-horses, hoop-la, and other side-shows (a Dun Cow by the way, is a greyish brown one). There was even a Dawley man named Gothamer, who had a travelling fair. He hailed from the 'Finger Road' area, and would return to his Dawley roots each winter, to park his fairground equipment during the 'off season'. 'Chapel Street' was another scene

Chapel Street, close to the place where the fair, circus and theatre used to visit.

of outdoor entertainment, specifically the big yard behind the 'Summer House' pub. Later in the century, the red-brick house belonging to haulier and coach proprietor Jack Ashley, occupied the site of the pub. It still does, and the garage that once housed his vehicles stood on the site of the yard. About twice a year, a fair would visit the 'Summer House' yard, and even greater excitement would be provided in the winter months, when an itinerant theatre made Dawley its base for the season. Wooden panels would be assembled to construct a 'theatre' on the yard. The productions were pretty serious stuff, in the main, including such grizzly tales as 'Maria Marten' (Murder at the Red Barn), and in deference to local interest, 'The Stirchley Murder'. Briefly, the story has it that in 1867 one Barnett Zusman, a Jew living in Ironbridge, was attacked, robbed and murdered at Lower Cross Meadow, behind St. James's Church. Two local men were charged, and one of them, George Harris was committed to Shrewsbury Assizes. It was stuff guaranteed to warm the blood on a cold night, and would have beaten watching television any day, but what wouldn't have? Incidentally, a Ketley gent. by the name of S.T. Morgan wrote a poem about the incident in 1909. For some reason, it was published in the 'Observer' newspaper in 1964, when it sparked more than a modicum of interest.

Everyday life was anything but Utopian, yet most people managed to put a brave face on it, and even enjoy it despite some rather basic living conditions. Take Hinkshay, for example. The long, terraced rows of cottages provided shelter for mine workers, and also employees of Stirchley Forge. They were a roof over the head certainly, but internally offered little room to spare, and scant facilities for their several occupants.

'Ladies Row' was the one you could see in its entire length, from the road leading through Hinkshay village. It ran parallel to the road, and was separated from it by a field which in later years was to become the home of Hinkshay United football club, and later still - the 'Ever Ready' battery works. The back of the row faced the field and contained a real curiosity - there were no back doors. In fact, there were very few back windows either, so that the residents enjoyed almost complete privacy from the prying eyes of any inquisitive cows, or whatever else may have frequented the grassy area. There were but two bedrooms to a house, with no running water or flush

toilets. Sadly, the toilets were situated at the bottom end (if you'll pardon the expression) of lengthy garden paths. Worse still, the loos were communal, there wasn't a separate one for each household, just a limited number serving the ten or twelve dwellings in the entire row. Quite how the practicalities were sorted out is a mystery. Even if there had been a booking system, that would not have allowed for any emergencies which might have cropped up. Two or three houses shared the same wash-house. There had to be a system in place for this amenity, since a different day was wash day for each of the families concerned.

Originally, clean water had to be carried in buckets from a natural spring, just below 'Single Row'. It was ice-cold when collected, but the water temperature on reaching home would depend on the time of year, the age of the carrier, and the number of persons stopping you for a natter on the way back. At some point in the early twentieth century Hinkshay residents were given the luxury of a series of cast-iron public taps located around the area, but it was still necessary to hump great bucketsful from the tap to home - although the journeys were presumably shorter.

Putting that part of Hinkshay together then, there was 'Ladies Row', as already described, and its neighbours 'Double Row' (a collection of back-to-back terraces), and 'Single Row' just to the left of it. This conglomeration of dark brick buildings formed a community of its own, on the eastern fringes of Dawley. They were built for an earlier age, yet continued to house families until the late 1960's. The community also boasted a shop, of sorts. A small shed beside one of the houses represented Albert and Mrs. Richards's general store. Home deliveries were also provided by means of a two-wheeled trolley. One youngster used to help out in his spare time, by pulling the trolley plus Mr. Richards around the district delivering general goods, including paraffin. The little Anglican Mission Church beside the main thoroughfare, and near the approach to 'the rows' was remarkably well attended at each Sunday evening Service. Frank Hargreaves played the organ while Joe Gittens primed the bellows. Lay readers such as Noah Chetwood often preached at the Services, and sometimes the white-haired, white-bearded and white-smocked Rev, Faulks would visit from Holy Trinity Church, Dawley. There was then, a real sense of community in that almost private enclave called Hinkshay, despite the dreary, surrounding pit mounds which clothed the landscape both there and at neighbouring Randlay.

Tucked away off the present-day beaten track, lay for many years another solitary community officially called 'Sandy Bank Row', but affectionately referred to as 'Dill Doll Row'. It was a long terrace of about twenty, dull brick houses lying in the flat valley between Doseley and Pool Hill. They survived from the days of the Industrial Revolution until the mid-twentieth century. To find the site today, you would need to leave the road, as the boy did in Chapter 2 of this book, near the high, brick railway bridge at Doseley, and walk past the front of the 'Cheshire Cheese' pub, following an unmetalled lane for a short distance. Soon, on the left, you would pass right by the place where 'Dill Doll Row' once hosted generations of Dawley families. The row was built in 1838 by the 'Coalbrookdale Company' for workers at Horsehay ironworks. Modern private housing now fills the site.

As at Hinkshay, the houses were small and mostly two bedroomed. The back bedroom had the privilege of overlooking the wash-house, close to the back of the house. This

time, each dwelling luxuriated in having its very own wash-house where water was heated in a boiler, and an oven where home-made bread was often baked. There was a tunnel-like entry at either end, and one in the middle of the row. You would walk down one of the entries, and then along a narrow brick pavement at the backs of the houses in order to gain access. Inevitably, the privies were to be found down certain garden paths, and there was the usual rivalry for such facilities, not to mention the horrors of negotiating the lonely pathway during dark and cold winter nights, as the need arose.

Such austere conditions proved no deterrent to the mating game. Some inhabitants of 'Sandy Bank Row' managed to rear some extremely large families. One such brood numbered twelve off-springs, an incredible ten boys, plus two girls for good measure! Thankfully, three brothers eventually volunteered to enlist for the First World War, that was one way of getting a bed to yourself, and one of the girls went into service. That still left an awful lot of bodies for a two-bedroomed house. How were they accommodated? Various permutations were tried at bed-times. The older boys showed their status by sleeping side-to-side, while the younger ones (using the same bed, of course) would either sleep two at each end, with their feet meeting in the middle, or else side-to-side along the edges of the bed. Whichever way they tried, the risk of asphyxiation could never have been too far away!

Yet another remote, traditional, enclosed society was to be found on the western fringe of Little Dawley, at 'Holywell Lane'. Local people referred to it as 'Hollowell Lane' for some indecipherable reason, just as they persisted in referring to the nearby Springwell Mound, as 'Springewell Mount'. Clearly, Little Dawleyites had developed their own vernacular, and nobody was going to wean them off it.

There was, and still is, a well at the entrance to 'Holywell Lane', whether a Holy one or not, and again a community survived in the lane from the early industrial days until the 1970's. It hid itself away beyond the 'Doseley Dodger' railway line, and the little settlement of Gravel Leasowes with its 'Pop Bottle' chapel, on a rocky lane leading to some undulating countryside. The dwellings, being squatter cottages, sprang up in haphazard fashion, yet merged to form a solid community alongside the rough lane.

Being somewhat separated from Little Dawley, it's not surprising that 'Holywell Lane' once had a small shop amongst the motley collection of cottages. Mr. & Mrs. Lewis Franks ran the little business from their cottage at No. 5. Essentials such as sweets and packets of wash powder were dispensed from its precincts. Others made some extra cash by harnessing the natural amenities of the area. A Mr. Darrall fashioned walking-sticks out of ash and holly from the woodland. Another Mr. Franks achieved a useful income from breeding and selling rabbits. A one-month old rabbit would set back an enthusiastic boy the sum of 4d., whilst 6d. was needed to buy a six-month old specimen. Given the propensity of rabbits for getting on with it, one wonders how many enterprising youngsters cottoned-on to the fact that their rabbit hutches could in turn, become 'factories' for breeding their own stock for sale. Since those were the days of presumed innocence, perhaps the children simply concentrated on enjoying their pets as mere companions.

An abundance of skills seems to have permeated the early century denizens of 'Holywell Lane'. Harry Rowlands, a T.B. sufferer, was particularly good at making tin and copper whistles. He also made

kites. Ben. Barker developed into an accomplished, local political orator on behalf of the Liberal Party. Abraham Barker could be a master of double-speak. After a gang of four or five lads had dug his garden for him, he would say to them, *''ow much dun yo want? Them as asks, shanna `ave and them that dunna ask, dunna want!'* It was surely part of a tongue-in-cheek game, and we can assume the boys were awarded what Abraham thought their efforts were worth.

A quiet spot near 'Holywell Lane', Little Dawley.

Several generations of the same families would inhabit some of the cottages. There were Baileys, Maidens, Lewis's, Skeltons, Evans's, and Rogers's amongst others, and there seemed to be people of those names in the Little Dawley area throughout the twentieth century, as there had no doubt been long before. Since the dwellings were not 'company houses', it's not surprising that the workers of 'Holywell Lane' were engaged in a variety of occupations. Some worked as far away as the Sinclair iron foundry, in Ketley. Presumably they got there by train from Doseley Halt. Others worked at Coalbrookdale ironworks, or in the various local pits, brick and tile works, and so on. The wife of one of the inhabitants would regularly take her good man a cooked meal to his workplace at

Lightmoor brickworks. He was sometimes heard to say, '*Mary, has thee brought me a puddin'?*' If she said 'No' he would reply, '*well, yo can tek it back then!*' The same man's idea of paradise was to pour a small quantity of whisky into a little bottle, carry it to the secluded natural spring called the 'Bath Spout', near Doseley Church, top it up with the cool spring-water, and knock it back exclaiming '*that's beautiful that is*'.

It seems that while the men folk were away earning an honest crust, some sort of hierarchy developed among the women left at home to see to the mundane chores of keeping the house straight. Natural qualities of leadership emerged, and one lady was known by all as 'Cock of the walk', while another was respected as 'Cock of the midden' (refuse heap). Presumably, if you chanced to visit those respective pieces of territory during daytime hours, you would soon become aware of a presence, a keen pair of eyes observing you and ensuring you did not get up to anything untoward. Shades of early 'Neighbourhood Watch', perhaps.

There were two local sources of clean water. The good folk living near the end of the lane furthest away from Little Dawley, carried their supply from a well (now dried up) just beyond the lane to Stocking Farm.

Those at the other end patronised the so-called 'Holy Well'. Unfortunately, it was apt to dry up during hot summers, and the poor people had to walk a round trip of about two miles to the Bath Spout. Even Bath Spout water would have lost its coolness by the time it arrived at 'Holywell Lane'! What about those who were living in the middle of the row? Did they toss a coin to decide whether to go 'uppards' or 'downards'? Did the cocks of the walk or midden determine who went to which well? We can be sure the issue would be sorted out so that everybody would know exactly where they stood.

Local Methodist chapels played an important part in the lives of many working-class families. In the case of the 'Holywell Lane' community, there would be a regular, three-quarters of a mile trek to the 'Big Penny' chapel at Little Dawley. Although built in 1837, the chapel is unlikely to have been patronised by many 'Holywell Lane' folk until the closure of the much closer 'Pop Bottle' chapel in 1903. Raymond Lewis, who worked at the Ash Tree clay pit near Lightmoor, turning weathered clay in readiness for tile or brick-making, led a young men's Bible Class at the chapel. However, his great forte was choral music. He was a leading singer in several local choirs, including Little Dawley Methodist Church choir. He later distinguished himself as a highly skilled conductor of the renowned Hadley Orpheus Male Voice Choir, coaxing them to competitive success both in England and 'the lion's den' in Wales. They even won first prize at the Welsh National Eisteddford, in the 1920's.

As befits a small, rather cut-off community, folklore about 'Holywell Lane' abounds. There was the old gentleman who, on returning a dictionary loaned to him by a kindly neighbour, pronounced, '*I've bin tryin' to read it, but I conna mek ends or middle on it. Theedst better 'ave it back!*' Then there was the fellow who boasted that he never, ever went to bed, and another old chap who seemed to do nothing else but carry a bag full of bottles of beer from the 'Crown Inn' Little Dawley, for the benefit of various thirsty neighbours. When the effort became too much for him, or a huge thirst got the better of him, he would slump under a hedge, and sleep it off! A communal storage for pig-swill used to nestle in the ground, near the lane. People would empty their discarded potato peelings, cabbage leaves and who knows what else, into the five-foot deep brick receptacle, and there the inviting mixture lay until ladled out as required by the local pig keeping fraternity.

The overriding picture emerging from all of the above, is of a variety of scattered communities dotted around the Dawley area. Each lived a fairly self-contained existence, whereby a visit to Dawley 'High Street' and market would be a real event. A trip to anywhere beyond Wellington would be highly unlikely. For many working families, there were no flush loos, and there was no electricity or gas (apart from in the pig-swill pits). Lighting came from oil lamps, and heating from coal or wood fires. Amazingly, this was provincial Britain in the same century that gave us the atomic bomb, space travel and sliced bread!

Lawley Bank, on the north-western fringe of the town, rejoiced in being composed of several smaller enclaves, each with its own distinctive name. 'Higgs's Hole' was a gaggle of cottages, mostly arranged into a sort of square. It lay in a dip on the edge of Lawley Common, just off 'Station Road' at its mid way point. Most of the inhabitants were mine-workers families. Some of them worked as far afield as the Stafford or Woodhouse Collieries, near St. Georges until the General Strike of 1926 saw them return to the smaller Dawley pits. Nothing remains but a fragment of the old lane, near the former Len. Ashley vehicle depot. Even this little portion may perhaps disappear when the Lawley Common development is complete. Nearer the Methodist Chapel end of the road was Ladygrove. Its dwellings (mostly cottages) occupied a lane almost opposite present-day 'Avondale'. The lane, leading to 'Old Office Road' survives but only one, somewhat modified, house at the far end is still with us. At the beginning of the road to The Rock, Prince's End still nestles on

the left-hand side opposite the 'Poacher's Pocket' pub restaurant (formerly the 'Wrekin View'). A lane, some steps and a short row of surviving cottages now share the area with some late twentieth century housing. The settlement is reputed to have hosted an early century jam factory. People say it was still in production during World War I, and rumour has it that the luscious substance was fed to 'our boys' at the battlefront. If this is so, it's nice to think that Lawley Bank made a contribution to the war effort, besides supplying man-power to the Front. Given Prince's End's elevated position, you would think the jam factory's sweet aroma would have been shared with much of the rest of Lawley Bank, on a windy day! A gentleman by the name of Watson Howells apparently lugged the product by horse and cart to Lawley Bank railway station, on the first stage of the journey to its ultimate destination.

The word 'fold' seems to have been manufactured in Lawley Bank, since so many of its inhabitants lived in one. There was Barn Fold, (or 'fowd' in the native tongue), opposite the Baptist church. The C.J. Williams Funeral Service buildings stand on part of the site. Leading off the road containing Lawley Bank's small shops, between the Methodist and Baptist churches, a few more folds hosted workers' families. On the same side as the former Methodist buildings was the entrance to Stoney Fold, (now occupied by modern dwellings including one street called 'Croft Fold'). On the opposite side lurked Reynold's Fold and Powis's Fold (the 'Powis Place' maisonettes now 'mark the spot'). For good measure, Shepherd's Fold still slumbers behind the mature houses along the road to the 'Poacher's Pocket'. In the agricultural world, a fold is an enclosure for protecting animals, so we will assume that in the human sense, at Lawley Bank etc., a fold is a small group of dwellings, off the main road, and practically creating its own individual community.

Like so many of Dawley's suburbs, Lawley Bank was essentially a 'pit village' since most of its working population found employment in either local pits or those a bit further afield. Several of the smaller pits in the area were 'gin pits', and that doesn't refer to some illicit beverage consumed at break times! A 'gin pit' would be roughly thirty yards deep, and the coal would be hauled up the shafts, using horse power. The beast would get its job satisfaction from walking round the pit-head in constant circles, duly attached to a drum, which in turn cranked the rope bearing the spoils to the surface. At the end of it all, the poor animal probably felt as if it had been on the gin. It's no wonder the men had a job catching the horse, to start work on a Monday morning!

A remnant of an old mine shaft at Lawley Bank, unearthed during open-cast operations during the 1980's

Should you ever develop the urge to dig yourself a nice little coal-pit, you may be interested to learn how such things were done years ago. First, decide how wide you would like the hole to be, then cut some turf out of the unsuspecting field, to the desired width. Next comes the really hard bit. Grab a pick and shovel and start digging downwards into the exposed ground, in the general direction of Antarctica. When you've managed to dig to a depth of between ten and fifteen feet, have a rest and arrange for some brickies to come along and start bricking-up the sides of the hole. When you have got your breath back, continue digging until the prized coal seam is reached. It doesn't sound too complicated - it just takes a lot of effort, know-how, and determination. That was how it was done at the small pits in the area.

Now that we've got the pit dug, we need to begin to appreciate just how unpalatable the work was 'at the bottom of the hole'. The object of the exercise was, of course, to get quantities of good coal from the depths of the earth, and bring it to the surface so that it could be transported to waiting end-users, whether industrial enterprises or domestic customers. Lumps of the black stuff would be hewn from the coal-face, and loaded into tubs. These were cast-iron trucks with small wheels, which when fully laden, were pushed along rails and down a slope towards the pit-bottom. The busy fellows at that spot (known as 'jiggers'), would pull to one side an empty tub newly arrived from the pit-head, and hook the loaded one onto a wire rope. A bell was rung to inform the pit-head that all was ready for another cargo to be winched upwards. Some of the coal from the 'gin pit' in 'Station Road' was taken to the goods yard at Horsehay station, for further distribution. Some was consumed by the Shrewsbury Electric Light Company, and was collected twice a day by a 'Sentinel' steam wagon. In some pits, underground lighting was simply supplied by candles placed within a ball of clay. One of many hazards down the mine was the appearance of black damp, when the arrival of a tell-tale smell at the coal-face would prompt a sharp exit by everyone in the vicinity, before a lack of oxygen caused a catastrophe.

People going about their normal business in the Lawley Bank area, would probably not suspect that they were either walking or perhaps, sitting above a coal-mine. The fact is, the underground roads had to run, as far as possible along the coal-seams. The mine-owners usually enlisted the services of surveyors (or 'latchers') to tell them not only where the best seams lay, but also the limits to which the roads could be run so as to avoid encroaching on someone else's land, or causing subsidence. The 'Station Road' coal-face, for example, wormed its way towards Lawley Bank chapel, while the one at Clare's Lane pit, which had a steam-winding engine, burrowed under the fields to the top of Rock Hill.

Life was often harsh and uncompromising, and again, it's difficult to appreciate that such a way of life existed during the same 'civilised' century that ultimately brought us Concorde, for example, and Boy George. A youngster might have found himself in chapel four times on a Sunday - though not necessarily from choice! In fact, the local chapel was often the focal point of the village's social life. There were Wesleyan Guild meetings, Bible Study groups, choir practices, Christian Endeavour meetings, Tract meetings, Youth clubs and so on. If you wanted to, you could find something constructive to do at the chapel on most nights of the week. Lawley Bank Methodist Chapel was one of those which had the blessing of a visit from the celebrated Dr. Parkes Cadman. You may remember that he was the Old Park man who married a Lawley Bank girl, and made good in the U.S.A. as a dynamic preacher. Not a man to forget his roots, Parkes Cadman would cross the Atlantic to preach at special Services in his home locality, from time to time. When P.C. was in the pulpit, the chapel would be bursting at its seams, with local people eager to listen to his every word.

Coal fields do not only breed chapels of course, they also beget characters of the down to earth (naturally), and amusing kind. The Lloyd brothers who lived in a cottage in 'Station Road', not far from Higgs's Hole, are still talked about with affection today. 'Little Billy' was known to just about everyone in Dawley. Even as an adult, he stood no more than four feet tall 'in his stocking feet'. In the 1950's, if you didn't see, or indeed hear, Little Billy Lloyd in Dawley 'High Street' on a Saturday morning, it would be like Christmas Day without Santa Claus. His cheerful chatter to anyone who passed by, and his rasping cackle, were as essential to the High Street scene as butter was to bread. Curiously, even in that sixth decade, Billy had the appearance of a pit worker of the turn of the century. Flat cap, small scarf knotted at the neck, long jacket, and hob-nail boots. He always carried a shopping bag which seemed to be almost half his own length, and practically touched the floor. Even as a youngster, Billy took part in the annual Dawley Carnival, and in later years often dressed up as the diminutive Gordon Richards, Oakengates's national Champion Jockey, albeit riding a donkey! Nearer to his Lawley Bank home, the young Billy could often be heard singing a ditty called 'That Little Shirt my Mother gave me'. In Billy's case, any shirt other than a little one would have engulfed him! He made himself useful by collecting newspapers and parcels from Lawley Bank railway station, destined presumably for shops up in the village. George 'Banger' Lloyd was Billy's brother, and in his spare time became a referee at local amateur football matches. Stories of 'Banger's' eccentricity on the field of play have become part of Dawley folk lore. One of the oft quoted anecdotes concerned a match involving the Baptist chapel team, and played on a field near the railway tunnel. A player disputed the validity of the goal allowed by 'Banger'. The ref's terse reply was *'thee look in the 'Pink Pairper' ter nate, and theet see whether it was a goal or not!'* Some clever clogs once asked him what would it be if the ball stuck on the top of the cross bar - *'a bloody miracle'* was 'Banger's' prompt reply!

Less than a mile down the road from Lawley Bank to Ketley, lies the old mining settlement called The Rock. Several of the original dwellings, together with the little Primitive Wesleyan Chapel still stand, and are duly occupied today. They rest at the top of an incline, huddled for protection from the encroaching army of modern housing now clothing the surrounding slopes. The Rock is a traditional neighbourhood amid a sea of modern, New Town urbanisation.

The Rock Methodist Chapel and Sunday School room.

The Rock's story is that it simply grew out of necessity, when both coal and clay pits were developed there about a couple of hundred years ago. Squatter cottages, and one or two larger houses built by the landowner, the first Duke of Sutherland, make up the bulk of the buildings. The Rock stood surrounded not only by pit clutter, but also some attractive, open

countryside, with views of the brooding Wrekin to the west. It was an isolated community, not altogether sure of whether its loyalties lay with Ketley, a mile or two beyond the bottom of the slope on its northern flank, or with Dawley, a couple of miles to the south. For much of the twentieth century it was, for administrative purposes, within the auspices of Dawley Urban District Council.

The chapel was built in 1861, on borrowed money. Material had been carted from the nearby rock-hole, to provide the foundations. Despite working five and a half days a week, and seeing little daylight in winter, the local mine-working and iron-working populations of the early nineteen hundreds, were still bright eyed enough to attend a six a.m. prayer meeting at the chapel on a Sunday morning. Later, many would turn up for the morning service, and also evening worship. The only real 'put your feet up time' was on the Sunday afternoon. On occasional summer Sundays, the various local Methodist congregations would band together for a 'Camp Meeting'. This was an outdoor jamboree of hymn-singing, bible readings, and sermon held on an old pit mound known as 'Camp Meeting Hill' between Mossey Green and Ketley Bank. Older people are always telling us what glorious summers they had in 'the old days', so perhaps we can assume the sun always shone on Camp Meeting Sundays.

The Rock boasted its own very able brass band, and it played at the chapel before both morning and evening worship. This must have made the atmosphere unique among Dawley area chapels. The band, in fact, became the forerunner of the eventual Dawley Brass Band, which entertained the public on all sorts of occasions, later in the century.

In case people think that the mines were only a danger to the brave men who toiled down below, the Rock has a story to tell which proves otherwise. One Sunday evening after the service, Billy Sheldon, a life-long stalwart of the chapel, visited his uncle and aunt at their cottage in the village. He was astounded to find them gaping at a hole in the floor of the cottage, half under the kitchen window, and half under the door. The building, and others nearby, had been constructed over a former pit-shaft, and water from the old pit had gradually destabilised the ground to such an extent, that the earth literally opened up beneath them.

Also on the northern fringe of Dawley lay the village of Old Park, somewhat equidistant between Dawley and the Oakengates area. Like The Rock that stood a couple of miles to the west, Old Park grew out of the nearby industrial activity. We already know something of the Old Park Iron Works, and it will come as no surprise to learn that the area sat on considerable reserves of coal, leading to the sinking of a proliferation of, mostly shallow, pit shafts from the late eighteenth century. The village centre mostly straddled a long slope leading up from Mossey Green. It boasted two Wesleyan chapels, one at each end of the slope. The 'bottom' chapel gloried in the name of 'Mount Zion', and the other, not surprisingly, was known as 'Hill Top'. Apart from numerous cottages, the village also had a little shop or two and one or two bakeries. In fact, as the twentieth century progressed, Old Park was looked upon as the virtual 'bakery capital' of the surrounding area. Daily deliveries of the most delicious, unsliced white bread were made around much of the Dawley district from the Old Park bakeries. The delectable aroma of the warm loaves was almost as satisfying as the taste. There were several bakeries around Dawley in the early nineteen hundreds, but their reputation didn't seem to spread as far as the likes of Rowe or Willis of Old Park.

Terraces of industrial workers houses, including 'Forge Row', and scattered, outlying cottages, made up the rest of Old Park which, like so many of Dawley's satellites, seemed to be a community enjoying an identity all its own.

At the beginning of chapter 17, we mentioned that, removed as it was from the scene of the big national and international events, Dawley's life in the early nineteen hundreds was, nevertheless, affected by what was going on elsewhere. It will always be so.

Imagine Monday morning - washing day, and the lady of the house is up to her elbows in soap suds in the outside wash house. There comes a knock on the back door. A doorstep salesman stands there with an armful of posters for sale. When told that they are pictures of Lords Roberts and Kitchener, the good lady immediately dries her hands, and finds a few pennies to purchase these 'must have' portraits. She dutifully hangs them on the living room wall for all to see, knowing that husband Charlie and all the family would be both proud and elated to have such illustrations of the great British Army's Boer War heroes smiling on them from above the settee. It was like pinning a large picture of your favourite football team on the wall on Cup Final day. Staunch patriotism was very much alive, even in a small backwater such as Dawley, and occurrences like the one described above, did happen there. Harry Poyser of Finger Road, Dawley fought in the Boer War, and in readiness for his return from that arduous campaign, a garland of flowers was constructed above the gateway to his house. He was truly feted on his arrival at 'the Finger', and someone even arranged for a talented local lady vocalist to delight his ears with a rendition of 'Home Again, Home Again From a Foreign Shore'. Having come through the ravages of the Boer War, Harry would have been well able to cope with the rousing reception he received.

THE PIG ON THE WALL POSTCARD

The beast that gave Dawley its 'Pig On The Wall' reputation

If a person from some other part of the Wrekin area asked you where you came from, and you replied 'Dawley', the invariable retort would be *'Oh yes, the place where they put the pig on the wall to watch the band go by!'* That reputation seems to relate to a spoof postcard produced way back in 1909, by an enterprising photographic studio. Around 1903, William Baldwin established his sons Ted and George in a studio at Langley Square. They later moved to a wooden structure in a garden behind a row of cottages in 'Old Vicarage Road'. So busy were they trading in this relatively new phenomenon called photography, that for a while they also admitted Charlie Bartlett of Madeley into the partnership. It was in 1909 when they produced the print that became immortal, and apparently gave Dawley its 'Pig On The Wall' renown.

Readers will recall that 1909 was the year when Dawley's memorial to Captain Webb was unveiled, and the Baldwin studio decided to mark the occasion with a tribute of its own. A postcard was designed which was a concoction of separate images, giving the impression that a somewhat obese pig had joined a Dawley fellow perched on the top of a pig sty wall, for the express purpose of watching Captain Webb's celebratory procession going by. Of course, it was nothing of the sort. What seems to have happened is explained below.

A chap named Ern. Fletcher kept a pig in a sty at the back garden of his pub ('The Red Lion') in Little Dawley. Sure enough, when the beast heard Mr. Fletcher coming down the garden, it would raise itself up placing its front trotters on top of the wall, knowing that feeding time was imminent. At some stage, probably in the late 19th century, a photograph was taken of the pig adopting his famous pose, with Ern. Fletcher seated proudly on the wall to the pig's right, and a rather rustic looking be-whiskered gentleman standing at the pig sty gate to the animal's left. The Baldwins got hold of this picture and 'doctored' it so that someone else was seated on the wall in the same attitude as Ern. Fletcher, the rustic gentleman was removed altogether, and the star attraction - the original pig - remained proudly in position atop the wall. A head and shoulders portrait of the Captain filled most of the space where the rustic had stood. In the bottom right hand corner, a brass band was leading a group of marchers along the road, and it sort of looked as though the pig and his human companion were looking down from the pig sty wall and onto the scene. Clever stuff, although closer examination of the picture seems to indicate that the procession in question was none other than part of a Dawley Sunday Schools Demonstration Procession complete with banner, being led by a Salvation Army band. A pub certainly stands in the background, but it is the 'Queens Arms' at 'the Finger', not the Little Dawley pub. The assumption is that the group of marchers represents the Stirchley Wesleyan Sunday School contingent, who were certainly not marching in honour of Matthew Webb. Some places in the Black Country have also been credited with pig on the wall traditions, but, thanks to the initiative of the Baldwins, Dawley has a postcard to boost its claims even if they are somewhat 'tongue in cheek'!

In 1911, King George V was crowned at Westminster Abbey. Even if it had happened at Dawley Parish Church, the event couldn't have been celebrated more enthusiastically than it was in the East Shropshire town. Celebrations were official and highly organised, including an impressive carnival procession, and singing by the children. The people of Dawley Bank were 'urged to co-operate to erect an archway or two there'. Does this mean that the good folk of that district were a bit rebellious, or for some reason traditionally unwilling to go along with what happened in the central part of Dawley? An official handbook was produced (price 1d.), and it was printed by Tom Weaver from his small printing and stationery business in the High Street. As well as providing a graphic run down of the events of the day, the programme also gave a fascinating glimpse of the type of 'excitement' enjoyed by local people on big occasions, in those days. An outdoor dance on the Council Fields in Doseley Road, would 'as the darkness comes, be lighted up for a grand final frolic!' A huge bonfire had been constructed at Heath Hill, which was Dawley's highest piece of ground. At dusk the bonfire was lit, and people craned their necks to see if Dawley's blaze could outdo that emerging from the summit of the Wrekin beacon. Spare a thought also for the indefatigable members of Dawley Town Band -they had one heck of a day. Not satisfied with leading the carnival

procession and accompanying the children's singing, they rounded off with a programme of no fewer than fourteen tunes, with 'Rule Britannia' and the National Anthem thrown in for good measure! A note in the programme asserting that 'the band will receive its instructions from Mr. J. Clayton only!' seemed to suggest that a pretty tight rein had been kept on them, for some reason - perhaps to ensure they had at least a bit of recreation themselves.

CAPTAIN WEBB'S MEMORIAL

Dawley's most famous son was undoubtedly Captain Mathew Webb the Channel swimmer. By 1909, some thirty-four years after his historic achievement, and twenty-six years beyond his untimely death at Niagara, the town had a tangible memorial constructed. It took the form of a white concrete monument that stood proudly at the junction of 'High Street' with 'King Street'. This became Dawley's focal point, and traffic was able to pass either side of, or around it, rather like London's traffic used to circumnavigate 'Eros' in Piccadilly Circus. It was thus positioned at the 'bottom end' of the High Street fairly close to the site of Webb's birth place, and with the 'Lord Hill' hotel as a back drop. The monument was four sided, and on each side there were a couple of steps leading to a drinking bowl served by cast-iron taps in the shape of a lion's head. The bowls and taps were attached to the main pillar of the memorial, which consisted of panelled sides with inscriptions and medallions, and pedimented gables decorating its upper part. Capping all of this were three, bulbous gas-lamps growing out of a single stem. It really was a memorial in keeping with the earlier, Victorian idea of how these things should be. It possessed a restrained dignity, yet had a practical function of benefit to the community. It provided a free drink of water to refresh

The Captain Webb Memorial in its original form.

the passer-by, and lit his way home after dark. Much later, it suffered the indignity of removal from the main thoroughfare altogether. It was tucked away to adorn the front of the branch offices of the former Wrekin District Council, near Paddock Mound, to the rear of the 'Lord Hill' pub. Someone must have thought this would be an honourable place for it, but of course, it meant the monument was nowhere to be seen from the very High Street in which it was originally installed! Nowadays, it is back in its original position at the bottom of the now pedestrianised 'High Street', complete with a more modern lamp at its head. The water taps no longer work, but even if they did, it's doubtful whether they would be put to their intended use.

THE DEMONSTRATION

If there's one annual event which Dawley people remember throughout their lives it's the yearly Sunday Schools Demonstration. It figured in most people's experience whether as participants or onlookers. It ranked with your first day at school, Father Christmas, or the first new potatoes of the season. You knew it would come along every year, and it is remembered by successive generations of Dawley folk as

an inextricable part of their lives. A child of the early twentieth century would have to qualify for a ticket to join the procession, by putting in a minimum number of appearances at Sunday School. Then, on the big day, it was on with your best clothing, have your mug tied around your neck (to be used at the big tea-party after the march-not for use in case of sudden travel sickness!), and off to the Sunday School building. You were then ready to form up behind the huge banner, so that the great trek could begin. The Brandlee Sunday School's banner exhorted 'TRAIN UP A CHILD THE WAY IT SHOULD GO'. That somehow seemed to set the seal on the purpose of the proceedings. On one occasion, at the open-air Service on the 'Meadow Road' field, it seems that both band and choir had different ideas as to when exactly a community hymn should begin. One observer reckoned *'the band was half-an-hour before the choir'*. The respective conductors apparently held a different opinion as to whose baton had the privilege of bringing in the congregation.

On returning from the Service, children would be treated to bread and butter, home made cakes, and mugs of tea on a field near their home chapel (Anglicans did not join the extravaganza until the 1920's). There would be sports and dancing, and prizes to be won. For children who had little in the way of treats or outings during the year, the Demonstration marked a real 'red letter day'. One poignant occurrence took place on Demonstration Day, 1914. While the children were busily tucking into their tea, the news came through that World War I had started. An immediate cloud was cast over the proceedings, and it is said that at Moreton Coppice Sunday School festivities at Horsehay, several members of the band who were playing background music had to put down their instruments and leave immediately, because they were Army Reservists.

CHARACTERS

It's perhaps not generally well known that Dawley had a Town Crier until about 1909/1910. Jack Evans had the distinction of being Dawley's last such messenger, and the familiar 'Oyez!' accompanied with the shrill ringing of a handbell, would precede an announcement of any worthwhile item of local or national news. Noah Ball, who, with his brother Clifford, ran a grocery business in the High Street during the pre-supermarket days of the 1940's and 1950's, kept the redundant crier's bell in his possession for many years. He lived at 'Harp Lane', Dawley.

Another character in the early part of the century was an old gentleman named Mansell Greaves. He had earlier enjoyed the extreme privilege of being a shoe-maker to Queen Victoria. For some reason, he put himself out to grass at Dawley, and spent the twilight of his career helping keep the feet of its citizens suitably clad. Whilst mending a shoe, he would keep a supply of sprigs in his mouth, removing and hammering them in one by one, as required. Had he chanced to sneeze during such an operation, any customer standing by would surely have gained a surprise introduction to the art of body piercing, as well as simply having his shoes mended! A patron who brought a dirty pair of shoes to Mr. Greaves would be told, *'if you'd cleaned these shoes they'd have been lighter for you to carry down here!'* One wonders whether he developed that phrase whilst ministering to good Queen Vic.! Perhaps not, for she would surely not have been amused.

With work harder to come by, poverty was very much 'on the map' for some Dawley people, and especially the elderly who had no pension to help them through their latter years. In those days, instead of 'going on the Social' it was a case of swallowing your pride, and falling back on the Parish Relief. One elderly Lawley Bank woman recalled the days when she was a young girl, charged with the errand of collecting her Grandmother's Parish Relief. A Mr. Moule dispensed the handouts from his house in 'Chapel Street', Dawley. The girl would sit patiently in the kitchen awaiting the crucial word, *'next!'* to be yelled in her direction from the living room. On being told that Granny was unwell that week, the adept Mr. Moule would also hand over a loaf of bread (*'don't pick it!'*), and vouchers for a quantity of beef and brandy. These latter items had to be collected from 'High Street' shops, and were used to make Granny some beef tea. Considering that Granny lived at Old Park, it's likely the girl herself would need reviving after completing her journey, although one assumes she wasn't treated to a helping of the 'Parish Relief medication!'

There was often pressure on children of poorer families to leave school early, and start earning as soon as possible. To qualify for this concession, the child had to obtain a 'Labour Certificate'. This would record that he or she had had a good attendance record over a certain number of years, and could be allowed, if required, to leave school at an earlier age (perhaps as early as eleven years old). As ever, most boys would seek jobs in the mines, while girls went either to the pit bank, or into domestic service. Lancashire was a popular destination in the latter case, since there were more domestic vacancies in that part of the world because many Lancashire girls found ready employment in the cotton mills. The Dawley girls would not only find jobs in the 'Red Rose County', but often husbands as well, so that they settled 'up North' for good.

Chapter Twenty

DAWLEY AND THE GREAT WAR

By 1914, the human race had stumbled into a World War situation. There can be few places in Britain that didn't supply and lose young men to the war effort, at the sharp end. So it was that large numbers of men from Dawley and the East Shropshire coal field joined the war that would 'be over by Christmas' in that fateful year. One amusing story of uncertain origin, concerns a reluctant hero from Dawley who was doing his best to convince his doctor of his unfitness to go to war. He claimed to be suffering from some sort of permanent injury to his arms. When asked by the medic as to how it was affecting him, the fellow replied, *'well, before I `ad me accident, I could lift me arms rate up `ere* (fitting the action to the words), *but now, I con only lift `em this `igh!*

Among the many casualties was a man from Burroughs Bank. In peacetime, he had become well known as an expert poacher. He also supplemented his earnings from the local pit, by delivering milk around the cottages of Burroughs Bank and The Finney, during the evenings. Following his call-up, he was to leave the Little Dawley backwoods for ever, as he was killed in action overseas. A man from the 'Finger Road' area suffered from shell shock long after the conflict was over. Thus, not only did the war cause suffering on the field of battle, but also it cruelly left many of its participants with a legacy of life-long torment which often robbed them of their dignity.

On the home front, war inevitably causes shortages of some of the necessities of life. Some Dawley people walked the eight miles to Wellington and back so that they could queue up outside such stores as the 'Maypole', in the hope of buying some margarine. The commodity wasn't rationed in WWI, but was obviously in short supply.

When at last the Great War ended, relief was enormous and universal. In celebration, Horsehay Works gave several, loud blasts on its hooter that could be heard through much of the surrounding district. Its Managing Director, Mr. Simpson, gave the workers a half-day holiday. The company also gave every employee a savings certificate worth 15 shillings. One energetic young man swiftly converted his certificate into a pair of football boots, costing 14/11d. For several years after the ending of the war, many local firms commemorated Armistice Day at the eleventh hour of the eleventh day in the eleventh month. When it coincided with a working day, work came to a temporary halt for two minutes. Randlay brickworks was one of many places to honour the occasion in such a way.

1914-1918

THE DAWLEY OUR PARENTS
GREW UP IN

The dreadful war was over. The politicians, notably Lloyd George, soon found as politicians always do a phrase to fire the imagination of the people. They were going, so they said, to turn Britain into *'a country fit for heroes'*. Like many others across the nation, Dawley people must have hoped that with the war at last out of the way, prosperity would soon be around the corner. Instead, our parents grew up during the 1920's against a backdrop of huge unemployment, massively swelled by the ranks of returning soldiers. The country's unhappy miners came out on strike for three months during 1921, because their employers reduced their wages and flouted safety regulations. Worse still, a nine-day General Strike took place in 1926, bringing the nation to a virtual standstill. Neither event did much to improve the lot of the protesters.

The newspapers reported that somebody called Adolph Hitler had formed the National Socialist (later Nazi) Party in Germany, and that Benito Mussolini had created the Fascist Party in Italy. It's doubtful whether such tit-bits of information caused even a ripple of interest in Dawley, yet as we all now know, they were events which would have a shattering impact on the whole world in later years. For the well heeled, the twenties brought the dance sensation called 'The Charleston', traditional Jazz and fun-seeking girls who became nicknamed 'flappers'. Scientific progress, including the development of radio communications and the discovery of penicillin, was gathering pace also.

How were Dawley people affected by all of this? It seems that only the things that jeopardised their 'daily bread' had any noticeable impact. Life was a struggle for many families, yet this was nothing new. The wisdom and experience of earlier generations who had suffered the deprivations of the late 1800's, had been passed down to their children, and hence to their grand-children. The daily living environment remained uncannily similar to what it had been for years before, although little by little changes began to creep in. Thankfully, we have the recollections of those who grew up in that post-war era, to help build a picture of what Dawley life was like as the 1920's and 1930's gathered pace.

One rapturous change that settled itself comfortably into the lifestyles of ordinary Dawley folk in the 20's, was the arrival of the town's first real cinema, 'The Cosy'. It wasn't so much an arrival as a conversion job, since the building had originally been constructed for some sort of army training purposes during the First World War. It was a long, shed-like edifice largely made of dingy, black corrugated metal, with a somewhat gothic, black and white frontage tacked on. This made it look like a cross between a mock-tudor mansion and an eastern temple. The conversion took place round about 1921 and, despite the uninviting exterior, the appearance of Dawley's first 'proper' cinema caused huge excitement within the population. The entertainment, both actual and unintentional, made 'The Cosy' a legendary part of the Dawley scene for decades.

One of the early films shown at 'The Cosy' was a silent version of 'The Four Horsemen of the Apocalypse'. On most occasions, musical accompaniment was supplied by pianist Jack Brimstone, of Lawley, sometimes supported by Howard Withington on violin. Part of the fun for the customers came when the hard-working musician failed to keep pace with the film. The obliging audience would give him an admonitory shout, and if the piano broke into a gallop a tad too late, Mr. Brimstone's ears would be assaulted with a gleeful, choral cry of *'not now Jack - theest too late!'* When the sound of gunfire was required, the enterprising cinema owner would persuade a couple of resourceful lads with sticks, to run along either side of the building, dragging the sticks over its corrugated flanks. They created one hell of a din, which those on the inside couldn't fail to appreciate. How on earth he got them to synchronise with the on-screen action, goodness knows. At least Jack Brimstone had the advantage of seeing the screen! To those living within a hundred yards of the cinema, the sound must have convinced them that Armageddon was at hand. Nevertheless, it seems the 'stick artists' would be rewarded with a free seat when their percussive talents were not required.

A visit to 'The Cosy' was not just a question of sitting down in the dark and watching a film. It was an occasion, a much loved experience which (probably once a week), temporarily lifted an otherwise humdrum existence onto a different plain. On the way to the cinema, some folk would stop off at Emma Colley's nearby little shop. Her speciality was bread-pudding. A slice would cost a half

penny, and picture goers would often enter the cinema armed with two pence for the ticket and a fist full of bread-pudding to munch during the show. It was worth saving up all week for that little brush with 'paradise'. Some people felt 'The Cosy' was a bit of a 'flea-pit', and not as agreeable a venue as the Town Hall had been. Despite this, 'The Cosy' really caught on with many people, and played its part in expanding the horizons of Dawley people, for nearly half a century.

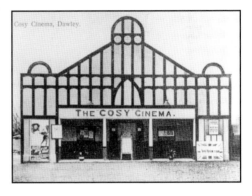

'The Cosy' cinema in its early days

THE DRUGGAN

We now have to mention a topic which is a bit unmentionable. Because the majority of houses were without flush toilets, something had to be done about the material consigned to the depths of the outdoor privies. Some enterprising householders would dig a shallow, circular hole in the ground, then wheelbarrow loads of ash and dump them in the cavity. The contents of the 'loo' would be emptied onto the ash and discreetly covered with yet more ash (thank goodness for coal fires!), so that the whole lot could conveniently be carted away. Most people didn't want, or simply were unable to adopt, such an elaborate strategy, and instead relied upon the services of one of Dawley's real characters - Mr. Jack Hadley. There is not a person who has lived in Dawley during the bulk of the twentieth century, who doesn't know about Jacky Hadley and his celebrated 'muck druggan'. You will not find the word 'druggan' in the dictionary, but Dawley people know that it was the vehicle dragged through the town by a tired cart-horse, in order to empty the outside toilets. The vehicle was under the capable charge of Jack Hadley and his loyal side-kick Tom (Razzer) Kitson.

Emptying the loos was basically night work, and so the polite name for the 'druggan' was 'the night soil cart'. Imagine walking home in the early hours in some remote district of Dawley. Hear the dull plod of a heavy horse as it loomed through the mist, and the clanging of buckets. Finally see the glow of a hurricane lamp gradually illuminating the dour faces of Jack and Tom, as they sat benignly on the front of the 'druggan'. Strangers would have been fearful that the grim reaper was coming to collect them. Local people would simply realise that one of Dawley's key, nocturnal pageants was simply being acted out. At the end of a particularly busy shift, the 'druggan' could still be seen ministering to a few unemptied privies, after daybreak. Little boys would yell to each other, *'eres Jack Hadley and the druggan cummin`!'* No matter what juvenile verbal abuse was thrown his way, Jack would remain unmoved, seated on his vehicle, stoically gazing to the front, and smoking his pipe. In those days the 'druggan's' contents were dumped in a far-flung field, somewhere apparently in the Horsehay area. The apparatus was returned to its shed at Portley Corner, the horse trundled into its field, and Jack walked home to his cottage near the Castle Pool, where he lived alone with his memories of another night's work well done.

Just what made a man dedicate himself to a

job like that? After all, manning the 'druggan' was the man's life! He actually devoted himself to emptying other people's stinking toilets, night after appalling night for most of his working career. What would have happened to Dawley if there had been no Jack Hadley to see to this most unsavoury of tasks? The answer is unimaginable. Jack Hadley deserves to be remembered for eternity, as the man who saved Dawley from disappearing beneath a sea of human waste. The earlier part of Jack's regime created a further legacy. The 'end product' (if you'll pardon the expression) was tipped in various old fields around the district. It was allowed to stand for a few years, before the addition of a covering of soil. Consequently, tracts of fertile agricultural land were created, for which certain local farmers were eternally grateful. An efficacious mixture of ash and 'night soil' created the field near the Park that eventually became the council Playing Fields. The quality of the wild mushrooms that used to grow in the field was exquisite. Now we can appreciate the reason why!

MARCHING AND SHOPPING

A group of Demonstration marchers.

Needless to say, the Sunday Schools

'Demonstration' was still introducing itself to new groups of Dawley's youngsters, and its appeal showed no sign of waning. In fact, during the 1920's, the Anglican churches decided to join in, so that even more pairs of happy feet than ever were making the journey to the Meadow field and back. The programme for the procession had to be re-scheduled so that Holy Trinity, St. Leonard's, and St. Luke's could be dovetailed into the existing routes by joining forces with the nearest Non-Conformist marchers, at some appropriate point along the way.

If there's one place in Dawley at which to gauge the true flavour of the town and its life, it must surely be 'the Street'. This was the place where just about everybody in the area came sooner or later for essential shopping, and for chat. It was a kind of unofficial meeting place for people who liked to natter about this and that, and feel all the better for the experience. Between the wars, the 'High Street' shops were fairly small, rather specialist affairs, so that you still had the traditional butcher, baker and, probably, candlestick maker. You knew exactly where to go for whatever you wanted, and you knew who exactly would serve you, with some friendly (in most cases) chat thrown in at no extra charge. In fact, most of the traders were characters in their own right. They had become household names (at least, in Dawley households), which were as familiar to local people as were the names of the stars of film who graced the screen at 'The Cosy'.

One interesting feature of the town's shops was their remarkable continuity. For instance, some businesses were passed down from father to son. Some premises which had been used for a particular purpose, a stationer's for example, continued under new management in exactly the same line, as if there was a regulation written in the municipal rule-book saying they had to be so used.

Colin Evans, the draper and outfitter, took on the business previously run by his father, Reuben. In his latter years, Reuben Evans suffered with some physical disability (perhaps rheumatism or arthritis). Pottering about the shop became a real trial for him. He was practically doubled up. Bending down and trying to reach something, he could be heard to wail, *'if the Lord wants me, why dunna 'e tek me, not keep me `ere in purgatory!'* . One of his tasks was to measure out and cut lengths of material, which he would do with precision while his glasses were perched on the end of his nose. His wife sold hats while all this was going on in the same shop, and she continued to do so even after Mr. Evans had died, and their son took over the main business. The Frank Bache news agency business had also been passed down from father to son. It seems that at one time, the shop had belonged to the next door butchers, and rented to the Baches for something in the region of 4/0d. a week. Bemrose the chemist also passed down the family line. The elder Bemrose had been a fine local preacher, but having to work late in his dispensary meant that he was unable to attend mid-week church meetings, and therefore did not qualify for a permanent place on the Methodist quarterly preaching programme. Harold Wright's chip shop had in an earlier life also been a chippy, owned by a man who ran a similar establishment near the 'Pear Tree Bridge' inn at Oakengates. Mr. Wright subsequently bought the Dawley business from his predecessor. At one time, Dawley was blessed with a handful of chippies, including one run by Mrs. Blocksidge in a little shop at the end of a row of cottages where the Rest Room now stands. Another one was run by a widow Mrs. Prime, and her daughter, at the bottom of the High Street. A bag of chips cost one penny then.

There were other chippies in outlying areas, and all this suggests that in the earlier part of the century at least, fish and chips were very much 'a poor person's meal'. It probably indicates how low was the pay of the brave souls (no pun intended!) who caught the fish from the deep, and those who painstakingly picked the potatoes. Thomas Weaver's news agency and printing business was eventually sold to Harry Briscoe, and in about 1930, to George Bullock. The latter gentleman kept things pretty much as they had been. He even allowed Mr. Weaver to remain living at the shop following the death of Mrs. Weaver. When Mr. Weaver died, the Bullocks took up residence, having vacated a property near the 'Lord Hill pub'. Mr. Bullock served in the main shop, and for a while, Frank Briscoe operated as Registrar for Dawley Green, in the little adjoining shop that had once been Mrs. Weaver's millinery emporium.

'High Street' characters didn't come much more notable than Herbert Slaney-Jones, the dependable *'if I haven't got it, I can get it you'* man. Of course, it was marvellous to have a store in town where you knew you could get whatever bits and bobs you needed to mend your mangle, or fix a wind-blown drainpipe to the kitchen wall. Nevertheless, there was more to a visit to Slaney-Jones's dimly lit store than merely collecting some essential piece of hardware. The very transaction of buying and selling was laced with 'entertainment', and it was all part of the game for the customer. Watching Herbert's eyes skimming over the rows of tiny, wooden drawers behind the counter, then lighting up when he promptly located the exact item and size you had asked for, kept the customer spellbound with fascination. You rarely left Slaney-Jones's shop empty handed. Then came the 'piece de

resistance'. Leaning on the counter to hand over the requested article, Mr. Slaney-Jones would take you into his confidence and tell you something like *"ere you are my dear that will be ten pence to you, but to anybody else it`ud be a shillin`'*. To a boy buying a cricket ball on his first visit, Mr. Jones would say *'well it's a shillin` really, but you can `ave it for a tanner'*. You always knew he was going to say something like that, but you still felt you were leaving the shop with a bargain. It certainly bettered today's 'three for the price of two' claims for grabbing customer loyalty! By contrast, Mrs. Slaney-Jones sold fine china at an adjoining, glass-fronted shop. Herbert's brother was skilled in engraving brass plates, so most of the local undertakers would make a beeline for this gentleman at the same premises, to have the name of the deceased written for them on a plate which was later to be screwed onto a coffin.

One butcher's shop was apparently not enough for the carnivores of Dawley. Instead, there were about five, dotted intermittently along the street. It seems they each tended to specialise, so that Clayton's for example, was a 'pork butcher', causing beef addicts to make for one of the others, further up the street. Thursday morning was Doomsday for up and coming pigs, since they were duly slaughtered at Clayton's very early on that day. Customers wanting the best cuts were at the shop door soon after breakfast, and felt that their early rising had been fully justified. Curiously, Clayton's was also noted for the delightful aroma of freshly ground coffee. As a sideline, they ground the beans on the same premises, and patrons would be greeted with the intoxicating fragrance as soon as they entered the doorway. Perhaps it also helped to put the hapless pigs in a good frame of mind as well.

Well-known farmer of yesteryear, Joe

Brown, who variously farmed near 'Old Vicarage Road', and at Stirchley Lane, once owned a slaughterhouse just off the High Street, in 'Chapel Street'. For good measure, there were two (unconnected) butchers named Bailey, and we mustn't forget Dockley Lewis also, who later passed on his business to his son Jack. In Dockley's day, there were two Lewis's trading in the High Street, so his rather distinguished first name came in handy in helping customers to avoid confusing the two. As if there weren't enough 'meating houses', Mr. Watts ran a small butchery business in the shop from which his son Charlie later sold bread and cakes.

A LOAD OF COBBLERS

Nowadays, when we possess a pair of shoes that begin to show signs of wear and tear, we simply sling them into the rubbish bin - the people of the 1920's and 1930's, and later, had other ideas. They would take the clapped - out footwear in search of a cobbler, who would be only too glad to knock them into shape again. He would tack on a fresh heel here, or a new sole there, and generally resurrect the shoes so that they would be fit for several hundred more miles, before finally being discarded. As well as having several butchers to the square yard, Dawley had a liberal sprinkling of shoe-repairers, who managed to earn a satisfactory living from keeping the population suitably shod. Of course, some people mended their own shoes, especially 'working shoes', but if you wanted a really professional job doing, or were finding the demands of the garden too time-consuming, off you went to the cobbler's to let him do the job for you.

So who were those good people who spent the lion's share of their lives dedicated to keeping Dawley feet comfortably on the move? Well, of course there was Preece's in the High Street. Will Preece succeeded his father by cobbling and selling footwear at the same premises, and his grey moustache and white hair helped make him a familiar part of the 'High Street' scene. Surprisingly, there were three cobblers to be found in the 'Finger Road' area, so it's more than likely that each part of Dawley had its own posse of shoe-menders also. At 'the Finger' or more precisely, the bottom end of 'Southall Road', yet another of Benjamin Preece's sons, Sam, throve as a shoe-repairer and shoe-maker. Clearly this sort of thing was indelibly entrenched in the Preece blood. Sam was very skilled at his job, and enjoyed friendly conversation with his customers whilst busily turning a sow's ear of a pair of shoes into something of a 'silk purse'. The 'Finger Road' cobbling fraternity also boasted a Mr. Downes, and Billy Balmer, who despite only having one leg, became known for the high quality of his workmanship.

BLACKSMITHS

In order to keep the Dawley economy going, it was not just the proletariat who needed to be responsibly and regularly shod, but also that indispensable leviathan of the transport world, the horse. Two of the best-known blacksmith's premises were to be found at 'King Street' and 'Finger Road' respectively. The 'King Street' enterprise was next to a half-timbered cottage that stood smiling at the nearby 'Lord Hill' (where the public loos now stand), and was therefore clearly visible from the High Street. For much of the first half of the century, horses pulled coal wagons, milk floats, bread vans, goods from railway stations, and so on. Mr. Millward's endeavours at 'King Street' helped for many years to keep the hooves on the march. There was, however, another string to his bow.

He was a more than competent Methodist local preacher, and one evening, while he was busy at the smithy, he received an urgent request to lead that evening's Temperance Meeting at High Street Methodist Chapel,because the intended speaker had 'cried off'. Mr. Millward was the only one who could save the situation, and he readily agreed to step into the breach.,

The Merrington family occupied the same house at the lower end of 'Finger Road', for well over 100 years. The Merrington blacksmith's business was a complete hive of noisy activity, up until the early 1920's. For one thing, Merrington's shod the horses for most of the local farms - up to twenty horses would sometimes be queuing up at 8.00 a.m. One wonders whether Bert Merrington also ran a lucrative side line in manure provision to local gardeners, since by the law of averages, a bevy of static horses were bound to provide quite a large 'tonnage' of the stuff on his property. Sometimes, huntsmen would duly arrive at Merrington's, have their horses re-shod, and carry on with the hunt.

Fred Beckett made cartwheels (not of the gymnastic sort!) on part of Merrington's land. There was a bit of joint enterprise involved with that, since Mr. Merrington produced metal hoops suitably heated up, which were then levered onto the wheels produced by Mr. Beckett in his workshop up the yard behind the smithy. The hoops would be allowed to cool and create a perfect fit for the wheels. Merrington's also manufactured pit chains, to be dragged by horses to the local pits. It is said that it was the falling chains (not made by Merrington's or any other local firm) which had caused the fatalities in the tragic Springwell pit disaster of the 1870's, when they fell onto the fallen miners, as they lay dazed on the pit bottom.

GROCERS AND BAKERS

As well as having its feet protected, the other thing the human race deems essential is getting its stomach regularly filled with acceptable supplies of nourishment. There were little shops dispensing groceries in many of the suburban districts, but the two 'big boys' of the High Street were Smith and Greenhall. Smith's had quite a large 'quality' shop, which added wines and spirits to the list of general provisions stocked at the store next to the junction with 'Meadow Road'. Mr. J.R. Smith, the proprietor, lived at the bottom of 'High Street' (roughly where Tranter, Lowe the accountants now operate), and it is said that when he suffered an illness, he had sawdust spread on the road to deaden the noise of the traffic. It hardly needs saying that Mr. Smith was another of the street's real characters. From time to time, he would appear in the shop from behind the scenes to ensure that everything was running smoothly.

Perhaps Smith's was most notorious for baking bread at the building opposite the cottages in 'Meadow Road'. One man recalls that as a young boy, he was sometimes enlisted to help out at the bakery, and was paid 6d. for pushing holes in the dough, using a curious piece of wood with spikes attached to it. What the operation did for the quality of the end product is known only to those in the trade - one thing is for sure, Smith's bread was highly valued by the customer. When production finally ended at the bakery, some people took to baking their own bread, because they feared that nobody else's would come up to standard. As a result, at least one former customer continued baking his own bread until the early twenty-first century. Imagine - he never knew the utterly bland taste of modern sliced bread. Some people have all the luck!

The demand for Smith's bread around the district was such that a horse drawn delivery van was used to distribute the highly prized loaves to patrons living in the far flung areas. The delivery-man was quite small in stature, and was sometimes the butt of mischievous rhymes from children encountered en route. His response, presumably if he was impressed with the quality of the verse, would often be to toss a cob in the direction of the juvenile bard, as a token of appreciation. Sometimes, he would have a boy assistant sitting alongside him at the front of the van.

A somewhat dubious story tells us that one breadman on reaching the end of his run after delivering in Horsehay, nipped as of habit, into a pub in the village, and downed rather more pints than was advisable. While that was going on, some local youths, being fully aware that the delivery man was over-occupied with quenching his thirst, took the horse out of the shafts of the van, and led it into a nearby field. When the man eventually decided he had room for no more liquor, he went outside and discovered his loss. Returning to the pub in something of a haze, he said to the barman, *'Is my name ___ ___? Cos if it is, I've lost me `oss. If it inna, I've found a bread van!'*

Taking warm bread around the district by horse and van, seemed to be something of a local pastime. Besides the firms already mentioned, there was Reynolds of Little Dawley (who also owned cottages at Southall), H.B. Williams of Horsehay (Mr. Williams also found time to play the organ at the Horsehay Pool chapel), Darralls of Dawley 'High Street', Ruscoe of 'Finger Road', Davies of 'King Street', Payne of Malinslee, as well as the Old Park bakers. As if that wasn't enough, both F.L. and R.N. Moore of Madeley had the temerity to steer their horses and their loaves in the direction of Dawley, as well. You do

wonder whether some people really did live by bread alone.

OTHER TRADERS

In contrast to all of this, Greenhall's seemed to have a rather more detached air about it. Certainly it was (by Dawley standards) a quite large concern, dealing mainly in groceries, cigarettes, etc. Its main business involved supplying most of the small retailers in the district from the warehouse adjoining the shop, next to High Street Methodist Chapel. One of Greenhall's several employees was Mr. W.L. (Bill) Woolley, who dealt with much of the clerical work, and later on, actually took on the business when Mr. Greenhall called it a day. Harry Sutch of Wellington occupied the little shop next to Greenhall's. He had another shop near Wellington's 'Cock Hotel' at that time also. Mr. Sutch sold and repaired bicycles, and his employee was Billy Taylor of Madeley. By a strange coincidence, Billy Taylor subsequently took over the Sutch business in the post World War II period. That part of the street seemed to be a good training ground for upwardly mobile employees!

Walker's also sold groceries at a shop almost opposite the Post Office, with a further little shop in 'King Street', near the 'Terrace Lodge'. Walker's had another string to their bow, since they also owned horses and wagons. The high-spot of the year for some Dawley folk, was an annual horse and wagon trip, courtesy of Walker's, to the Half-Way House on the Wrekin. There, a sticky bun and a bottle of 'pop' were consumed before the intrepid travellers tackled the ascent of the summit, this time relying on 'shanks's pony' rather than Walker's horse. The owner of Darrall's the grocers, would regularly travel by pony and trap from his shop in Oakengates to the branch shops at both Dawley and Bridgnorth. He would hardly have had time to do much else!

The name 'Variety' Phillips is one that lingers long in the consciousness of older Dawley people. Given the amount of hardship in the area, that's not too surprising. Luxury was a word that only a minority of the population could talk about with any degree of understanding. William Phillips could sell you just about anything - provided it was second-hand. Hence, he soon became re-christened 'Variety' by his faithful customers, since it was to his shop they hastened to purchase practically anything from a pin to a battleship, and which had had at least one previous, careful owner. Eventually, he took to selling brand new furniture, and many a newly wed couple would place a modest deposit on a three-piece suite. They would then sign-up to pay the rest on the 'never-never', in the small room at the rear of the shop.

The unsung heroes of the town were the proliferation of little shops hardly announcing themselves, yet highly regarded by their regular patrons. For instance, a Mrs. Skelton kept a small shop near the 'Royal Exchange' pub, roughly where the Rest Room now resides. She made and sold her very own Dandelion and Burdock 'pop'. That beverage was immensely enjoyed by the younger generation in particular, especially on hot summer days. Its quality was remembered years afterwards, as being of the best. Little shops abounded both in the main part of the town, and in the outlying districts. In many cases, they were only able to survive by allowing customers to put their charges 'on the slate', until the next pay packet, or 'dole money' instalment arrived.

Chapter Twenty Two

DAWLEY'S LITTLE COMMUNITIES

MORE ABOUT DAWLEY'S VARIED COMMUNITIES – AND WHAT WENT ON IN THEM

A peek at the lifestyles of ordinary folk during the inter-war years reveals a gradual move from a nineteenth century simplicity, to the tentative dawning of what we might call 'the modern world'.

The Little Dawley area managed to hang on to much of its semi-rural charm throughout most of the century. For a good deal of the time, it still had fields and woods, pools and streams, together with small tracts of farmland for grazing or crop growing. Youngsters growing up in the 1920's would often be reminded of the area's recent industrial past. There would be stories of how grandparents and even great-grandparents had toiled for long, arduous hours in the local pits. The names of the pits, Springwell, Top Yard, Deepfield, and the By Pits were indelibly printed on the mind. The now defunct mines had become an eternal part of the village's culture. The efforts of brave men who returned to the pit to rescue ponies in danger of drowning from the encroaching flood waters, were part of its folklore. Local people would also learn that the 'black diamonds' that once were so painstakingly harvested from the bowels of the earth, were then trundled along narrow railway lines to the Darby ironworks and furnaces at Horsehay, Lightmoor and Coalbrookdale. Amazingly, you can still see the brick bridge that carried the 'ginny' rails over a now defunct canal, soon after beginning the descent from Little Dawley to Lightmoor. We should all be grateful to those dedicated local organisations who had the historic structure superbly restored for posterity, in 1994.

Young lads would play near the derelict engine-houses and chimney stack of the By Pits, just behind the Methodist chapel. When eventually they were demolished, the bricks were cunningly used to build the kilns at Doseley pipeworks. Part of the By Pit's wall had to be demolished by a local resident, in order to accommodate a garage at a nearby property. An elderly citizen walking by at the time asserted, '*if you come across tuppence when you take that wall down it's mine, because I hid it when I was a kid!*'

Dawley Urban District Council eventually set to, and filled in some of the Little Dawley pits with ash extracted from the inevitable ash mounds around the mines.

As a reminder of the village's rural traditions, everyone also knew where 'The Pound' was. A partly walled enclosure stood opposite 'Ivy Farm' on the road to Gravel Leasowes and Doseley. It was the official collection point for stray animals of the district, and had survived the centuries as the pound for the ancient Manor of Dawley Parva. Even so, some people could recall that in the not so distant past, owners could be fined either half-a-crown, or five shillings before reclaiming their long lost creatures.

The Sheward family of Little Dawley could proudly claim to have been involved in both the haulage and blacksmith's businesses for something like 200 years - a quite remarkable feat. In the late nineteenth century, Mr. John Sheward was often consulted by the Coalbrookdale Company when it wanted genuine guidance on the purchase of horses. In the early twentieth century, the family business was often the first one people looked to when a group needed to travel together to some event or other. Horse-drawn, seated carts known as brakes would be used to whisk teams of footballers or cricketers to away matches. Eager punters would be driven the long distance through Corvedale to a session at Ludlow races. Sunday School outings were yet another service catered for by the business.

In earlier days, horses were used in the funeral business. To some extent, things seem to have come full cycle these days. In the early part of the century, horse-drawn transport for both funerals and weddings was highly organised and co-ordinated. For funerals, it was a case of black horses and brass harness, whereas for weddings, it was brown horses and silver harness. A poor person, and there must have been plenty of those about, would be transported to his or her funeral by horse and flat dray. The better off would make their last journey in a horse-drawn hearse. Whilst we're on this cheerful topic, let's not forget that the human participants in the solemn pageant (that is to say, the live ones) were also required to dress the part. At one time, top hats, livery coats with brass buttons, black boots, breeches and leggings were standard issue for funeral personnel. Heaven help them on a blazing hot day! To complete the sense of co-ordination, the horses would sometimes wear black ear-caps. For weddings, white ear-caps with tassels were the order of the day, the nags also being embroidered with white ribbon. Things were never quite the same again, when the age of the horseless vehicle finally took a

hold.

ROAD HAULAGE

Lorries began appearing upon the scene around 1920, and some of the earlier ones tended to be steam-powered. Johnston Brothers of Doseley quarries had one, and it was limited to five miles per hour.

Two of Dawley's well-known haulage contractors, namely Harry Price and John Sheward greeted this new age by acquiring a few lorries apiece. Inevitably, some degree of rivalry sprang up between them, and the Sheward camp loved to tell of an incident involving the firms' respective steam wagons. The rivals shared a Doseley quarry contract involving a journey to Stafford. On the return, Price's vehicle was in the lead and appeared determined to keep it, neither stopping to take on more water nor empty the fire-box ashes. Near the 'Cock Hotel' at Wellington, the Price wagon finally protested at its unsympathetic treatment, in the only way it could. There was an explosion, the lead plug had melted in the fierce heat, and the safety valve and a pile of ash fell to the ground. There must have been one red-faced lorry driver, trying to avoid his opponent's gaze as Sheward's 'tortoise' eventually overtook Price's 'hare' and made it home before dark. Doubtless, Price's could counter with a similar victory over the foe, but the incident shows that the age of healthy competition was very much alive even in the twenties.

It may come as a surprise to learn that many of Shropshire's so-called 'main roads' were relatively narrow, unmetalled 'cart tracks' until shortly after World War I. When the motor vehicle caught on in a big way from the early 1920's, so the roads had to be widened, strengthened with stone hard-core, and of course, topped up with a surface of tarmacadam.

A gentleman by the name of Samuel Woolley who was born at Childs Ercall, but eventually settled at Spring Village near Horsehay Common, on the fringe of Dawley (having been appointed bailiff of Horsehay Farm), played a leading role in bringing the highways up to standard. He showed commendable enterprise in snapping up a steam-roller plus a brace of 'Peerless' lorries (solid tyres and all) from the War Office. They were sold as surplus to requirements after World War I had ended. He then set about finding some work for the vehicles to do. He managed to contract himself to Shropshire County Council, which was embarking on a road improvement scheme throughout the county. Many Shropshire roads were upgraded by this joint venture, and among those close to the East Shropshire area, were the Ironbridge, Buildwas, Cressage route, and the Cressage to Shrewsbury thoroughfare.

NT2551. One of the American 'Peerless' lorries acquired by Samuel Woolley of Horsehay.

Steam power being what it is, you can't just jump aboard a steam-roller, switch on the ignition and race off down the road heading for something that needs flattening. On a typical Monday morning,

Mr. Woolley would be out of bed at the disgustingly early hour of 4.00 a.m., in order to light a fire in the roller's firebox. Gradually, a head of steam would be produced, with sufficient pressure eventually built up, enabling the wonderful giant to carry out its intended function. By 7.00 a.m., the rest of the workforce would have assembled at the Horsehay depot, ready to do battle on another Shropshire track way. Not all of the road-men were purely local, some travelled up from Ketley and Hadley in order to join the happy band of road-builders.

Of the original lorries, one was red and the other grey. Samuel Woolley's son William drove one of them, and Fred Langford of the Potteries the other. Incredibly, the tailboard of the red lorry survives at the bottom of the immaculate garden belonging to Samuel's grandson Alan, at Hartshill in Oakengates. For the compulsive vehicle-spotters among us, it's worth revealing that the ex-War Department stock had to be registered with Shropshire County Council. One of the lorries was then given the Shropshire registration number NT 2551, whilst the steam-roller bore the number NT 260.

BUSES

Mention early forms of omnibus travel to an elderly Dawley person, and in a split second, the name Bert Poole will be uttered from eager lips. For many years, Bert lived in a small, wooden bungalow behind a low wall and hedge at the bottom of 'High Street', almost opposite the Webb Memorial. Rather like Samuel Woolley, Bert Poole was a pioneer blazing a new trail, in this case in the local provision of public transport during the 1920's. He owned two buses, a straight forward, canvas topped charabanc, normally driven by Mr. Poole himself, and the one that all the old-timers always remember, the 'pill box'. This black bus had variously been described as a box on wheels, or a toffee-tin on wheels. You got into the bus from the back, and a Mr. Purcell from Horsehay had the privilege of being the regular driver.

Bert Poole seemed to have a great sense of public duty where his buses were concerned. Men who had to travel weekly down to Wellington in order to 'sign on' at the Labour Exchange (Dawley seems never to have had one of its own), would be conveyed there and back for 2d. On Thursdays and Saturdays, the famous 'Toffee Tin' would run once in each direction to Wellington, coinciding with the market. Imagine the depth of chatter on those weekly bus runs, as a complete load of Dawley people passed the time away on the journey having all the latest gossip over, as the bus clanked its joyful way along the A442. All good things must come to an end of course, and at some stage during the mid-1920's, the inevitable hand of progress drew Mr. Poole's enterprise to a

A 'Midland Red' bus stands opposite Bert Poole's bungalow and bus depot.

close. The Birmingham based 'Midland Red' bus company was busily pursuing its conquest of Midland counties. One by one, local bus firms were succumbing to the big company like British Tribesmen surrendering to the advancing Roman army. The 'invader's' tactic was to run 'Midland' buses at the same time as the existing local services. It wasn't long before Mr. Poole put his hands up in resignation, and sold out to the giant newcomer who was able to run services more frequently, and to more destinations. For some reason, the 'Midland Red' was not interested in the Dawley to Oakengates route operated by Darrall's of Malinslee, perhaps because of the often narrow and pot-holed roads. Darralls' Leyland buses were garaged at the old 'Engine House' near Malinslee Church, and were for many years able to continue their services undisturbed.

COMMUNITY LIFE

As a century moves on, circumstances change, and so inevitably must the environment in which people have to live. The twentieth century was a time of constant change, and it's interesting to observe how the way of life in Dawley's assorted communities was forced to adjust to what was going on.

Take Lawley Bank, for example. The place which was once swarming with pits, and a virtual town of its own, could still boast five butchers' shops and two large grocery businesses, Reynolds and Brice, plus a variety of pubs through the 1920's. By that time, however, most of the pits had gone, and people began to move to other parts of the district and beyond. Traders were now having a struggle to keep going, and it's amazing that a few of them actually managed to survive into the 1940's and early 1950's.

Little Dawley also remained an essentially self-contained community through the first three decades of the century, despite a tailing-off of its mining and agricultural activities. At one time, the 'Unicorn Inn' was still brewing its own beer, under the supervision of the incumbent, Mrs. Wilde. There were two farms near the centre of the village, and a third (Sheward's Ivy Farm) lay just around the corner on the road to Doseley. Of the village farms, Jack Gough's stood where Little Dawley's short row of modern shops now reside. Presumably, the houses now spilling down the slopes towards the Castle Pools and Wide Waters have the privilege of occupying once productive farmland. A bit further down the road from Gough's, and on the opposite side, Jack Price had a farmhouse. Both farms changed hands during the first half of the century. Gough eventually sold out to Powell, while Price's farm went to Wall and Corbett. When Wall left, the Corbetts kept it going. It may have been their cows that used to litter the road in such unladylike fashion during 'bicycle boy's' childhood. If it wasn't, we'll have to blame the Powells. Either way, farming the surrounding fields couldn't have been such a paying game as time wore on. At one point, Mrs. Corbett took in lodgers, apparently from Lancashire, but eventually both farms disappeared from the scene completely during the post-Second World War era. 'Corbett Close' at the northern approach to the village marks the location of the former farm.

Opposite the Methodist Chapel at the centre of the village, Bright and Jones sold groceries from a small shop that later become a 'chippy' for a short period. A little further up, Reynolds bakery was busy mixing dough, and it continued baking up to the late 1940's. Reynolds also had a grocery store, somewhat larger than the Bright and Jones affair, about fifty yards higher up the road. The property became the late Graham Bufton's cycle shop during the latter part of the twentieth century, and is now a private house.

The 'Crown Inn' had stood back from the road, just above the chapel. Despite its historic origins and absorbing history, it became 'a pub too far' at Little Dawley and had to close, ultimately being put out to grass as the Estates Office at Blists Hill Museum, Madeley. Completing the village's commercial life, Mrs. Williams kept the little post office in her dwelling at the end of a row of cottages, just below the chapel. Alas, the homely post office barely survived the 1940's, though the row of cottages remains albeit in an updated condition.

Until the early twentieth century Little Dawley's devoted population could still boast some three Methodist chapels. The one at Gravel Leasowes ('Pop Bottle') had certainly ceased before World War I, and the chapel on the Lightmoor road ('Fat Bacon') had gone by World War II. The story goes that 'Pop Bottle' was a breakaway chapel from the 'Big Penny' at Little Dawley, in the late eighteen hundreds. Soon after closure of the chapel, the property was converted into two houses. It must have been a strange sensation for the local people who moved into what had, for some years, been a place of worship. It still stands, in modified form, amid the mix of properties

'The Wide Waters', showing part of the old sluice mechanism, Little Dawley.

comprising present-day Gravel Leasowes.

The fascinating realisation that dawns on you when looking at the different pockets of the Dawley area as they existed in the 1920's and 1930's, is the fact that each separate community represented its own exclusive little world. There would be small shops catering for most every day needs. A visit to Dawley 'High Street' would be an important weekly event for many. A trip to Wellington or Shrewsbury would almost be a journey to the other end of the world. Horsehay was very much a case in point. Two shops stood at right angles to the dominant Horsehay Works, near Horsehay Pool. Joe and Bessie Ball owned the smaller of the two. It was essentially a general store (what they didn't stock, you could probably live without), but Joe's forte was his toffee making, whilst Bessie relieved the monotony by producing home made boiled sweets. After Joe's death, Bessie continued serving the local community as 'Grocer and Sugar Boiler' well into the 1950's. Next door was the 'Co-op', the 'Ironbridge and District Co-operative Society' to be a bit more exact. For many years, the manager was a Mr. Ted Bradburn, who later became his own boss by quitting the Co-op to open his own little outlet at Coke Hearth, in Coalbrookdale. Horsehay's shopping facilities were a bit scattered, effectively mirroring its living accommodation. Howard (H.B.) Williams ran a successful general store in 'Woodhouse Lane', and there was a bakery attached, Mr. Preece being the baker. We can see that it was possible to buy 'Horsehay bread' as well as 'Little Dawley bread' and 'Old Park bread', and so on. It would have been nice if each village bakery had had the village's name embossed on the crust, or somehow lettered through the middle, seaside rock style, so that visitors could buy it and take it home as a nutritious reminder of their stay. There was yet another small general store cum-sweet shop, at Horsehay, this time on the corner of 'Woodhouse Lane' and 'Wellington Road'. Whilst it was convenient to be able to pop around the corner to buy your groceries and sweets, it's no wonder the generation growing up between the wars had such immense need of false teeth, by the time they reached middle-age! Being a village full of ironworkers and miners, Horsehay needed some pretty central watering holes as well as grocery stores. The 'Forester Arms' was the most central, situated on the junction of the roads to Dawley and Lawley. The 'All Labour in Vain' was also nearby, while the 'Traveller's Joy' lay in a dip at the bottom of 'Woodhouse Lane', looking up at Horsehay Works. For good measure, the 'Station Inn' ensured that travellers between Horsehay and Dawley had no reason to die of thirst, as they made the one-mile journey connecting the two. All of those hostelries seem to be doing well, even in the present day.

We've often mentioned that Dawley was characterised by its plethora of little, tucked away, self-contained communities. Horsehay had its own little gem on the outer fringes. This was Spring Village, a collection of cottages close to Horsehay Pool, and backed by the open expanse of Horsehay Common. It was thus a bit separated from the rest of Horsehay, and would have grown out of the need for accommodation for the miners and others who came to work nearby. Not to be outdone, the village-within-a-village still managed to have at least a couple of small shops, selling the bare necessities to a ready-made local customer base.

Enos (commonly referred to as 'Een') Bott had a cottage cum-small general store straddling the border between village and common. Strangely, close by was yet another little shop where Jim Ball sold cigarettes and other 'essentials'. It seems curious to have two, practically competing shops in the same stretch of the same tiny community. Mr. Bott had a further activity, however, since he also travelled around the Dawley district most days of the week, dispensing paraffin, candles, sweets, and so on, from a horse and cart during the 1920's and 1930's. 'Een' Bott would have a different destination each day, as he sought to cover most of the area, bringing the goods to the consumer. While Mr. Bott was on tour, his wife served in the shop. She had a reputation for generosity, and canny young children would time their visits to the store to coincide with her incumbency. They knew that this way, they would get a bigger helping of sweets to the pennyworth than would otherwise have been the case.

Generosity of spirit was not confined to the Bott side of the commercial divide, however. Some lucky youngsters who called to collect their fathers' regular cigarette rations, were able to persuade Mrs. Ball to let them check various packets of 'Woodbines' for cigarette cards they still needed for their collections. Those packets would be put on one side, ready for the errand boys' next visit. While Bott's speciality was paraffin, Ball's was cakes and pikelets, and those delicacies were freshly made in the cottage adjoining the shop. Why do such idyllic days have to pass into complete oblivion?

Horsehay may well be described as a village even today. There are some lucky cottages overlooking either the pool or the common, and it is still surrounded by a certain amount of countryside, but for many years it was essentially a place where people came to work. The expansive premises of the 'Horsehay Company Limited' provided employment for over three hundred people, and dominated the view from just about every angle. In the early part of the century, the Simpson-owned Company had made quite a name

for itself, by sending steel bridges and overhead cranes to such distant places as South Africa and Argentina.

No Company is, however, impervious to the economic misfortunes of its host nation. By the end of the 1920's, trade at Horsehay had slumped quite badly. Some workers found that they had been unable to accumulate enough stamps on their cards to qualify for 'labour pay'. They were out of work, and out of pocket, and this would have a knock-on effect on Dawley's retailers. Some ex-Horsehay employees moved, at least temporarily, to distant parts of the country, some as far away as Lincoln, in order to find suitable employment. Horsehay-trained workers could justly claim to be among the most highly skilled in Shropshire, and other employers would be only too pleased to take them on. For those staying on at the company, there was the need to put up with whatever alternative work the company's hard-pressed management could provide. By 1935, the firm had started making moulds for engineering components as a way of keeping the company breathing. Some of the company's choicest offerings were displayed at the British Industries Fair in Castle Bromwich, Birmingham, in an attempt to spread the word about Horsehay's new product line to a wider industrial audience. Even though the nature of the work was not entirely to the liking of some of the workforce, they knew that it was simply a case of 'take it or leave it'.

Another 'tucked-away' Dawley enclave was called 'Southall'. It lay slumbering just off the junction of the A442 main road and the minor road to Little Dawley. It was little more than a clump of miners' cottages, surrounded by abandoned pit mounds whose surface was becoming increasingly clothed with encroaching trees. By the 1920's, some of the cottages, probably built by the 'Coalbrookdale Company' a hundred years earlier, were in the private ownership of John Reynolds of Little Dawley. One woman and her family had to live there by courtesy of the Parish Relief, following the untimely death of the main bread winner. Another family, unable to scrape together the rent, was promptly evicted by order of the Court. The cottages themselves were small yet, in their way, quite comfortable to live in. Some were in short rows, where there was one outside washhouse to each pair of dwellings. Diplomacy and patience would thus be important qualities on washdays! The settlement was too small to have its own shop, but close enough both to 'Finger Road' and 'Old Vicarage Road', to not be too inconvenienced by that state of affairs. Children would play games on the nearby mounds. Some adventurous boys would often make the trek to Little Dawley, and join forces with other lads in a communal game of football on Springwell Mount, using a proper lace-up ball.

While Southall quietly looked after itself at the south east extremity of Dawley, Brandlee lived its own little life just to the north west of Dawley's centre. Some of the old Brandlee still remains, including a row of cottages in a half-hidden area between the top of 'Doseley Road' (near the Roman Catholic Church) and the beginning of 'Station Road' (virtually opposite 'Morton Court'). Much of Brandlee was gathered around a nearby hill, and it owed its existence to the proliferation of coal-pits that broke out like an unwelcome rash during the nineteenth century. On the one side of the hill, the so-called White Brick Works with its distinctive chimneys was still working at the turn of the century, while at the other, facing 'Station Road', was the Brandlee Methodist New Connexion chapel. As we know, the chapel came into existence during the nineteenth century, largely due to the enthusiasm of a manager of the 'Coalbrookdale Company's' Horsehay Ironworks. It remained a well-supported place of worship for many years,

until closure was forced upon it in the late 1930's. The chapel had been a bit of a hot bed of stirring hymn-singing, and has even been credited with the writing of an unofficial 'Dawley carol'. The four-verse carol (author unknown) begins with the words:

*'When marshalled on the nightly plain,
The glittering host bestood the sky.*

The carol goes on to tell how the star of Bethlehem guided the writer through his or her sea of troubles. There was at least one further carol said to be peculiar to Dawley. Its origins are unknown, and it tells of someone's personal encounter with the Saviour. The first two lines are:
*'Whilst nature was sinking in silence to rest,
The last rays of daylight shone dim in the west.'*
For some reason, its chorus wished everyone a Happy Christmas.

A view of Brandlee, looking towards 'Doseley Road' and 'High Street'.

The last organist at Brandlee chapel was Harry Boycott. Mr. Boycott seems to have been something of a child prodigy, since at 11 years of age he played the organ for the Sunday School Anniversary. Presumably, some of the children on the platform, and certainly all the choir members, would have been older than he was.

Dick Jones the undertaker and builder at Brandlee, traded under his father's name of Ben Jones. He was one of at least five undertakers in Dawley at that time. Dick was a total character. There is a story that after one of many funerals he arranged at Little Wenlock Church, he was invited to have a drink with the bereaved family before leaving for home. *'Ar, Missus'*, he replied, *'we 'ud better 'ave one to wash 'im oer Jordan!'*

It's hard to speak of Malinslee in the same breath as Brandlee or Southall. Present-day Malinslee seems little more than a rather sprawling dormitory, near the fringe of Telford Centre. Nevertheless, in pre-and immediate post-second world war days, it was every bit the little self-contained community as were the others. During the 1920's and 1930's, the properties all spoke of earlier times, including St. Leonard's Church which overlooked the entire scene. There were brick cottages, some in short rows, and the occasional detached house strung out along 'Church Road', with 'The Wicketts' pub for company. Many of those buildings are alive and kicking today. Typically, the cottages had no running water, and the loo was way down the bottom of the garden. Downstairs, there would be a parlour, and a living room leading to a built-on scullery where the washing-up was done. The wash house was outside. The absence of running water meant that the strong men of the house had to hump bucketsful of cold water from the hydrant down the road, and pour them into the copper the night before washing day. Sticks were lit under the copper to produce a fire to heat the water. If you thought the cold water carrier had it rough, spare a thought for the lady of the house, who had to pummel the washing in a large tub repeatedly, using a long, wooden 'dolly'. In fact, the tub was affectionately known as the 'dolly tub'. If that wasn't enough exercise for one day, there then followed the tiresome business of scrubbing stubborn stains with a bar of soap, and using a wash-board. Finally, every item had to be put between the wooden rollers of a heavy mangle, the dear lady, of course, having to turn the large handle until every drop of moisture had surrendered.

Another pub, the 'Park Inn', used to lurk in a quiet lane running parallel to 'Church Road'. The beer was 6d. a pint. The Thompson family lived in, and also kept a fish and chip shop in 'Church Road'. The nearest 'proper' shop was a brief walk away, at the junction of 'Bank Road' and 'Church Road'. Here, Leslie Hollis sold all sorts of things, including paraffin, sweets (as ever), bread and so on. Children eager to spend their pocket money could invest 1d., and receive in exchange a variety of old favourites including bulls-eyes, kay-li suckers, and gobstoppers, all poured into separate little bags.

Just past the Church gates, and the Institute building at 'Church Road', was a lane to the right leading to a row of rather different-looking (stone) cottages. Their official address was also 'Church Road', but they have enjoyed the nickname 'Skylight Row' for many a year. Nowadays, they form part of 'Brunel Road'. It appears that when the young Gertrude Plant, a resident of the said cottages, got married, a local newspaper reporter noticed windows in the roof of her family home. He referred to the entire place as 'Skylight Row', and the name was happily adopted for posterity. Miss Webb, from St. Georges was the owner. The rent was 7/6d. per fortnight. People who had lived there have described the cottages as nice, three bedroom dwellings, each with a cellar that never got wet. The experience of some folk living in 'Church Road' itself was a little different. The cellars in those, privately rented cottages could sometimes fill up with unwelcome water. Once, on the far side of the cellar a man had become marooned by the flood and was rescued by resourceful family members who hauled a tin bath down the cellar steps. They launched it on the water, and pushed it in the castaway's general direction, so that he could row himself back to safety!

As far as the rest of Malinslee was concerned, there were a few mineworkers' cottages beyond 'Skylight Row', including those at Little Eyton Fold, and some further cottages at Moor Farm. Otherwise, it was a case of fields and pit mounds. Spout Mound and Pottuck Mound were among the more prominent of them, and there were others in the vicinity of the present-day 'Moor Road'. Although many of the pits had long since been abandoned, people still dug their own little 'adits' into the hillsides in search of free bucketsful of domestic fuel.

'Skylight Row', Malinslee.

The nearby farmland could also provide a bit of mild excitement. It was not unknown for adventurous lads to nick swedes from the fields, adding to their intake of fresh vegetables. Frank Taylor, who farmed part of the area, once wheeled two dead, new-born calves out of his field. Some gypsies who happened to be passing by, told him to hang the bodies over a beam in the cowshed, and the problem wouldn't recur. He did, and apparently it didn't!

EDWARD PARRY

Rev. Edward Parry's name has already flitted through these pages, and his imperious influence was still very much a part of the Malinslee scene in the 1920's and 30's. Most Malinslee people of the period have some entertaining tale or other to tell about the redoubtable clergyman. He really was the 'squire' of Malinslee, being landowner, and, of course, vicar all rolled into one. He was a forceful presence throughout his little empire, and not only on a Sunday, either. People called him 'Sir', and practically stood to attention as he approached. If he told a passing boy to take his hands out of his pockets, he would be obeyed instantly. One day, a boy was carrying a bucket of water from a hydrant near 'Church Road'. Along came Parry, who instructed the boy to '*go and ask them to give you another, and balance yourself*'. Clearly, the vicar didn't want any unbalanced teenagers in his parish!

Parry the farmer kept a horse and two cows, which were fed with hay scythed by some willing parishioner, from the long grass in the churchyard. Incidentally, it appears that the main burial ground at the churchyard occupied a field once donated to Rev. Parry by a Mr. Jones of Lawley Bank Post Office. The vicar also cultivated certain tracts of land, including a patch near the pump pool, along the lane leading to Old Park. A couple of fellows were employed one morning, wheeling heavy, rain- sodden clods of earth from the nearby mound. Parry, patrolling his territory, alighted upon the scene, wearing a white smock and straw hat. With his distinctive deep and commanding voice, he yelled, gesturing towards the heavy wheelbarrow, *'put it down, put it down, move those clods to the back, it's pushing the wheel into the ground!'* The weary blokes complied, then one said, *'righto sir, weer dust want 'em?'* *'Over there put them over there'* the vicar ordered.* *'Righto sir'* came the response, whereupon one of the workmen having become overtaken with mischief, 'accidentally' flung one shovel-full in Parry's direction, transforming him into the one-hundred and second dalmation! This resulted in one of the few occasions when the vicar was heard to 'cuss' in public!

What was he like on a Sunday, you may be asking? The answer is, pretty much the same, domineering personality he was through the rest of the week. His sermons were not noted for their brevity, and he wouldn't hesitate to interrupt his own address by telling some restless boy to *'take that sweet out of your mouth!'*

Chapter Twenty Three

THE THINGS PEOPLE GOT UP TO

THE DEMONSTRATION, CHOIRS, CONCERTS, CINEMAS, GAMES AND PRANKS, FLOWER SHOWS, CHRISTMAS

It's good to discover that the annual Demonstration was still weaving its exhilarating spell over new generations of Dawley youngsters. The procession was an achievement of precision planning. Things had to go strictly according to the programme, so that getting the various Sunday School groups from different geographical areas to dovetail into the march at the right place and the right time was like plotting a military campaign. Nevertheless, it worked. One elderly lady recalls taking part with the Stirchley Methodist Chapel. On their enthusiastic tramp to the Demonstration field, the Stirchley contingent met up with their 'Finger Road' counterparts at 'Finger Road', not surprisingly. The augmented group then trudged to Portley Corner, where they were joined by fellow footsloggers from Little Dawley. Sometimes, a band would lead the marchers from Stirchley, and the Little Dawley lot would have to fall in behind Stirchley.The next year, the situation would be reversed, and Stirchley would have to follow Little Dawley and its accompanying band. Those groups approaching Dawley from the Portley direction had the misfortune of having to climb Dun Cow Bank. How those poor buglers managed to keep bugling whilst climbing such a steep gradient, one can only guess at. Then it was a short downhill jaunt to the big field in 'King Street', nowadays occupied by 'Attwood Terrace' and what we still like to call 'The Royal' cinema (in truth 'The Royal' bingo hall).

After the open-air service, there followed the excitement of processing along the town's main High Street, watched by a huge audience of onlookers. That was a once a year experience, nay privilege, which gave the marchers a feeling of brimming importance. For the Stirchley group, it was a case of trekking past the park in 'Doseley Road', down the 'Gander Fields' to Portley Corner, and along 'Finger Road'. Finally, they would arrive back at the Sunday School building for a grand tea. Not too grand mind you, because soon afterwards the children would be led to a field at nearby Wallows Farm, for sports and games. It was a real day to savour and remember.

It's thought that it was not until the 1920's, that the Anglican Sunday Schools began taking part, but once they did, they stayed with the event until the end of its days. One C of E girl was first allowed by her mother to take part at the age of about five or six. Mum made a silk dress especially for the Demonstration. Roses were freshly picked from the garden, and carefully arranged in a little wicker basket for carrying in the procession. An excited bunch of Sunday School scholars would congregate at the schoolroom near Dawley Parish Church, awaiting the arrival of the troupe of Wesleyans from Little Dawley. Following the main event, there would be a 'bean-feast' in the grounds of the vicarage which was, of course, nowhere near the church, but close to the National School, off 'Doseley Road'. Again, there would be games and competitions, and prizes to be won. Our girl remembers going home carrying a papier mache bird on a stick, plus a fist full of pennies. She has described the entire event as the most wonderful day of her life up to that point.

It's only fair that adult churchgoers should also have their share of excitement. Sunday School Teachers would walk in the Demonstration procession, at the head of their particular contingent. Apart from anything else, some persons of high stamina levels were needed to carry the school's banner, which was supported by a long pole at either end.

A Sunday School contingent from Stirchley chapel assembles at the Demonstration field.

CHOIRS AND 'HOME MADE' ENTERTAINMENT

Whilst weeknight church meetings of various kinds continued to be well supported during the first half of the century, it was the chapel and church choirs which tended to attract adults in greater numbers. There was also a social element attached to choirs. Choir practices were, apart from an opportunity to exercise ones lungs in the musical sense, a chance to chat in a relaxed way about this and that, and there were annual choir suppers and summer outings to enjoy as well.

East Shropshire's reputation for fine choral singing has been well known for over one hundred years, and Dawley was very much at the centre of it. Every Non-Conformist chapel, it seems, had a choir, and a good one at that. The choir's main job was to lead the singing at Sunday worship. This they did quite lustily. In local parlance, they would often 'bost it' especially where the hymn had a rousing tune. You could well imagine the rafters being raised throughout the district on a typical Sunday evening. There would also be annual Sunday School Anniversaries, and Choir Sermons where the choirs would play leading parts. The Anglican churches would also be well served by their choristers.

That wasn't all, however. There was a Dawley Male Voice Choir, even a Little Dawley Male Voice Choir, and eventually a Dawley Philharmonic Choir (so that the ladies could get a look in, as well). These 'specialist' choirs generally recruited from local churches and chapels anyway. There was a time when Dawley and District Male Voice Choir, under the direction of George Holleyhead, was sixty voices strong. They often rehearsed in the schoolroom at Lawley Bank Methodist chapel. They did well in competitions at Music Festivals such as Chadsmoor, near Cannock.

Dawley Philharmonic Choir first saw the light of day in 1930. It was very much an amalgam of members of the various local church choirs. What a brilliant idea to pool all of that talent into one whacking great mixed choir. Whoever thought of it should have been awarded a medal. A committee was duly formed, and an accompanist chosen. She was the same Miss Mary Jones who once kept the music and stationer's shop in part of the converted Market Hall entrance in Dawley 'High Street'. All it needed was a talented conductor to weld all those voices into a successful unit. In their infinite wisdom, the committee appointed

Dawley Philharmonic Choir

one of the choir's founders, Bert Gregory (no relation to the author) to that vital post. Mr. Gregory remained conductor for some 21 memorable years. He really was the right person for the job. A man of the highest integrity, both musical and otherwise, Bert Gregory also possessed the subtle skills needed to get the very best out of the singers. The choir soon built for itself an enviable reputation for quality, delighting audiences in concerts (often for charity) at church halls, and even the Music Hall at Shrewsbury. 'The Bluebird' was one of the choir's favourite pieces, and virtually became its signature tune. Like the male voice choir, the 'Dawley Phil.' won awards at Music Festivals, being regular performers at the once renowned St. Georges festival. They even brought the

First Prize away from a competition over the border in Wales. Regular rehearsals were held in the Methodist Schoolroom in 'Chapel Street,' although the final rehearsal before an open-air contest generally took place on a piece of spare ground behind the draper's shop of Colin Evans (himself a choir member), in 'High Street'.

It seems the inter-war years were the golden age of 'home-made' entertainment. In Dawley, besides the impressive choirs, there were numerous talented individuals who strutted their stuff at church and chapel concerts all around the district, on a fairly regular basis. Among them were Emanuel ('Man') Holleyhead of The Lodge, near Malinslee who later lived at the chapel cottage, Stirchley. He was a fine soloist who would sometimes team up with George Hollis of 'Bank Road' to sing 'Watchman, What Of The Night', and other favourites. Then there was Ern. Heighway, a modest yet multi-talented man, who could not only sing but also perform musical gymnastics using a set of spoons, wooden finger-held clappers, and even a large saw. Billy Hollis of Jiggers Bank, near Horsehay, was another master of the musical saw. There were many others and although the much enjoyed local concerts continued into the immediate post-war years, their days were, sadly, numbered. The unstoppable impact of the fast-developing cinema industry, and later the captivating presence of television within the home itself, led many people to settle for nothing less than professional entertainment. Nevertheless, the passing of the 'church concerts' is a cause of much regret. They were social occasions, get-togethers where people could enjoy watching familiar faces displaying their talents, and, of course, where they could catch up on the latest gossip over a cup of tea during the interval. How much flair has subsequently remained undiscovered, one wonders, since the disappearance of those fertile outlets?

PAYING TO BE ENTERTAINED

Live entertainment was not confined to church and chapel halls. The ever drab-looking Town Hall continued drawing in certain types of audiences. If the sight of two, game Dawley men furiously boxing one another around a ring, bleeding but refusing to hit the canvas, was your idea of fun, then the Town Hall was definitely the place to be on fight nights. On another night, Tommy Allworth's local dance band would provide a more soothing experience. Tommy was also a gifted artist. Amongst other things, he painted the advertisements on the safety curtain at the cinema. 'Jack Ashley's taxis', and 'Play up Eddie, Church

Road, Dawley' (whatever that meant), were two of the adverts that vied for your attention before the picture show began.

For youngsters living on the outskirts of the town, a family Saturday evening visit to 'The Cosy' cinema was an eagerly awaited event. Pocket money would usually stretch to the purchase of a chocolate bar from Frank Morgan's shop, near the picture house (they even had 'Aero' in the late 1930's!). Seats at 'The Cosy' were mostly 9d, although one shilling would entitle you to occupy the back rows, which were separated from the rest by a short gap and a low, wooden divider across the front. After the escapism of the picture show, there was sometimes a visit to a nearby fish and chip shop. There was nothing like a hot, vinegar-sodden *'penn'orth'* to take the mind off the long walk home.

One person recalls that 'Sonny Boy' featuring the incomparable Al Jolson, was the first 'talkie' film to arrive at 'The Cosy'. Certainly, a non-talkie featuring a singing Al Jolson would not be much use, let's face it. Colour hit the screen at 'The Cosy' a little later, in the shape of an all-singing, all-dancing extravaganza (pre-dating Fred and Ginger) whose title seems to have been erased from people's memories.

Whilst family visits were commonplace during the evenings, it was young ones only on Saturday afternoons. Tuppence would get you into the special children's show, and one penny would buy you a bag of sweets to suck while you were enjoying the performance. A cinema visit was a special occasion, whenever it took place.

Demand for the cinema had grown to such an extent by the late 1930's, that a second emporium was constructed at the corner of 'King Street' and 'Meadow Road'. This was 'The Royal' cinema which fronted 'King

Street'.

GAMES AND PRANKS

Money being at a premium, and opportunities for ready-made entertainment still fairly limited, it was largely a question of 'make your own fun' for most of Dawley's population including the rising generation. Lads tended to go for such legitimate games as Tip Cat, Tin Can Murky, Whack Horse, (a very robust romp, that one), spinning cigarette cards to get one on top of another, and the inevitable marbles (by gaslight in the dark evenings). Informal games of football or cricket would be played on local fields and pit mounds. Girls would prefer Hopscotch, skipping, or perhaps Hide and Seek, or sometimes just nattering in a group under a gaslight or seated on a wall.

Winters were often hard and kept people in doors. Board games such as Ludo, Snakes and Ladders (often received as Christmas presents) were popular pastimes with which neighbouring children could join in. Reading and card games were enjoyed, and some resourceful youngsters would learn the piano and give 'concerts' in front of the family at the fireside. Some girls learnt to sew, and produced their own frocks, others made small dolls out of handkerchiefs.

In the modern world, we have hooligans and muggers and people who generally think it's their duty to behave badly in public places. There have been skinheads, mods and rockers, teddy boys and so on. Older people have seen them as a kind of organised threat to their peaceful way of living. What all this ruminating is leading up to is that in young people, there has always been a certain roguishness, a need to cock a bit of a snook at authority, or the adult world in general. It existed in the first half of the twentieth century, without a doubt. The difference was that there was a line that should not be crossed. There was an in-built respect for one's elders.

Pranks there may have been, but they were little more than harmless fun, a moderate letting-off of steam. In small-town Britain at any rate, there were no menacing gangs to frighten the life out of vulnerable members of society.

Let's be straight, butter <u>would</u> have melted in the mouth of a Dawley youngster - living in a semi-industrial environment would have seen to that. The difference was that their skylarking would be quickly over and done with, forgiven, and forgotten by most victims, perhaps with a wry smile of reluctant admiration. With a sentimental relish, older residents have confessed to some of the antics they got up to as

House at 'Church Road' with Bake House and Wash House attached.

children, although they would certainly not have owned up to them at the time. There was the night that the gas lamp failed to work in 'Church Road'. Unable to play their usual game of marbles, some 'resourceful' boys relieved the boredom by tying a length of black cotton to a shoebox, suitably stuffed with nothing of value. Along came an unsuspecting adult who bent to pick up the box, which was yanked to safety by the lurking lads. Even a group of girls were not averse to filling an empty sugar bag with soil, sealing it and placing it in the middle of the road (not 'Church Road' this time). A dear lady returning from a shopping expedition at Dawley, and thinking she had had the good fortune to discover a 'freebie' bag of sugar on her walk home, promptly picked it up and carried it home in her basket. In another location, thick thread was used to tie together the knobs at the front doors of two adjoining cottages. An intrepid youth knocked on one of the doors, then joined his comrades concealed behind a low wall, to watch the spectacle of two increasingly irate neighbours struggling without success to open their doors.

Of course, not all pranks were as comparatively innocent as the ones described above. Even where someone got carried away and really overstepped the mark, however, they would live in fear of being found out, as respect for adults including the local 'Bobby', was still deeply ingrained in a young person's psyche.

FLOWER SHOWS

Grown-ups, of course, were able to think of much more constructive things to do. Since most Dawley homes had sizeable gardens attached, it's no surprise to learn that growing flowers and vegetables was a popular pastime among the adult fraternity. Comparing notes as the various seasons wore on, was a major topic of conversation throughout the district. Some keen types constantly strove for excellence, so that the desire for some kind of 'flower show' reached a crescendo in the early 1930's. John Robert Harris was the man who 'grasped the nettle' so to speak, by organising Dawley's first (apparently) show in a lean-to adjoining the diminutive Finger Road Methodist Chapel. The chapel also boasted a Men's Own Choir, which for some reason sang at the chapel on Sunday afternoons. It seems to have started as some sort of men's fraternal meeting, with visiting speakers spouting on some interesting topic or other. From this, sprouted the choir, and later the flower show. The choir later moved to the Town Hall for more singing and visiting speakers, and subsequently to the Methodist Sunday Schoolroom in 'Chapel Street'. Where the choir went, so the flower show followed since roughly the same group of chaps was involved in both.

August Monday, in those days the first Monday in that month, and a Bank Holiday, was the day the flowers were put on display. This was also of course, Demonstration Day at Dawley, and the show would start immediately after the grand parade had passed through the High Street on its way home. What a 'master stroke' that was! The centre of the town would already be swimming with onlookers, so why not encourage this captive audience to crowd into the building and admire the displays, rounding off a really good day in the Dawley calendar?

Dawley Flower Show's fortunes fluctuated with the passage of time, and had to be resurrected during the late 1930's. At that point, along came Mr. John Wooding senior (father of the Oxford graduate John Wooding, who later ran a grocery store in the High Street). Mr. Wooding had a delightful garden of his own in 'King Street', and was always very willing to pass on tips to other aspiring gardeners, whilst showing them around his empire. The general feeling was, *'what Shrewsbury can do, Dawley can do also'*. Shrewsbury Show was, and still is, <u>the</u> big horticultural event in Shropshire. Dawley enthusiasts, dismayed at the tail-off in its own event, felt the time was right to re-launch it by aiming big. Under John Wooding's guidance, Dawley Chrysanthemum Society was born. Floral displays would be concentrated purely on the chrysanthemum, whilst vegetable growers would be able to show off their specimens as well. Of course, the event never managed to rival Shrewsbury's, but the impetus given to it by Mr. Wooding and others ensured its long-term success. Competitions were open to gardeners living within a twenty-mile radius of Dawley, and it really meant something to be a prize winner at the Dawley show. Furthermore, Dawley was one of only a few places in Shropshire where you could win a prize for simply growing chrysanthemums.

For the chrysanthemum grower, producing blooms for the show was virtually a year round occupation. As many as sixty or seventy ten-inch pots would be carefully nursed in the grower's greenhouse, just to get a few blooms worthy of putting on display on August Monday. It's good to be able to say that the Society still exists, even though some of its long-term members now find the fiddling and bending required by the all-year pursuit of perfection, a bit beyond the pale now. They meet monthly at the 'Dun Cow' annexe, and are still entertained by visiting speakers spouting on some interesting topic or other. The convivial evening is brought to a close by the introduction of a buffet supper. The annual show now takes place at Dawley Christian Centre, in the centre of the High Street. Thus, one of Dawley's traditions continues to flourish. Some members actually show at National events, also. One of them, who was a novice when he joined the society, has been so well tutored by his new found friends, that he has risen to the rank of official of the National Chrysanthemum Society, and has won two gold medals for his services to that illustrious body.

CHRISTMAS

No one in the Western World will need telling that the Christmas season is special. Most elderly Dawley folk will tell you that their Christmases were really wonderful, and nobody would doubt the fact. When you look more closely at the way the festive season was actually spent by working-class people, you realise that simplicity was the keynote to a memorable time. Perhaps we in the modern world could learn a thing or two from that message, or has the 'high tech' computer game, digital T.V., hi-fi system age in which we live taken us too far to turn back?

Christmas morning started when your parents told you it did. Even so, it would be reasonably early, as a child's sense of excitement would soon be ready to bubble over. The first job of the day was to explore the contents of the stocking which had been ceremoniously hung over the bed rail the night before, and was now magically bulging with good things which had materialised during the hours of sleeping. Most people had one main, if unspectacular, present - a board game of some sort, perhaps - and a collection of smaller ones. The smaller items ranged from nuts, an apple and an orange, (quite a treat in those days) to a shiny new penny-just imagine the amount of sweets to be purchased with that! A girl might also dig a new hair ribbon out of the depths of the stocking, and a boy a large handkerchief perhaps. The thing is those seemingly mundane items were the sorts of things a child rarely had during the rest of the year. Money was generally pretty scarce, and the gifts didn't come all that cheaply either.

After breakfast, it was quite usual for groups of children to meet up on that enchanting morning, and set off on a carol-singing jaunt around the neighbourhood. It was a traditional thing, an accepted part of Christmas Morning, whereby neighbours would place pennies and halfpennies on a plate in anticipation of a visit from the juvenile warblers. Christmas Day just wouldn't have been the same without it. One young boy, who lost his father when he was only three years old, found the carol singing an economic necessity. His first port of call was the house of the lady next door, and she, in exchange for a sincere rendition of 'Brightest and Best of the Sons of the Morning', would hand over a sixpence piece, no less. Thus encouraged, he would embark on an ever-expanding musical tour of the district, eventually finishing up at the Nedge Farmhouse near Shifnal! He would have exercised his larynx to such an extent en route, that there would have been precious voice left to say 'Thank You' for the donation received at the latter venue. The sad fact is that because there was no longer a breadwinner in his family, he had no real Christmas presents, and had little more than the bare essentials throughout the rest of the year. The exhausting carol singing excursion was a means of compensation for what he had missed out on.

On the subject of carol singing, we should mention that it was also the custom of local chapel choirs to tour the area during the evenings leading up to the festival, and give their renditions whilst gathered around the front doors of certain selected residents. They got to know the places where they would be well received, and generously rewarded. Cash donations would in some cases be used to supplement much needed choir funds, in others it would be given to a suitable charity. Either way, the householders who were blessed with a visit, looked forward to the annual spectacle of well-muffled choristers grouped in the half-light, and sending the magical sound of traditional carols into the cold evening air. One chapel choir visited a cottage in 'Finger Road' and had to squeeze within the cramped confines of a walled front lawn. Unfortunately, the men on the back row were forced to lean on the wall and found to their horror, that part of it collapsed under their combined weight. After thanking their host for his contribution, and receiving such plaudits as *'Good Show, Good Show'* at the quality of their performance, the group trudged on into the night, not daring to reveal what had happened to the wall!

Christmas, apart from being a commemoration of the birth of Christ, was the supreme time of year for getting together, and relieving an otherwise miserable time of year with some family fun. Christmas dinner (for people fortunate enough to have one) would be a much enjoyed experience, usually involving just the immediate family. A chicken or cockerel, specially fattened up for the occasion by the householders themselves, would provide the centre-piece at the table. Once the grand meal was over and done with, the rest of the day would be the time for joining forces with others. Admittedly, some would snooze away the afternoon, while others welcomed grandparents, uncles and aunts, and so on for what the Irish might call 'a bit of a hooley'. Games would be played, with which everyone had to join in - just because it was Christmas! Great mirth would be shared from watching awkward people doing things they were simply not cut out to do. Imagine Granny, for instance, trying to throw a rubber ring at a ring board fixed to the kitchen door, and you will see what I mean.

For some families, it would be at teatime that the get-togethers started. Neighbours and friends, young and old, would often be part of the throng. After tea, there would be an evening of home-made entertainment. Board games (fresh from Santa Claus's delivery service), Blind Man's Buff, and so on would be played with much laughter, the sort you only seemed to get at Christmas. When it was time to slacken the pace, there would always be someone who could knock up a carol or two on an upright piano, or perhaps a scratchy violin. The evening just went its course, with laughter and conversation being the essential ingredients. How on earth did television manage to muscle in on such a perfect state of affairs, in later years?

Boxing Day saw another round of visits to relatives and friends, and Dawley at least, had a special tradition that belonged to that day alone. That was the arrival of the 'Molly Dancers'. The title seems to be a Dawley corruption of the general term 'Morris Dancers', but it's questionable whether the Dawley Boxing Day performance was quite the same as that seen anywhere else. The 'Molly Dancers' always seemed to arrive after the Boxing Day lunch had been consumed, and the crockery put away. A strange band of perhaps three or four youths with blackened faces, and wearing rather battered top hats would suddenly materialise in your back yard, as if they had dropped there from another planet.

From descriptions given by various observers, it seems there was more than one troupe of 'Mollies' going the rounds. It is said that some wore small bells strapped to their legs, some used tambourines, or wooden clappers, or a mouth organ, or even a concertina to accompany the song and dance routine. Two large sticks would often be knocked together to help the rhythm along. The common thread was the blackened faces and tophats. Nobody seemed to recognise the entertainers, so that they would literally be curious groups of mystery men, sometimes allowing their audiences to join in with them. It is thought that one such bunch came from Dark Lane,

but one person who confessed to the author that he had, in fact, been a regular 'Molly Dancer' during his youth, was very much a Dawley man. His great uncle had been keen to pass the tradition (not to mention a concertina) down to him in the late 1920's, to ensure the thing kept going. From that, we can deduce that Great Uncle had himself been a Dawley 'Molly Dancer' in the mid-to-late eighteen hundreds. Goodness knows how many generations of those mystery men had preceded him. The apparel, the dance routine, and the distinctive song they sang must have remained unaltered over a very long period, and were certainly in evidence during the 1940's.

Whatever memories people have of the 'Molly Dancers', one strand remains consistent - the distinctive song they performed. The words went like this:

'SOMEBODY'S IN THE HOUSE OF DINAH,
SOMEBODY'S IN THE HOUSE I KNOW,
SOMEBODY'S IN THE HOUSE OF DINAH,
PLAYING ON THE OLD BANJO.

RUMPSY, DUMPSY DOO DI DAY,
RUMPSY, DUMPSY DOO DI DAY,'

The verse would be repeated several times but what the heck it all meant (and who wrote the ditty) nobody seems very sure.

The happy band or bands took their gig to all parts of the Dawley area. The object of the exercise was to raise much-needed cash, so perhaps the entertainers came from less well-off families. Some even carried a large tin bath around in order to collect the pennies. Most people would be happy to reward the performance with a few coins, and farmhouses were known to be particularly lucrative stopping off places.

Chapter Twenty Four

DAWLEY COUNCIL MAKES ITS MARK

AND UP GO THE HOUSES

A community has to be run by somebody. Basic amenities have to be provided, and the general fabric of the place needs to be maintained at a civilised level by some municipal body, while the population dutifully gets on with the engrossing business of everyday living. We've said earlier, that Dawley's seat of government became an Urban District Council in 1894. In time, the council took responsibility for such diverse activities as drains and sewerage (yes, Jack Hadley and Co. were council employees, and the celebrated druggan was a council asset), street cleaning, housing allocation and maintenance, pot hole filling, and so on.

The council's first offices were then conveniently stationed at the Market Hall entrance, where the round-arched windows are. You climbed up one or two steps to get to the door - its seems the Victorians always felt you should climb a few steps to get into an important building. It was a sort of homage, which ordinary people were obliged to pay towards officialdom. You had to know your place. The premises were later to become Mary Jones's stationer's shop, and later still, the Gas showroom. Today, they are occupied by a cafe. By 1935, the council had outgrown its first home, and it upped and went to 'King Street', occupying a large, red brick house (previously inhabited by Mr. Hal Simpson of Horsehay Works), near the 'Ring-o-Bells' pub. It stayed there for a long time, and even allowed the Welfare Office to share the building for a while. The council offices remained at 'King Street' until 1968,

when a sort of Civic Centre was built on the Paddock Mound. Alas, the march of progress overtook the D.U.D.C., in 1974. The nationwide local government re-organisation decreed that the council, which had expanded its empire in the latter years to reach such places as Hollinswood, and Cherry Tree Hill near Coalbrookdale, was to be no more. A new blanket authority, initially known as Wrekin District Council, took over administration of virtually the whole of Telford, so that eighty years of purely local administration disappeared overnight.

'King Street' from the 'Ring-o-Bells', and showing the gabled former council offices.

The 'Ever-Ready' battery-company, that had a branch factory on the former Hinkshay United football field in the middle part of the century, successfully applied for a Grant of Arms in 1956. This gave the Dawley council a rather impressive coat of arms, symbolising the fusion of the three, traditional Dawley parishes, and a maritime crest commemorating 'Captain Webb the Dawley Man' (as John Betjeman persisted in calling him in his poem). The Latin words *'TRINIS CATENIS VINCTUS'* completed the design. They may not have conveyed much to the local ratepayer, but the words gave an instant touch of class to a previously unassuming authority, and actually meant 'three together conquer'.

Housing was mentioned as being one of the council's charges, and the period between the wars saw the authority taking the matter very seriously indeed. It wasn't so much a case of a huge population explosion, after all, even in 1891, some eighteen per cent of Dawley parish's houses were unoccupied due to industrial decline. The problem was that most of the population was living in dwellings created up to one hundred and fifty years earlier, to cater for the then booming working community.

'New Road', Dawley. Some of the first council houses built in the town.

Most of the premises were considered sub-standard by the 1920's. Young married

couples were often living with parents, other families or other types of rented accommodation. Conditions were simply too cramped, and in many cases, insanitary. Even so, it took until 1927 for something to happen. For the next nine years, the council managed to fling up some 370 houses on five sites, sandwiched between St. Leonard's Church, Malinslee, and 'New Road' to the south of Portley Corner. More were added soon afterwards.

The council houses built during that time had a solid and permanent feel to them. They became the backbone of Dawley's housing stock through most of the remainder of the twentieth century, being modernised with central heating, double-glazing and so on, during the later decades. Their names became familiar to all around. The order in which they went up was roughly - 'Finger Road' (The Ley), and 'New Road' between 1927 and 1930, with more at 'New Road' in 1935/6, making sixty in all; twenty six at 'Portley Road', near the High Street (1931/2); sixty four at 'Alma Avenue' and 'Rhodes Avenue', Malinslee (1933/4); one hundred and twelve at 'Johnston Road' and 'Ardern Avenue' off 'King Street' (1936/9); forty eight at 'Attwood Terrace' on the old Demonstration field (1937/8). Most houses were built as semi-detached pairs to a standard, government approved design, using bricks and tiles manufactured locally, and local labour wherever possible.

Some resourceful person, or persons, at the council offices, would have been designated the task of inventing suitable names for the various housing developments. One obvious ploy was to use the names of council officers, or councillors, who had distinguished themselves in the course of keeping Dawley 'ticking over'.

Let's start with 'Johnston Road'. The Johnston brothers decided to quit London and start a business in Dawley in 1915. These were the Johnston brothers of Doseley pipeworks fame. The company has been spinning large drainage, sewerage and various kinds of water pipes at Doseley quarries, at a rather dusty site near St. Luke's Church, Doseley ever since. It has provided employment in the area for the best part of one hundred years, and you can still see huge articulated lorries toiling up Doseley Bank, and making their lumbering passage towards the nearest motorway, heavily laden with great circular, grey pipes even today. In the early days, one of the Johnstons so integrated himself into Dawley's society, that he became chairman of the council. He must have made a good job of it, because he's been immortalised in the name of the road in question.

Another illustrious council chairman before World War II, was Mr. Alma Rhodes. Whether he got his first name from the battle of Alma is not known, but he was so well thought of in Dawley that two neighbouring streets were named in his honour. So it is that 'Alma Avenue' and 'Rhodes Avenue' proudly commemorate the celebrated man, as they lie contentedly close to St. Leonard's Church, at Malinslee. Similarly, 'Attwood Terrace' perpetuates the name of the former Councillor Attwood, (of Malinslee Hall). The tradition of remembering past Chairmen in that way has continued through the post-war period.

Whilst we are talking names, when it comes to 'Finger Road', we could argue over that until Gabriel blows his final call. The simplest explanation seems to be that it was all down to a pub in that area called 'Peter's Finger'. Now why give a Dawley pub a name like that? Some say that it relates to old pictures of the first Pope (St. Peter) raising his finger to give a blessing. Incredibly, there is apparently a place in Wiltshire called Dawdley, which also just happens to have a pub named 'Peter's Finger'.

One long-time Dawley resident has said he understood that at some point in the town's history, a form of property tax was payable on certain privately owned buildings. The local tax collector was named Peter. When a homeowner was about to spend his money, someone would say to him, *'well be careful, or Peter's finger will be on you!'* The implication was that Peter would soon be pointing at you, if you hadn't enough cash left to pay the tax. Presumably, the building where the levy was collected was the building that eventually became the pub Christened 'Peter's Finger'. The pub was believed to have dated from 1782. People going to the pub would say, *'we're going to the Finger'*, and the whole district was somehow pleased to adopt the name for itself. The pub was demolished in 1906, to be replaced during that year by 'Haughmond Villas'. That dwelling still stands at the beginning of 'Southall Road', close to the 'Queen's Arms pub'. The house has the old pub's date plaque incorporated into the chimney.

The transformation begun in the late 1920's and carried on through the 1930's, gave central Dawley a virtually new set of clothing. As we know, most Dawley folk were living in properties built somewhere between the late 1790's and the mid-nineteenth century. Fairly humble cottages, terraced rows and so on festooned the area from the times when the great 'coal-rush' got seriously under way. With World War One safely behind them, the Dawley council decided it was time to do something about the increasingly overcrowded and unhygienic conditions under which many people were living. The problem was that large-scale house building was simply too expensive, so it wasn't until 1927, when the Government poured some decent money into local authority coffers for the purpose, that Dawley U.D.C. got cracking in earnest.

In 1927, up went the first of the line of houses built along one side of 'New Road', and the process continued into the early 1930's. Between 1927 and 1930 the first houses at the so-called 'Finger Road' were built. By 1936, the 'New Road' houses had acquired a new neighbour at 'Finger Road' (actually, it was off the true 'Finger Road', and near to where the senior citizens' development known as 'The Ley' now stands). The properties bordered two sides of a tract of grassland traditionally called 'The Ley', where children often played their summer games. Together with the 'New Road' dwellings, this ensured that the field was surrounded on three sides by council housing. Talking of 'New Road', there were enough bricks to spare from the project to allow local resident Mr. Bob Briscoe, to have a property built from them. Mr. Briscoe owned a bungalow and smallholding in the vicinity, and even kept a cow in the field behind them. To illustrate the still semi-rural environment of the 1930's, Mr. Briscoe, having milked the cow, was a familiar sight as he carried buckets of fresh milk using a yolk around his neck in classic rustic fashion. He would tap on the windows of 'New Road's' houses, and his ready-made customers would have their jugs filled to the brims. Wasn't he thankful for the council's initiative! Completing the pastoral scene, a threshing machine would be stored overnight in Mr. Briscoe's drive during the summer, ready to be used by local farmers for gathering in the harvest. A sloping field just south of the High Street became 'Portley Road' during 1931. One historian has conjectured that the name 'Portley Road' may relate to some ancient 'castle gates or portals'. All we can say for sure is that the road was fairly close to an existing area known as 'Portley', consisting of a field and some cottages situated where today stands the junction of 'New Road' with the A442. We will assume the 'ley' part of the name refers to an ancient field, just as it does in the names Dawley,

Lawley and Doseley etc. As for the first part of the name, well we may never really know its origins.

Portley Colliery and its pit mound had stood where fir trees now overlook Portley Corner, a road junction controlled today by traffic lights where 'Springhill Road', 'New Street', 'Finger Road' and 'New Road' now manage to collide with one another. If they'd had the time, the house builders at 'Portley Road' would have been able to wave at the fellows busily planting fir trees just across the way. The council, to its credit, decided to camouflage the defunct pit mounds of the former Paddock and Portley Collieries, by planting shoals of pines all over the large, offending humps. The vast mound of the old Parish Colliery, 'New Road's' companion, came in for the same treatment. The results of the planters' efforts can still be admired today, bringing a little touch of 'Norwegian woodland' to Dawley's landscape. A lot of unemployed labour was used on the project, and the workers set to in 1928 and continued planting until about 1934. In fact, if a man had been 'on the labour' for a certain length of time, he would be obliged to join the tree planters, or else be cut off from receiving any more unemployment pay. The tree-planting work, whilst unpaid, was the means of qualifying for further aid. You were then able to visit the Receiving Officer, Mr. Frank Moule, who promptly gave you a note telling you where to go in order to claim food.

A Mr. Houlston held the position of Means Test Officer. This entailed touring the district to verify people's financial situations. No mean job, you may say. It certainly couldn't have been easy. Just imagine having to tell somebody who had one of those honky-tonk, upright pianos in a corner of the parlour (the focus of many a good Christmas sing-a-long), that it would have to be sold or there would be no help with the family budget. The job must have been full of such discordant notes!

'Alma Avenue' and 'Rhodes Avenue' gave St. Leonard's Church at Malinslee some much-needed company. Perhaps they helped to fill the pews somewhat, as well.

South of the church, quite a large tract of land gave way to the street known as 'Ardern Avenue'. During 1937/8, the historic field which had proudly hosted the Dawley Demonstration for some forty years, finally disappeared to be replaced by a combination of 'Attwood Terrace' and 'The Royal' cinema.

Naturally, there was no shortage of people to populate these spanking new houses. The Housing Act of 1930 had empowered the council to earmark a number of the older cottages and terraces as slums ripe for clearance, so they had to go. Families moved from the likes of Dark Lane, Rough Grounds, Old Park and so on to the council estates. Recently married couples were also among the lucky ones to get a new house. If you did manage to get one (and not everyone was so fortunate), you really felt that you had arrived. You had become the proud tenant of a brand new, nice-looking relatively spacious and well-built property that had running water (cold, of course), and a flush loo located within or at least closely attached to the house itself. Ordinary people had never lived amid such luxury. Imagine no more long walks down the garden on freezing cold nights in search of the privy! The habit of a lifetime had been curtailed at a stroke, and nobody minded.

'Ardern Avenue'

143

'A pig on the wall view of Dawley'

WAR AND PEACE

Chapter Twenty Five

HOW DAWLEY SURVIVED
WORLD WAR II

On 3rd September, 1939, the unthinkable happened. Britain and France found themselves plunging into conflict with Germany, and ultimately, World War for the second time in 21 years. The untidy political mess left over in Europe, and especially Germany, from the 'settlement' of World War I had boomeranged to such an extent that the old foes simply had to slug it out again. Once more, young men and women, including many from Dawley, were either called-up or volunteered to fight for the cause of 'right over wrong'. If you volunteered, you had more say in where you were deployed. If you were called-up, you more or less went where you were told. Although the casualties were somewhat less than the astronomical losses of the First World War, millions died during the six year conflict up to 1945, and many others were scarred for life. So it was that Dawley and East Shropshire men sacrificed their lives in such diverse areas as France, Germany, Italy, Greece, North Africa, the Far East, the North Sea, and so on. You'd think the world would have had enough of war, yet it still goes on in one form or another, and probably always will.

Dawley men had to register for call-up at the labour exchange in Oakengates. One man from Sandy Bank Row, Doseley, was encouraged by others to register as a plater's help, a protected occupation, and thus avoid call-up. He couldn't tell an untruth, and registered correctly as a welder. He was duly called-up, but was subsequently killed in action, becoming one of the many who didn't return home from the fighting.

Dawley could hardly claim to have been a war zone, yet it couldn't help being affected by what was going on elsewhere. No battle was fought anywhere near its boundaries, yet it felt the impact of the war perhaps a little more keenly in some respects, than it had during World War I. A world event of such monumental proportions ushered in a new and different era in the experience of most people, so it is possible to talk of 'war time in Dawley', and we can build a picture of how the town was affected by the situation.

The main thing to be done was to get ready in case there was some form of attack. The development of air transport since World War I for example, meant that all parts of Britain had become vulnerable to attack from the skies. Quite early on, an important meeting was held in the Town Hall in order to form a Dawley branch of the Home Guard. Mr. Joseph Simpson, of the 'Horsehay Company Limited' chaired the gathering. The meeting was partly made up of old soldiers who had fought and suffered during World War I in such places as the Western Front, Egypt, Gallipoli, and the Dardanelles. What they didn't know about fighting for King and Country was hardly worth knowing. It seems, however, that Mr. Simpson's ride was not a smooth one, for there is talk of friction at the meeting between him and a former 'time-serving man'. Nevertheless, things were straightened out, and a Dawley battalion was duly formed, with Mr. Simpson in overall charge.

The battalion was split into smaller platoons, each group having its own particular function. One was nicknamed 'The Tankbusters' (it's not readily apparent as to why), but its main job was to keep an eye on Horsehay Works where, unknown to Hitler, gun mounts were being made to help the war effort. Duty squaddies would take it in turns to patrol the works at night, with rifle on shoulder just in case. The platoon's H.Q. was a room above the weighbridge at the top end of the works, not far from Horsehay railway station. Percy Bullock, a Manager at the works, ran an Intelligence Section, at a different location. Mr. Bullock also did most of the clerical work for the Dawley battalion. Other platoons had very humble beginnings such as a cottage at Single Row, Hinkshay, before graduating, in that particular case, to a room at the 'White Hart' pub. There was also an Ambulance Section led by Frank Jones of 'New Road', and based, rather luxuriously, at the Town Hall. One of the latter platoon's more unsavoury tasks was to spend a particular Sunday afternoon visiting Malinslee railway station, Dark Lane, where an injured man was mysteriously lying in the Waiting Room. Since the trains didn't run on Sundays, the man's predicament was all the more unusual. The resourceful men dragged the twenty-two stone victim over the railway bridge, and down to Dark Lane Chapel. By that time, they had deduced that his injuries were pretty serious, and Frank Jones himself came to see what had happened, so the man was carted away by an ambulance from Shifnal. All in a day's work, you may say, but there would have been a few weary limbs and back muscles among the platoon members following the afternoon's events.

One Dawley man who worked at the John Maddocks Foundry in Oakengates, was invited to join the Oakengates battalion. Being an existing and proud member of one of the Dawley platoons led by Billy Edwards, he retorted *'No, I'm gunna guard Dawley. The Jerries are not gunna shoot me in Oakengates, if they'n gunna shoot me, they'n gunna shoot me in bloody*

Dawley, not Oakengates!'

If you think the antics of television's 'Dad's Army' troop are a bit over the top, if you'll pardon the pun, the reality as far as some sections of the Dawley battalion were concerned, was even more hilarious. You have to appreciate that many of the men were simply ordinary blokes with no previous experience of military discipline or procedures, and who simply wanted to 'do their bit' to help. One man was so huge, that when his platoon went on manoeuvres in the local countryside, he found he couldn't get through the gaps in the hedges. He had to be given special dispensation to run around the hedge, instead of through it. He sounds just the kind of fellow to be a 'tankbuster!'

Members of The Home Guard: Dawley

Home Guard volunteers were required to undergo some basic training, in some cases at Dover. There is a dubious story of a Dawley man who was on night duty training on the White Cliffs of Dover, and found things sufficiently quiet as to allow him to sit on his rifle butt and light up a cigarette. While he was enjoying his peaceful smoke, a training Officer crept up behind him and prodded him in the back with the barrel of his rifle. The Dawley man turned around, startled. *'Now then, what would you have done if I'd have been a German?'* asked the angry Officer.

'You've no need to worry,' came the swift reply, 'I've already done it!'

The other worthy group of laymen dedicated to protecting life and limb, were the A.R.P. (Air Raid Precautions) Wardens. Their main responsibility was to deal with fires in the event of an enemy raid. Their regular meeting place was a room in one of the buildings in 'Burton Street', and another industrialist, Mr. Mulroyd, manager of Johnston Brothers, Doseley, was the man in charge. In one training exercise at Malinslee, the wardens lit a 'demo' fire, then found that the hose wouldn't reach it. Undeterred, the stalwart officers promptly and carefully moved the fire closer to the hose, to give them some valuable practice in putting the thing out! One nightly routine involved touring the district in pairs, checking that all housing was properly 'blacked out'. People were obliged to cover their windows at night, with some black material in addition to normal curtains, so that no chink of light would be visible to the enemy flying overhead. Most folk purchased a sort of roller-blind made of fairly stiff, black paper. Each evening, before interior lights were switched on, out would come the blinds from their daytime hidey-holes, and onto the window recesses they would be fixed. How the shops managed to supply exactly the right sizes is hard to understand. Some people simply taped dark crepe paper to their windows but either way, it was a strict obligation to seal off any hint of light from within the house. If a warden spotted a transgressor, he would knock at the offender's door and issue a stern reminder that the matter be put right forthwith.

DANGER IN THE AIR

Dawley seemed to be on a regular Luftwaffe flight path to and from Merseyside. As a squadron of bombers approached (usually after dark), the distinctive air-raid siren fixed to the police station building, would wail its fearful warning, and the population braced itself for the possibility of an attack. German bombers made a distinctive 'vrum vrum' sound, and you could always tell when a bunch of them was overhead. Even today, older residents can recall the stomach-churning feeling that accompanied the howling siren, the silent wait, then the droning of the enemy planes as they flew over. When they'd gone, the all clear was sounded, but when they returned from discharging their deadly cargoes, the procedure was repeated. People could breathe more easily when the final all clear echoed over the rooftops. The town was completely dark, of course, since even the street lamps remained unlit. If the enemy decided to bomb Birmingham, or perhaps even Coventry some fifty miles away, people living in the higher parts of Dawley could clearly see the crimson glow etched eerily in the distant gloom to the south. Some brave souls even went outside to watch German planes drifting in and out of the glare of searchlights as they pressed onwards towards their destination.

No bombs were dropped on Dawley, but there is plenty of evidence of some falling nearby. One German bomb dropped close to Lawley School, leaving a huge crater in the ground. Of course, bombs could fall accidentally, and it was also the practice to get rid of any 'undelivered' devices at some point during the return journey. Another such stray exploded near the Wrekin (it was loud enough to be heard in Dawley), and yet another landed in woods near Lilleshall. Bombs were dropped in anger, however, at Allscott Sugarbeet Factory, and in the Ironbridge Gorge. Ironbridge Power Station was an obvious target, and for that reason it was defended by anti-air craft guns whose brick emplacements can still be seen today. One is near Buildwas Abbey, the other close to Cressage bridge.

One Saturday morning in the early days of the war, a Dawley woman working at the 'Merrythought' toy factory at Dale End, Coalbrookdale, rushed out of her office on hearing an unusual sounding aircraft flying low along the Severn valley. When she got outside, she saw a German bomber flying so low that she could see the pilot, and the distinctive emblem of an enemy aircraft. Some buildings then obscured her vision, but she heard the deafening sound of bombs exploding on the Benthall Edge side of the River Severn, just a short way along the Wharfage. She returned to the factory, only to find a colleague normally noted for his bravado, busily cowering under the table! A Horsehay pupil at Coalbrookdale High School was summoned, along with others, to the school that same Saturday morning. Their brief was to paste sheets of muslin onto the classroom windows, to prevent the glass from shattering in the event of a German attack. Their efforts were none too soon, as the sound of two huge explosions tested the efficiency of their workmanship. Presumably, the plane was interested in fouling up the power station, but had taken a dislike to the menacing guns. Instead, they must have decided to leave the good people of Ironbridge with a souvenir of their visit. There are no reports of any casualties, or indeed of any other attempts at sabotaging that part of the electricity system.

Apart from bombs arriving on the ground, the planes themselves sometimes did the same thing. An R.A.F. machine crash-landed in a field just below Stirchley village. A lot of people went to see it, and the good old Home Guard was charged with the job of looking after it. Thankfully, no one was harmed. More tragically, a United States Air Force Fighter on a training stint from Atcham airfield was seen to dive low, and partly ablaze, towards the centre of Lawley Bank. It actually hit the ground on a smallish patch of grass that can still be seen just in front of the 'Bull's Head' pub. The pilot must have tried desperately to avoid nearby houses, and managed to hit the piece of land which once had been a bullring. A young silver birch tree currently stands on the spot where the plane crashed. It is said that the young pilot's watch was still on his wrist, and in full working order despite the impact. Sadly, its owner was not so fortunate. In the 1960's, his parents visited the scene, and presumably found some kind of comfort in knowing exactly where their son had lost his life.

Lawley Bank. The site of the World War II U.S.A.F. plane crash.

WARTIME VISITORS

Perhaps nothing could convince you more eloquently that a war was going on, and that something out of the ordinary was happening all over the place, than the sight of groups of servicemen milling around your own neighbourhood. The former Methodist Sunday Schoolroom at the top end of 'Chapel Street', was host to various groups of service personnel during wartime. It was a quite large building of dull brick, built in the 1860's, and stood virtually opposite the blue-brick Methodist chapel. Today, the site is part of the car park behind the 'Co-op Pioneer' supermarket. The unspectacular building was once alive with the sound of American

G.I's who soon became acquainted with the local population, especially the female element!

The 'Yanks' could often be seen riding their bikes around the district, and so well did they ingratiate themselves with the ladies, that some Dawley girls went back with them to the U.S.A. as brides! One American, billeted at the schoolroom in 'Chapel Street' regularly entertained at a dance hall in Wellington, under the name of 'Rinss Lee and his Rhythmagicians', and it is believed that he too married and took a local girl back to the States. The lifestyle of these ladies would have been transformed forever, thanks to the Second World War.

British Forces also occupied the 'Chapel Street' schoolroom at some stage in the proceedings. We may ask why so many soldiers were eager to reside in Dawley. The answer chiefly seems to lie in the persistent, unbelievably lengthy convoys that were forever wending their way through the town, along the A442 road. Where they were all coming from or going to, only the military knew. Frequent snakes of canvas-covered army lorries, some carrying goods, some carrying personnel, some also hauling huge and rather frightening cannon guns, and all escorted by jeeps, could often be seen crawling through the High Street. There would be a jeep at the front bearing a red flag, and one at the rear sporting a green one. The American jeeps would also have a large white star painted on the bonnet. Some convoys would be going north, while others travelled south. There were so many of them that you felt the entire war effort was being channelled through Dawley, and that it stood along the nation's most important artery for the movement of military equipment. Sometimes, a fleet of tanks would rumble noisily through the town. The staff at 'base camp Chapel Street' had to ensure the convoys were safely

directed through their section of the route. Signposts had been removed in order to confuse the enemy, so somebody had to guarantee that our chaps could find their way. Soldiers would travel from Dawley to some rendezvous point, sometimes using motor bikes, to clear the traffic and point the way so that the convoy could proceed smoothly along its journey. Some people say that the Dawley, and Lightmoor (stables) billets were also used as 'overspill' accommodation for the Atcham air-training base.

Dawley received other interesting wartime visitors. In an effort to boost the morale of people throughout the country, popular entertainers of the day used to travel from place to place, and give concerts at suitable venues. The newly built 'Royal' at Dawley was one of the chosen halls on the circuit, and special live shows were staged there about four times a year during the war. The shows were eagerly looked forward to and much enjoyed by many Dawley people. The pianist Semprini was among the star performers to visit 'The Royal'.

THOUGHT FOR FOOD

An everyday effect of wartime was a disturbing shortage of those things that nowadays, we pluck unthinking from the shelves of our local supermarkets. So many resources were being concentrated on the war effort that so many people had to 'make-do' the best they could, and get used to the idea of doing without some of life's material comforts. It was, after all, a small price to pay compared to the sufferings of our armed forces, not to mention the many civilians around the world who were being deprived of virtually everything they owned. The government issued ration books for such commodities as meat, sugar, butter, sweets and clothing, etc., which meant you could only have so much of them per month, in exchange for the appropriate coupon from the book. As far as food goes, people responded by intensive cultivation of their gardens. The authorities encouraged the nation to 'dig for victory,' using eye-catching posters for the purpose. Home grown vegetables and fruit were produced in greater quantities than ever before, and ingenious ways of storing some of them for the winter months were employed. Potatoes were stockpiled in earthen clamps, fruit preserved in special 'Kilner' jars, and so on.

Digging your own garden was one thing, while rearing your own pig was quite another. Nevertheless, that's just what some Dawley folk did, even those for whom the bacon sandwich had been the nearest thing to a pig that they had ever previously encountered. A modest Pig-Keepers' Association was formed at Hinkshay, using a room at the 'White Hart' pub for a meeting place. Such was the interest, that even people from Coalport attended the inaugural gathering. 'Official' pig keeping was quite a serious business. There had to be an elected chairman and committee. Proper record books were kept detailing the history of each pig, including the amount of meal it consumed during the year. Imagine doing that without the aid of a computer! The books also had to be properly audited. Dawley was now ready to 'pig for victory'. The plus side to all of this was that members were entitled to a double ration of meal with which to fatten their beasts and this presumably guaranteed a much better return for all their hard work. Special deliveries of foodstuffs were arranged, some of them arriving via Stirchley railway goods yard. Non-members had to try and buy scraps of food for their porkers from wherever they could, and it wasn't such an easy task at all - especially as there was a potato shortage.

A certain amount of wheeling and dealing would go on where scarce food supplies were concerned. Wherever there is a formal system of rationing of some commodity, you can be sure that someone will find a way around it. One large family that happened to be well acquainted with a friendly farmer were given his margarine allowance, since the farm was able to produce its own fresh butter. In general, people helped each other out, and there was often someone who would let you have a little of something that you needed more than they did. If you happened to be a trader, you had the advantage of being able to barter for the things you wanted. A man who supplied animal feeds to farms might well return home with new-laid eggs, or fresh butter. For all that, most people lived simply, but generally managed to cope.

'POST SCRIPT'

Once Pearl Harbour had been attacked in December, 1941, American and British forces were obliged to concentrate also on Japan as serious opponents to be reckoned with. Shropshire men found themselves fighting in the far east, and some were taken prisoner by the Japanese forces, with all that implied. A Dawley soldier who had been reported missing for some time, sent a postcard home from Changi prison in the Far East. When it eventually reached Dawley, the excited, early-morning postman mis-posted the card. On realising his mistake, he knocked on the soldier's family's door until the folks awoke to tell them about the card, then patiently waited for the other household to arise before retrieving the important piece of mail.

Chapter Twenty Six

'BICYCLE BOY'
BEGINS LIFE'S JOURNEY

The boy whose bicycle rides introduced us to the Dawley district in the earlier chapters, was a 'war baby'. As an adult, he now has but a few memories of his pre-school days, when he would have had no knowledge at all of the fact that a World War was raging. Instead, he accepted as normal that a child had to be regularly wheeled in a pushchair up to the Welfare Office in 'King Street', to collect a bottle of sticky orange juice, and a bottle of cod liver oil. Britain was clearly looking to its future by ensuring the rising generation grew up full of the right sort of sustenance.

A girl a few years older than the boy would volunteer during her school holidays to take pushchair and boy to her relatives' cottage at Heath Hill. The kindly aunt would ply the boy with slices of raw carrot, and he didn't see anything unusual in that either. It stands to sense that if you've never sampled a bar of chocolate, you're not to know how much better it tastes. In the early 1940's, carrots were often grown in people's gardens, but chocolate was hardly available at the shops. There are memories also of visits to his maternal grandmother's on hot, sunny days. His thirst was quenched with tumblers of a yellow, fizzy liquid made from mixing water with some lemon-flavoured crystals from a tin. That was the nearest thing he got to a drink of 'pop' in his entire early life. Another of grandma's treats was to peel an apple, dip it in the sugar bowl, and hand it to the boy who felt he was experiencing the ultimate in decadence.

When Mr. Simpson of Horsehay Farm opened his impressive house and gardens to the public for some charitable cause, the boy got a tremendous thrill from riding a huge, wooden rocking-horse in the children's room, the likes of which he had never before seen. All of this illustrates the point that in war- time, children of working-class families knew little of life's luxuries or indeed the things a contemporary child would regard as essential. They grew up during the early 1940's accepting this state of affairs as quite usual . Perhaps it gave them a better sense of perspective during the post-war years when things gradually became more plentiful. The boy's first day at school was remembered for the initial 'settling-down' session, when each child was put to sit at an individual desk, and given a small cardboard box containing a pile of coloured, wooden sticks. Perhaps it was a subtle type of aptitude test, because the boy found himself placing parallel rows of sticks in zig-zag fashion to create a 'road', and using the box and its lid as motor lorries ferrying yet more sticks along the road, to some mysterious destination. Clearly, ingenuity was not in short supply even though toys and other such children's delights certainly were.

It was during the latter days of the war when the boy became increasingly aware of the conflict. There were immediate outward signs such as the two air-raid shelters one at each end of the road in which he lived. They were strange looking concrete 'tunnels' each standing on a patch of waste ground. Only the top part showed above ground level, and you had to go down steps to reach the entrance whose doors seemed to be permanently locked. Going down the mud-stained steps to explore was not a pleasant experience, since the descent was accompanied by an increasingly obnoxious smell of dankness.

Surely, no-one would ever want to go inside such an objectionable construction, or was the smell created merely to deter inquisitive youngsters from hanging around there? People said the shelters were put there because of the danger from bombing raids, and there would be somewhere safe for the entire neighbourhood to go in the case of such a catastrophe occurring. Exactly who would give the order to go into the shelter, or who would decide which families should go to which shelter were questions that puzzled the boy. Also, who would hold the door keys, anyway? Presumably, these matters were in the capable hands of the local A.R.P. wardens, but you never got to find out, since the emergency didn't arise. Judging by the 'pong' described above, it seems a blessing for which all concerned should be thankful.

WARTIME LIVING

At home, breakfasts were enlivened with a substance known as 'dried egg'. It was a yellow powder which came in a tin, and was mixed with water to produce a fairly stiff substance, looking and tasting a little like scrambled eggs. It was used, so parents said, because fresh eggs were very scarce as there was a war going on. There was the nightly parental ritual of fitting up the rolls of thickish 'black-out paper' to the windows. They were removed again the next morning. One night, there was a knock at the door, and an A.R.P. warden informed the boy's parents that whilst on a patrol up Dun Cow Bank, he had noticed a telltale chink of light piercing the darkness. The offender was the boy, who had peeped out of the window to count the stars before sinking into bed, and promptly failed to seal the black-out totally on completion of that unimportant task. At least the A.R.P. man was on top of his job. The boy has vague memories of watching searchlights criss-crossing the night sky, and certainly recalls the wail of the air-raid siren. The

sound produced a frightening sensation, even though he never heard the humming of an enemy aircraft. It was the thought of what might happen that was so alarming. Some six or seven years later, a similar siren was used by the retained fire-service on a building near the boy's secondary school at Coalbrookdale. Each time the siren howled, the old feeling of terror from those war time days gripped the boy, and took quite a while to subside. His parents told him that earlier in the war, they would wheel him and his brother (in prams) into the small pantry under the stairs, on hearing the dreaded warning. They also told him of the night they stood on the brick steps of the house and watched in disconcerted horror, the huge and distant flames denoting the major blitz on Coventry. They had heard about it on the radio, and living in an elevated position, realised that it would be possible to see it despite the distance.

The radio was the thing people clung to for up to the minute news of the progress of the war. It was also used by 'Lord Haw Haw', the traitor William Joyce. He regularly put the wind up British citizens, including the boy's parents, by interrupting normal programmes with his demoralising messages of terror from German territory. Despite being Irish, he had a particularly nauseating upper class accent. *'Germany calling, Germany calling'* was always Haw Haw's opening gambit, and people knew they were in for a session of brain-washing until the BBC could manage to cut him off. The boy himself remembers the news-bulletin that reported the successful construction of a Bailey bridge over the River Rhine, by the British army. The report also said that this great achievement would hasten the ending of the war, and Germany would soon be defeated. The boy felt a wave of relief breaking over him. Up to that point, it had seemed to him that Germany was always winning. The sound of German voices or the tramp of marching German army boots as depicted on various radio programmes had always struck him with fear. Hitler had appeared a fearsome opponent, and an impossible nut to crack. The very name 'Berlin' seemed to represent the frightening epicentre of enemy power and evil. It took several post-war years for the boy to discover that peacetime Germany at least, had many places of beauty, and its people were as friendly as those anywhere else. It's unfortunate that wartime so vividly warps people's perceptions.

During the last couple of years of the war the boy's family enjoyed their first annual Summer holidays together. They were held on a farm perched above the western banks of the River Severn at Buildwas. In those days, seaside resorts were simply closed for business. The result was that the boy was introduced to the idyllic beauty of rural Shropshire. It was love at first sight, and the affair was never-ending. There were riverside meadows, sloping green fields, and thick woodland to explore. Magnificent views of the Wrekin and the Severn Valley decorated the pastoral scene. At the farm were cattle, sheep and poultry. Majestic Shire horses clomped their way to the fields each morning. Cornfields lit up the nearby countryside. Butter was made in wooden churns, within the farmhouse. This was an unhurried world bathed in rustic charm and serenity. Yet life is seldom perfect, for even there you could find stark reminders of the presence of wartime. The route from the railway station to the farm passed through a field containing a brick gun-emplacement, designed to protect Buildwas Power Station from attack. The power station itself was camouflaged. The ruins of the Cistercian Buildwas Abbey at the other end of the field were left to fend for themselves. The tank engines pulling branch line trains to Shrewsbury carried a row of red buckets hooked across the back

of the coal-bunker, in case of a fire emergency affecting the train. The bluntest reminder of all, was the night-time sight of orange flames licking upwards from the side of the Wrekin. A British plane on a training flight had misjudged the presence of the hill, and came to grief on its flanks. It was such an event that led to the introduction of the celebrated 'Wrekin Light' warning beacon, and it continued to draw attention to the much revered hill for many years, even after the war was over.

On the subject of aircraft, the names of the different warplanes were well known to the boy. With so many airfields nearby (including Atcham, Shawbury, and Cosford), it was not surprising that the daytime skies over Dawley were frequented by a variety of planes that he could readily identify. RAF fighters such as Spitfires and Hurricanes together with Mosquitoes were often seen. An American Lockheed Hudson with its twin fuselage was always an exciting sight, as was a plane towing a glider, or a whole group of aircraft flying deafeningly low in some sort of formation. There would be the occasional Wellington or Halifax bomber, also. It would be unusual to receive a visit from one of the huge Lancaster Bombers, they were mostly based in eastern England, but at least two Dawley men flew in such aircraft during the war. On certain occasions, their planes would be on training flights over Shropshire, and they managed to persuade the captain to do a detour over Dawley. Thus, Dawley was treated to the spectacle of a large and noisy, four-engined RAF Bomber making several low passes over the town, and even dipping its wings in salute to relatives on the ground. The son of Frank Taylor, the milkman, of Langley Farm, was one such Dawley airman, and the boy's own uncle another. The boy's grandmother resourcefully grabbed a white tablecloth to wave as her son's Lancaster roared above

'New Road'. Another uncle was in the army, and was at one stage stationed in Iceland helping supply British warships that were busily trying to keep the enemy under control in the North Atlantic. On one occasion, whilst on leave, he gave to both the boy and his brother a tin of Russian boiled sweets, legitimately procured from Britain's then allies. The boys had never seen boiled sweets before, and were the envy of their school friends who reacted as though they had seen the crown jewels!

The boy's memory pales a bit, but thinks that many warplanes continued flying over the town for some time after the end of the war. Through the medium of books, as well as radio programmes, such German names as Junkers, Heinkel, and Messerschmitt became almost as familiar as those of the British and American planes, though thankfully, the boy never actually saw an enemy aircraft!

A remnant of the former stable-block at Lightmoor, where also, some U.S Servicemen were billeted during World War II.

On the ground, as we have mentioned before, Dawley witnessed many elongated convoys of army vehicles lumbering along the main road and through the High Street. They were a particularly exciting sight for groups of children playing in side streets or fields, nearby. If a fleet of roaring, caterpillar-driven tanks happened to pass

through, the enthusiasm reached fever pitch. If you were at play, and someone heard the unmistakable sound of army lorries rumbling along the main thoroughfare, the shout *'Convoy!'* would go up immediately. With a sense of some urgency, a dozen pairs of clattering, juvenile shoes would race to the roadside, and their owners would stand in awe at the noisy, seemingly endless cavalcade. The bolder ones would shout *'Got any gum, chum?'* to the doleful faces sitting at the back of the army lorries. Often, the convoy would be British, and the soldiers rarely had anything to give away. British army lorries were often tall and powerful looking, and their engines emitted a sort of high-pitched whining sound which didn't seem to fit the image of such a towering giant. It was like listening to an adult male whose voice had still not broken. Sometimes, an American convoy would pass through. They consisted mostly of 'Dodge' vehicles, with long pointed front ends bearing a large white star. The question *'Got any gum, chum?'* was invariably greeted with a shower of small packages hurled by the occupants of the lorries. There would be a scramble among the youngsters on the pavement, to be the first to pick up one of the packages. In fairness, it has to be said that the goodies were always shared out around the crowd of children, so that everyone would have something from the haul. The Americans usually threw packs of chewing gum, or even more interestingly, cellophane wrapped packets of crunchy biscuits. Some say that even nylon stockings were thrown, but the boy has no recollection of that. The confectionery was just amazing. Chewing gum and biscuits were otherwise unheard of. To actually hold one of those American packages in your hand, and better still to have one of the sweet-tasting products in your mouth, was like being allowed a sneak preview of heaven, before it was all gone and life returned to normal once more. The interesting question is, if the children of every small town did as the Dawley ones did, how on earth were the United States Forces able to keep both Britain's youth and themselves suitably sustained throughout the war? Did some accountant at the Pentagon have to include in his calculations of the annual defence budget an amount to cover handouts to deprived British children, from convoys in the UK?

Youngsters, being possessed of vivid imaginations, used to enact supposed scenes from wartime battlefields among the gorse bushes of former pit mounds. One group would be the British, and set off ahead of the others who were the Gerries (Germans). There would be much lurking behind bushes, and ferocious skirmishes using broken tree branches or twigs representing machine guns and pistols. The sound of firing weapons would be provided by the mouth - a sharp 'kee-oo' for the pistol, and a rasping staccato 'A-a-a-a-a-ah' denoting a burst from the machine gun. There would also be the occasional *'Aghhhh'* from some poor devil who had been 'fatally wounded' during the combat. Sometimes, it would be the British against the 'Japs' (Japanese) since there were those among the gang who could effectively administer the 'Chinese Burn' to an opponent's wrist. This represented the torture meted out to prisoners of the Japanese army. Local children knew even about that. Sadly awful news travels fast in this world, even to a small Shropshire town such as Dawley, and you simply didn't have any idea of just how nice ordinary Japanese people actually were.

PEACE BREAKS OUT

Thankfully, the time came when, after some six years of conflict, the World War was finally over and Dawley celebrated with the best of them. The boy vividly remembers an event that took place at the top end of the road in which he lived. On a particularly dark night, a communal bonfire had been organised to which the entire street was informally invited. A huge throng of onlookers, including some from other parts of the town, assembled around the huge mound of tree branches, gorse bushes, waste timber and general rubbish, at a given time. From the direction of the High Street came a posse of young men each brandishing a stout stick whose top was covered in petrol-soaked rag. One by one, these giant 'matchsticks' were lit under supervision from some adult men. The torchbearers surrounded the sacrificial heap, and set it ablaze to the accompaniment of fervent rejoicing from the crowd. An accordion player emerged from the throng, and began stroking the keys. The people starting singing, 'Keep the Home Fires Burning', with a fervour that was full of both relief and rejoicing. No more would the air-raid sirens wail. The 'vrum, vrum' of German bombers would no longer be heard above Dawley's helpless rooftops, and the whole world could now sleep easily,, secure in the knowledge that the dreaded war was over. Those were the emotions that flavoured the singing. When the tune changed to 'When the Lights Go On Again, All Over the World,' there was cheering as well as singing. There was a tide of warbling faces, illuminated by the yellow flames of the hot and crackling bonfire. Both young and old seemed to share a common bond of jubilation.

On another night, the boy's father took him and his brother onto the Paddock Mound. An open space at one end of this otherwise fir-covered relic of the old mining days, provided a suitable vantage point from which to watch the spectacle of two blazing beacons. Just as news of Drake's emphatic defeat of the Spanish armada had been flashed across the nation by means of a chain of beacons in the reign of Good

Queen Bess, so the ending of World War II was marked in similar fashion. First, could be seen to the east, the distant flames at Sedgley Beacon near Dudley. The Wrekin then sprouted an orange blaze near its summit, as the string of beacons continued to spread further abroad. The night was silent, and the flares spoke a wordless message to the people, a message they had long waited for, sometimes doubting it would really come. Now they knew for sure that the war and all the horrors it had brought in its wake, was truly over for good.

At school, the event was marked in a two-fold way. The more impressive of the two as far as the boy was concerned, was the free bar of 'Fry's Chocolate Peppermint Cream' given to every pupil as a 'reward', so the Headmaster stated. This appeared to be the gift of 'Shropshire County Council'. If so, it had shown commendable wisdom, in the boy's estimation. The Year Two teacher had to break open a succession of grey, cardboard boxes to access the bars, and then call each class member to the front in strict register order. Not one child had ever seen such a product before, and everyone was excited at being literally 'called to the bar'. This confectionery remained one of the boy's favourite sweet meats for a long time. A longer lasting memento was supplied by H.M. Government - it amounted to an oblong card with a little cotton hook at the top, and bearing a message from King George VI, thanking the nation's children for putting up with the various inconveniences of war time so admirably. Everyone felt at least a foot taller at receiving such high, if mystifying praise. The boy's card remained hung on a nail in the lounge for several months.

It seems that whenever Britain has something major to celebrate, a rash of street parties invariably breaks out in nearly every town and village. The parties have become a national characteristic, happening automatically wherever there is a large number of children. Dawley had its street parties, and there was one in the street where the boy lived. It was a summer Saturday, and the entire afternoon became a journey into a world of unaccustomed excitement. Soon after lunch, all children had to assemble on Portley Flat. There, to the astonishment of the animated youngsters, stood a line of the most antiquated buses and charabancs you could imagine, some of them even had soft-tops. There hadn't been much call for day trips for many a long year, so evidently the coach owners hadn't deemed it necessary to update their fleets of vehicles. The boy had never even heard the word 'charabanc' before, let alone been in one. To the children's further surprise, they were informed by those adults who seemed to be organising the venture, that they were to be taken on a mystery trip, before returning for the street tea-party. This announcement only served to increase the sense of enthusiasm stirring within each young breast. The children were herded into the waiting vehicles, and the journey began. Nothing like this had ever before happened in the lives of these youngsters. The buses struggled then won the battle with the ascent of Dun Cow Bank, and moved in stately procession through the High Street. Surprised onlookers turned and waved at the occupants, who gleefully waved back as if members of the Royal Family on a victory tour of the Kingdom.

There was so much excited chatter and joke swapping on the trip that the boy hardly took notice of where they were going. Eventually, buildings came into view, and then busy streets. They were, so the driver shouted to the passengers, in Shrewsbury. None of the children had been that far from Dawley before, or seen a town of that size.

Through the main streets of the county's capital wound the motley convoy of coaches. Again, people stopped in their tracks to watch the Dawley cavalcade passing by. To his astonishment, the boy, who was now eagerly taking in the sights of the centre of the town, suddenly spotted his parents ambling along the pavement. They had apparently travelled to Shrewsbury by train. Banging his nose (accidentally) then his knuckles (deliberately) on the window, he managed to attract their attention. There was much mutual waving, and then the charabanc moved on and headed for home. Needless to say, the weather was kind, as it surely always was during one's childhood, so that a welcoming tea party took place at tables and chairs set out in the children's street, on their return from the Shrewsbury adventure. There were sandwiches of meat paste, cups of tea, home-made buns, and dishes of something called 'junket', a sort of substitute for blancmange, and whose name sounded rather like a German war plane.

Those were, of course, still the days of austerity. The children didn't realise that this was very basic fare. Nobody would have cared, anyway. They had had a surprise charabanc trip, and now a communal, celebratory tea party the like of which the street had never seen before, and never saw again. The folks who organised and financed it had given the children and, in turn, themselves, a marvellous day to remember.

Life was slow to get back to normal during the immediate post-war years, and there were still sporadic reminders of the conflict to be seen here and there. On shopping visits to Wellington, there was the sight of small groups of foreign soldiers, sporting the letters P.O.W. (prisoner of war) on the backs of their khaki shirts or jackets. They were apparently billeted in camps situated in some of the rural places surrounding the town, prior to repatriation, and could often be seen ambling along the town's shopping streets. British and American warplanes could still be seen flying over Dawley, and there were yet more army convoys passing through. Perhaps everyone was returning to where they had started from, concluded the boy.

One morning during the school holidays, and not long after the ending of the war, the boy was sitting on the mound near the 'Gander Fields' (now 'Springfield Road'), when a fleet of unladen, heavy lorries came along the narrow lane and formed a queue which completely blocked the road. First, one of the lorries would slowly trundle into a long, brick building at the bottom end of 'Chapel Street', which had at one time been part of a corn-mill, and in the immediate post-war years became the Ernie Clements cycle factory. There would be quite a delay, and then the lorry would emerge fully laden, tarpaulin covering the mysterious load, and lumber up 'Chapel Street', on its way to the main road. The next vehicle in line would crawl into the building via the narrow entrance, and so it went on. It was a slow performance, so that there still remained a line of empty lorries along the lane for some time. Other people noticing the unusual sight, would also stand and watch. Nobody knew what it was all about, and the cargo remained a secret. It was a completely 'one-off' incident, happening so close to the end of the war, and people speculated that something had been stored in the building during war time, and whatever it was had to be removed now peace was restored. If Spitfire aircraft could be manufactured at Sankey's works without the knowledge of Germany, then why couldn't a harmless looking building in Dawley be requisitioned for storing something equally important to the war effort?

Chapter Twenty Seven

PEACE IN OUR TIME
A LATE 1940S CHILDHOOD IN DAWLEY

'War babies' began their schooling at about the time the war was ending, or in some cases just after it had finished. They were the first flush of peacetime schoolchildren, enjoying life without the threat of imminent destruction hanging over them. They were the new generation for whom the allied forces had courageously fought, ensuring they could enjoy the fruits of a hard won peace. In many ways, their young lives tended to fall into a similar pattern to that of the previous generation, yet increasingly, they were touched by the gradual hand of progress, as the decade emerged from the rigours of war time. Perhaps a closer look at a fairly typical week in the life of our boy will help create a useful picture of post-war life in the Dawley area.

SUNDAYS

Sundays meant early breakfast, since there was the need to get ready for the hike from Dawley to Little Dawley Methodist Chapel. It was the place where his parents had met and married, so despite the distance to be travelled, that was the place of worship for the off springs, also. Nevertheless, Sunday breakfasts were a total feast. The frying pan sizzled with enthusiasm as bacon, eggs, sausage, tomato and even kidneys, on a good day, were arranged artistically within the vessel. It seems the return to normality so far as food was concerned, was not too slow in coming after the war. Early Sunday mornings and the intoxicating aroma of frying bacon (a new post-war experience for the boy), became inseparable companions. Even the thought of the sputtering delights within the pan, sent ripples of saliva through the

mouth. The meal would be enjoyed against the calming background of 'Chapel In the Valley' a special Sunday morning radio programme presented by the genial Sandy Macpherson. Sandy Macpherson was a well-known organist, who frequently entertained audiences on the wireless, with his well-chosen selections of good music. On Sundays, he would invite listeners into a mythical, little country chapel. He, of course, would be organist, and he would have characters such as Mr. Drewitt, the village postman, and his young daughter (whatever her name was) singing solos and duets, at appropriate moments during the Service. There would be a small congregation, lustily singing well-known hymns, and Sandy would describe the proceedings in his warm and comforting Irish tones. It seemed the perfect start to that 'different' day of the week. A plate of English breakfast and a taste of village life seemed somehow to gel in a way that set the senses moving in all the right directions. The end of the programme would invariably coincide with the final swiping of the breakfast plate, using a slab of locally-made white bread, and producing an agreeable cocktail of egg yolk, tomato juice and bacon fat. Fortunately, cholesterol had not yet been discovered! Incidentally, the boy once saw Sandy Macpherson in the flesh. He gave one of his highly popular concerts, suitably supported by local choirs and soloists, at the Methodist Chapel at the bottom of Station Hill, at Oakengates. It was as if the never-never-land had been miraculously brought to life. You could actually see the man sitting at the organ. He had suddenly become a real person, and not just a voice that came out of a radio set.

That evening was capped with a journey home, courtesy of the 'Stirchley Dodger' railway train. No matter that it was followed by a tiring hike in the dark, from Stirchley station to the centre of Dawley - the boy had enjoyed one of the biggest nights of his young life.

After Sunday breakfast, would come the first of three long walks to Little Dawley Methodist Chapel. May mornings were the most memorable. On a nice day, the tramp along field-paths (the heavily disguised route of former pit tramways) was accompanied by exquisite bird song and the intoxicating scent of 'May Blossom' wafting on the warm breeze, from countless hawthorn hedges. At the chapel there was a challenging climb up a curving flight of brick steps, before arriving at the Sunday School room. On entering the room, you had to produce your 'Star-Card', a little fold-over piece of card containing your name on the front, and a series of printed squares on the two inside pages. A man would open your card, then use a small, wooden stamper (frequently fuelled from an inkpad set in a tin box) to produce an ink star in the appropriate space for the particular session attended. A full, or substantially full, star card at the end of the year was a scholar's passport to some enviable free benefits. Chiefly, it meant you qualified for a gift on Prize Giving Day (a book suitably inscribed on the inside cover), and a place on the annual Sunday School summer outing.

There would be a half-hour worship session, which included hymns from the children's hymn-book whose soft covers had become so worn by the fingers of generations of scholars, that they had taken on the texture of tissue paper. At 10.30 a.m., the children's feet would clatter down the staircase, and file into the main chapel below, where an assemblage of adults had already gathered for the morning Service.

These Services were not always designed with youngsters in mind (it depended on the whim of the particular preacher). Worst of all, there would often be a lengthy sermon, beamed at the grown-ups, and which literally flew over the heads of the youngsters, who always occupied the front few rows of the chapel pews (boys on the left, girls on the right). So bored was the boy on one occasion, that he somehow managed to trap his foot in the narrow gap between a thick, metal pipe (part of the chapel's heating system) and the wooden division board, separating the left hand and right hand pews. Just when he thought he might have to stay in the chapel until called by St. Peter, he had the brilliant idea of unlacing his shoe, extracting his foot from it, then wrenching the reluctant piece of footwear from its 'shackles'.

The journey home was always made along the main highway, stopping off at the boy's paternal grandparents in 'New Road'. There, he and his brother were plied with cakes purchased the previous day from Watts's shop in Dawley 'High Street'. Variously, there would be Eccles cakes, or jam or lemon tarts, or crisp and sugary pastries with a dab of jam in a hole in the top. Further decadence was provided by the presence of such Sunday newspapers as the 'Empire News' and the 'Sunday Pictorial'. These weekly journals gave up-to-date reports of the major Saturday football or cricket matches, and news of the players' injury situations. Exactly why people should also want to know about the antics of show business personalities during their off-duty hours, the boy couldn't understand. He only knew that for him, the sports news couldn't possibly wait until Monday. The boy's grandfather was a branch secretary of the Boilermakers' Union. While the boys were busily putting jammy finger marks on the newspapers, granddad was using the dining table as a desk. He spent a good chunk of each Sunday catching up on union paperwork, having spent much of Saturday attending regional meetings in Wolverhampton. That, was true dedication.

Walking to and from Little Dawley was an exhausting business, and despite the interlude with the cakes, the boys had no difficulty in further demolishing a hearty lunch of roast meat and vegetables, backed up with home-made apple-pie and custard, on their return home. Soon, it was time to hit the trail to Little Dawley once again, using the field paths. The afternoon Sunday School session in the upstairs room chiefly consisted of hymns, prayers, and a story with a moral to it. On a good day, there would be white, printed sheets entitled 'Cliff College Choruses' waiting on the bench seats, along with the hymnbooks. The boy liked the cheery ditties from the sheet, including such anthems as 'I'M H-A-P-P-Y', and others of a similarly jolly ilk. They provided such a contrast to some of the hymns in the book. He had no idea what or where Cliff College was, but remained convinced it must have been inhabited by a constantly happy race of people, who were privileged to spend their lives singing with perpetual smiles on their faces. By the afternoon session, most scholars had got the sleep out of their eyes, and the numbers were supplemented with those who hadn't made it on the Sunday morning. Consequently, the 'audience' was a bit more animated in the afternoons, and sometimes the Sunday School leader would stop in the middle of a prayer, to loudly tell those who were too busy catching up on the latest gossip, to 'STOP TALKING, PLEASE!'. The final part of the session involved splitting into small groups, determined by one's age, where stories about inspiring people were read by a group leader.

When Sunday School was over, the boy and his brother then trudged home, using the main road again. This time, they called

at their maternal grandfather's cottage, near the Parish Church. Invariably, granddad would be snoozing in his wooden chair in front of an open coal fire. He would open his eyes as soon as the boys entered the parlour, and at the drop of a hat, so to speak, he would immediately launch into some amusing anecdote that never failed to keep the lads enthralled. He really was a natural raconteur. He had been a miner at Kemberton pit all his working life, walking to and from the workplace through the Castle Fields (the modern Aqueduct development now occupies the route). Like all miners of his generation, he would daily arrive home still covered in pit grime, and have to use a tin bath at the fireside in order to get clean again, before consuming the main meal of the day. At some stage in his career, he had sustained a nasty injury at work, and was temporarily 'farmed out' to the private owner's estate, near Buildwas. He and his equally blighted work mate, would be employed on fence-mending and hedge-laying tasks in and around the wooded depths of Buildwas Park Estate, until they were declared fit enough to return to the fray at the pit. In the course of this activity, granddad became friends with the tenant farmer, Harry Shropshire (what a wonderful surname to be blessed with!) and his family, of Buildwas Park Farm. It was through this contact that the boy's family came to spend their summer holidays on the farm during the early to mid 1940's. It's an ill wind, and all that!

The boys would arrive back home from Sunday School in time for early tea (four o'clockish on Sundays). Tinned fruit, and cake would be consumed in the company of Franklin Engleman, as the suave radio presenter took his microphone for its weekly walk 'Down Your Way' on the Light Programme. At half-past five, it was off to Little Dawley again, chaperoned by parents this time, and they always used the 'road route'. Evening worship began at six, and was very much an adult affair. Some of the sermons were so lengthy, that the boy's undoubted imagination would take over involuntarily. One of his more fanciful 'day dreams' involved looking up at the ceiling lights, about six in all, which were suspended from a considerable height on long cables. In his mind the boy assumed the persona of Tarzan, a real cinema favourite at that time, and saw himself swinging from one light bowl to another until the entire chapel had been traversed a dozen times. By the end of this excursion, with any luck the sermon would be coming to its conclusion, and it would soon be time to go home.

On the return journey, the family called at the 'New Road' grandparents. Here, the proceedings were dominated by a lengthy bout of 'Sunday night talk', as the adults chattered at length about what had been going on in Dawley during the past week. Comments something like *'You know, she married a Bailey from down the Cunnery, he had a gammy leg'* frequently decorated the flow of conversation. The boys were treated to another round of Watts's cakes, while the grown ups got their teeth into slices of Norgrove pork-pie. Grandma washed hers down (the pie that is, not her teeth) with a bottle of 'medicinal' stout. One yawn too many from the boys saw to it that the session broke up before too long, and then it was home to bed - another typical Sunday done and dusted.

THE SUNDAY SCHOOL'S 'THANKYOU'

There had to be some reward for all that dedicated trudging to Little Dawley and back. There were certain 'Red Letter Days' in the Sunday School calendar, and in those times when big treats were few and far between, such days stood out above most of the rest, year by year. Sunday School Anniversary Day was in early May at Little Dawley. Additional walks to the chapel on mid-week practice nights, added nicely to the total mileage covered on that route during the course of a given year. When the big day arrived, a surprising turn out of girls in white dresses, and boys in white shirts and grey trousers displayed itself to the congregation no less than three times during that Sunday. The huge, wooden doors on the right-hand side of the Sunday School upper room were opened for that one day only. The young choristers stood in selected rows-youngest at the front (they were not yet old enough to be self-conscious)-and oldest and tallest on the back rows. By facing through the gap where the doors normally stood, the children were looking down onto the main body of the church - a salutary experience the first time you tasted it. A printed programme (produced by G.H. Bullock of Dawley) containing all the anniversary hymns, and telling people this was the one hundred-and-what-not anniversary of the Sunday School, was handed to members of the congregation as they entered the church vestibule.

The listeners could follow the words from the sheets, whilst the scholars tried to recall them from the deep recesses of their memories. A 'special' preacher would be appointed for the day (the West Indian, Rev. Dudley Miller was one of the most popular), and the occasion was special to the adults in the church also. It was certainly a different sort of Sunday. While the children and choir were toiling through their final hymn (it almost always seemed to be number seven - 'Summer Suns are Glowing'), a steward emerged from a door at the side of the pulpit. He climbed the stairs to whisper something in the ear of the preacher - and handed him a scrap of paper. When the hymn ended, the preacher would say he had been asked to announce that the total collection for the day amounted to £_____. You could see some people whispering to each other in response to that. *'We've done better than last year!'* would be one typical comment. The children would be thinking ahead to the summer months, relieved that another good pile of money had come into Sunday School funds. The Sunday School would be able to afford prizes, and another annual outing. There would be much to look forward to in the time ahead.

Prize-Giving Day provided the novelty of a rather special Sunday afternoon. The entire ceremony took place in the chapel itself, so there was no need to climb all those steps, for a change. Parents were present, and a guest speaker led the proceedings and also gave out the prizes. Every young eye was fixed on the table at the front, which was laden with a pile of pristine books. There was excitement and suspense in wondering which of them would be coming your way. After some hymn singing and so on, and some appropriate words of encouragement from the speaker, would come the moment every eager child had been waiting for - the distribution of the prizes. The speaker descended from the pulpit, and stood by the table. In turn, starting with the youngest, the name of each child would be whispered to the speaker by a Sunday School official standing nearby, as the book cover was opened revealing the sticker containing the recipient's name. Some went to the front shyly, some went with a smile, some almost ran to collect their prizes. In every case, there would be the thrill of discovering the title of your new book, and seeing your name in copper plate writing on the inside label. In the days of immediate post-war austerity, this was exhilarating stuff. It had been well worth having that Star Card filled up. During the hard winters of the late 1940's, the boy attended Dawley High Street Sunday School, as this entailed a mere short walk from his home. In those years, he would stay on through the spring and summer,

and qualify for Prize Giving Day at that Church instead.

The Little Dawley Sunday School outing took place always on a summer Saturday. For the boy it entailed another walk to the chapel. The sight of two gleaming motor coaches busily turning around at the road junction near the 'Big Penny', and then pulling up alongside the enthusiastic throng of youngsters and Sunday School staff (plus parents in some cases), was guaranteed to create yet another wave of elation, courtesy of the Sunday School. Outings by motor coach to Rhyl, Southport, or Trentham Gardens were quite a contrast to those the boy's parents would have experienced. In their day, it would have been a slow clomp by horse and wagon (whatever the weather) to the likes of Bridgnorth or perhaps Church Stretton. To them, it would have seemed like a journey to the other side of the world.

THE DEMONSTRATION ROLLS ON

The other big Sunday School event was, of course, the annual Demonstration still going strong some seventy years or so after its inception. August Bank Holiday Monday was always the day for this unique occurrence, and as this sometimes coincided with the boy's family summer holidays at the seaside, he only took part on a few occasions. When he was involved he found himself as happily caught up in the excitement as any Sunday School scholar had ever been. In fact, for him it was a bit of a fitness workout as well. He would first have to walk through the fields to Little Dawley, before joining the march back to Dawley again. At the chapel, children would be getting together in a group, assembled according to their ages. Most of the girls would be decked out in white dresses, probably the same ones they had worn for the Anniversary Services, and carrying small wicker baskets containing summer flowers from the garden. On the whole, the boys would again tend to wear 'Anniversary gear' including ties and white shirts. The boy remembers one year when they were to be led by a band from Wellington, possibly belonging to some church uniformed organisation. The drummer had a sort of leopard skin sheet strapped to the front of his body, which seemed designed to protect him from the uncomfortable bulk of the huge base drum he had to play. Eventually, children, some adults and the band got themselves in order and the march began near the chapel gates. 'Boom-boom' went the drum, 'tan-tara' went the bugles, and, as a bevy of onlookers living near the chapel watched and waved, the Little Dawley cohort set off in the direction of Dawley. An immense, old banner at the head of the procession proudly informed the world that this indeed, was the Little Dawley Wesleyan Sunday School. The boy didn't exactly envy the poor adult men who had to carry the banner by holding on to its support poles for the entire journey.

The children were tickled pink to be part of such a parade. All along the route, little knots of people stood outside their houses to watch the procession. It made you feel important, though slightly embarrassed at the same time. Self-conscious boys would sometimes try to assuage their feelings by indulging in a bit of mild clowning. They would often be admonished by the girls, who asked them to consider what the people in Dawley 'High Street' would think of them if they acted that way later in the march. That was normally enough to settle the lads down. Just beyond the schoolroom near the corner of 'Holly Road' and 'Old Vicarage Road', the walkers were brought to a temporary halt, while their counterparts from the Parish Church joined

at the rear. The enlarged group then continued along 'Old Vicarage Road' and 'New Road' until they were stopped again near Portley Corner. By a masterpiece of planning, the parties from both Finger Road and Stirchley Methodist Chapels were waiting, and then the procession continued to make a concerted assault on the steep Dun Cow Bank. Somehow, the drummer was still boom booming, although his fellow musicians were allowed to save themselves until the final approach to the High Street.

Dun Cow Bank and 'High Street' were home territory to the boy, and being allowed to march along those main roads where busy traffic normally held sway, was a rather exhilarating privilege. For this day only, you were actually permitted the freedom of your own town centre, and became the focus of hundreds of pairs of interested eyes. It was a strange yet not disagreeable sensation. Near the Webb Memorial the parade waited for the folks from St. Leonard's, Bank Road, Dawley Baptist, and Lawley Bank Sunday Schools which were led by a different band. Then came the grand march along the entire length of the High Street. The first time the boy experienced the sight of the crowds filling the pavements on Demonstration Day, he caught his breath. He had had no idea that such large numbers of people would be interested enough to stand and watch a lot of Sunday School children processing through the main street on a Bank Holiday. Yet interested they were, so much so that the pavements on either side of the street were simply crammed with folk. Necks would crane forward first to read each successive banner as it came into view, then to look feverishly for familiar faces among the walkers. Suddenly, each 'demonstrator's' spirits were lifted. It had been a long, hard slog from the respective starting points, and now everyone felt a few feet taller as they caught the atmosphere created by the watching throng. It must be the same with marathon runners who have toiled agonisingly along a lengthy and often lonely course, only to enter a packed stadium or street of cheering thousands, so that at last their efforts were being recognised.

The lucky blighters from Dawley High Street Methodist were able to just tag on the end of the line as it passed by the junction with 'Chapel Street' (they simply didn't know what suffering was all about!). Theirs would have been a mere short stroll to the assembly ground in 'Doseley Road'. Somewhere along the line, the 'troops' from Horsehay Pool and Moreton Coppice Sunday Schools also got in on the act, though the boy was never quite sure how this came about, since they had marched into Dawley from the opposite direction to everyone else, omitting the High Street.

The post-war Demonstration Services took place on the Council Field, next to the public park. A guest speaker would address the congregation from the back of a lorry, using a microphone. There would be prayers, readings and hymns (always including 'Onward, Christian Soldiers'). Onlookers couldn't fail to see that the church throughout the Dawley area was still very much 'alive and kicking'.

The march back to the various churches was never quite as thrilling as the inward journey. A touch of 'deja vu' would set in. There was, of course, a further joint sally through the High Street. The bystanders were again massed along the pavements. What on earth had they been doing while the parade was at the service? Some had undoubtedly joined in at the field, but not all. According to tradition, the Sunday School youngsters were treated to a tea party back at their respective bases. Afterwards, allowing a suitable time for the digestive juices to do their essential stuff,

The Salvation Army Band playing at the Demonstration

sports and games would take place in a nearby field. The boy remembers one such occasion when the festivities were attended by a visiting, middle-aged American couple. The genial gentleman member of the pair gave the proceedings an unexpected boost, by announcing that he would be giving cash prizes to the winners of the various races. *'If you win a race, I will give you some money so that you can go buy yourselves some candy'*, he proclaimed to the scholars. The children looked at each other. *'Candy?'* they exclaimed, *'E must mean sweets. 'Flippin' 'eck, I 'ope me mom 'asn't used up all 'er coupons!'* Sweets of any kind remained on ration for several years after the end of the war.

OTHER FESTIVITIES

The one celebration at Little Dawley that really penetrated the boy's senses, was the Harvest Festival. There would be a long table between the front pews and the pulpit, laden with 'fruits of the earth' of all kinds. Healthy vegetables from local gardens, including potatoes, beetroot and marrows would mingle with cooking apples (what a pleasantly autumnal aroma they gave off), pears, tinned foods, and even a giant lump of coal, to provide an agreeable kaleidoscope of some of life's essentials. The centrepiece was a massive loaf, cleverly formed into the shape of a wheat sheaf. At the evening service, the combination of this magnificent array with its various colours and smells, the lighted church at the twilight hour, and the nearness of the surrounding semi-rural landscape, created a sort of magic which never failed to trigger the boy's imagination.

The final big Service of the year took place, not too surprisingly, on New Year's Eve. First, there would be a 'Social', that is an evening of sandwiches, tea and games for all age groups, in the upstairs schoolroom. Then, at 11.30 p.m., everyone descended the brick stairs to occupy the main worship area. A 'Watch Night Service' then proceeded, towards the end of which they always sang 'Standing at the Portal of the Opening Year'. That never failed to generate a feeling of excited anticipation within the boy. By the time the Service was over, the calendar had moved imperceptibly into another year. The relatively small congregation enthusiastically shook hands with one another, wished each other a 'Happy New Year', then made their way out into the darkness, and headed for home. The boy remembers those New Year walks back to Dawley. There was mystery in the air, a full moon lit the way, and the boy frequently looked up at it, glad of its light at such an otherwise dark hour. There had been no moon visible on the outward journey, and the boy used to feel that at mid-night on New Year's Eve, God had caused this pale circle to emerge from a cloudy heaven, to somehow bring in the New Year. It would also usher people safely home to their beds. It always seemed a particularly tiring walk home, but at least there was the comforting knowledge that a lie-in would be sanctioned on New Year's Day.

PRIMARY SCHOOL DAYS

Monday to Friday life for the boy was dominated by the business of getting to, attending, and getting home from school. He remembers breakfast-times, where scrambled eggs on toast suddenly became rows of little, yellow soldiers, each waiting to be anointed with tomato sauce. The entire operation was performed to the accompaniment of the 'Radio Doctor's' treacly voice spilling out from the wireless. Whether he was instructing the nation on how to cope with a severe attack of the 'collywobbles', or the treatment of lumbago, didn't much matter. A daily dose of his reassuring tone distilled a feeling of serenity that somehow helped the day to get off to a gratifying start.

Then, there would be friends to meet up with en-route for school. The half-mile walk entailed passing along the uneven road to Pool Hill. What a journey of contrasts that half-mile was. Walter Hart's two Bedford coaches slumbered inside an open-fronted garage, next to his impressive, red brick, detached house. Behind a long, high and dingy wall, the small gas works quietly got on with whatever small gas works quietly get on with all day. Then came the rear of a small house, curiously painted in black, presumably in sympathy with the wall. The main gasometer was just about visible above the wall. When its dome had risen to its maximum height, like a well-baked cake, people would say *'there's plenty of gas in the gasworks today'*. You would feel secure in the knowledge that your gas cooker wasn't going to give out, halfway through preparation of the evening meal. Opposite the 'black house' stood a stone wall with a curious, glazed brown brick incorporated within its flanks. Young school 'freshers' would be told it was a 'chocolate brick', and if you touched it, you would soon be receiving a bar of chocolate of your own. Somehow, it didn't seem to work for the boy.

It was near this location that Jack Hadley was occasionally encountered, making one of his last calls before completing his extended night shift. The druggan would virtually block the lane, so that the schoolchildren had to somehow squeeze alongside, fingers constantly pinching noses, in order to overtake the stationary vessel without too much suffering. All the while, they were praying that they would get well clear before Jack and his accomplices came on the scene, wielding a couple of full buckets!

To continue the walk you then had to turn left at a small group of cottages, and troop beside a wooden bungalow, near which the boy once encountered a lizard on the grass

verge. The route finally descended a narrow path known as 'the gulley', to arrive at some further cottages, and then reached the school.

Pool Hill School was the one that the Darbys had built in the mid-nineteenth century. It was the place where the boy's parents, and even his grandparents, had been educated. Externally, little had altered during all those years. Also the wooden topped, cast iron desks with grooves along the front to house pens and pencils, and a hole containing a ceramic ink-well bearing the name 'Addison', looked as if they had witnessed more than one generation of pupils. Even the lessons, in which there was daily choral reciting of 'times tables', writing in exercise books using pens with a wooden stale and a thick removable metal nib, appeared to have changed little since at least the days of the boy's parents. The individual small boards and slate pencils had, however, disappeared by the boy's

An early twentieth century group of Pool Hill School pupils. Note the smart uniforms worn by the boys.

time.

The boy's journey through the school has left him with little pockets of memories, begetting anecdotes of the seven years he spent there. As his first school Christmas approached, he was involved with fellow class members in the production of decorative paper chains, made from strips of differently coloured papers. The strips had first to be cut from a larger sheet, glued at one end, then fitted together to form the chain. The boy recalls that at least two lengthy chains had already been slung across the classroom walls, before he had managed to glue together more than about three links. He found it hard to understand why more glue seemed to end up on his fingers, than on the intended targets. He had to face the unfortunate fact - he had been born clumsy!

Year Two was the year of the 'Fry's Chocolate Peppermint Cream' celebration of the ending of World War II. It was also the period when the boy took his first, tentative steps in the miraculous process of actually reading words from a book.

In the third year, the class observed the daily progress of kidney bean seeds, which had been wrapped in soaked blotting paper, and placed in jam jars adorning the windowsills. The zenith of the seeds' ambitions was production of shoots and a pair of gradually unfolding leaves. Most of them seemed to achieve this without too much bother. In lieu of P.E. exercises, the female teacher would have class members joining hands in the playground, and circling as they sang 'London's Burning, London's Burning, Hurrah, Hurrah!' The boy found it hard to comprehend why they should be singing 'hurrah, hurrah!' at London's unfortunate predicament. On a more civilised front, there was dancing around the Maypole on the school field on May Day. Despite fairly intensive

rehearsals, the boy still managed to cause frequent, minor tanglings of the coloured tapes by taking wrong turns at crucial moments as the children tripped their way around the pole. Remembering the words 'Come lasses and lads, take leave of your dads, and away to the Maypole high............,' and co-ordinating the zig-zag dance movements proved a touch too difficult on the big day. On another occasion, an abridged version of 'Jack and the Beanstalk' was performed in the playground for other classes to observe. The boy played the part of the giant. He drew on his experience of cowboy films at the local cinema, to give an overly dramatic depiction of his death scene. He slumped to the ground in a slow, twisting movement, before treating the audience to an agonised cry of '*A-a-a-a-gh!*' before finally expiring motionless on the tarmac.

In the next class, much time was spent on a project relating to the wedding of Princess Elizabeth and the Duke of Edinburgh. A large chart was produced, recording the names of all the official guests, including the Marquis of Milford Haven, a name by which the boy was completely intrigued, even though he hadn't a clue as to who the fellow was, or where he actually came from. After school one day, while walking across the schoolyard, the boy witnessed some lads taking the caps off the heads of younger boys, who were patiently awaiting the arrival of their mothers. Up in the air would fly the caps, causing their owners to scamper after them. This cap - flinging seemed a rather good idea to the boy, a choice privilege reserved for boys who were a little older. He joined in, but a bit over-enthusiastically. His first and only victim's cap landed on the roof of the little brick porch at one of the school's side entrances. Suddenly, the pit of his stomach fell out, as he anticipated the fury of an enraged parent. Fortunately, the caretaker was summoned by one of the other older boys, a ladder produced, and the cap successfully retrieved in the nick of time. Some people simply have to learn the hard way!

The boy spent three whole years in his final class at junior school. Doubtless, many lasting benefits emanated from the earlier classes, but he was conscious of a fresh awakening of his interests during those final years at the school. The teacher was Mr. Alan Brown (known to all as 'Smoker' Brown, when he was not within earshot). He was a local man who had not long returned from serving in the army during World War II. The teacher was a disciplinarian, but at all times he commanded respect, and his skill at opening the minds of his scholars to the fascination of the world around and beyond them, was to have a profound and lasting effect on the boy. Mr. Brown knew exactly how to create in young people a thirst for knowledge. As a member of Mr. Brown's class, the boy discovered a modest talent for drawing, which had hitherto remained dormant. He also found that he actually enjoyed writing 'composition' (short essays), and singing, and above all, developed a curiosity about so many things, which has remained with him ever since. He didn't fully appreciate that teacher's impact until much later in life.

It was Mr. Brown who encouraged class members to subscribe to Arthur Mee's weekly 'Children's Newspaper,' a 'pandora's box' of fascinating information. Distribution of each brand new issue around the class caused a ripple of excitement in the boy, akin to the anticipation of a favourite meal. The school occasionally took part in musical concerts, one being at the 'Garrison Theatre' in Donnington. There was also a day trip by coach to Rhyl, as a reward for those pupils who had participated in a grand concert in the school's own hall. There were football matches against other

schools, and an absorbing project on the Festival of Britain in 1951 (which event the boy subsequently visited).

One of the great pleasures of those Junior School days was eating school dinners. That was a delectation previously denied the boy's parents, who either ate sandwiches at school or went home for lunch. Tables and chairs were set out in rows in the main hall, and you had to queue in order to be fed. A team of cheerful ladies wearing blue uniforms would fill your plate with whatever was on offer. There was no choice available, but the meals rarely failed to satisfy. Irish Stew would be ladled out of a great pot, or meat and veg. deftly deposited onto the waiting plates. Puddings included something called 'rice substitute', tapioca pudding, and treacle tart with custard. Whilst you were waiting to be called to the serving table, you would ask those returning with steaming dishes, 'what's for pudding?' *'Frog Spawn'* might be the reply. If so, you knew that tapioca was on the menu, but it didn't matter what it was, lunch time was a lively event at the school, and you did your best to enjoy whatever the cook decided to produce. In fact, the kitchen was at one end of the chief teaching block, so that as the morning progressed, an increasingly distracting aroma would escape from the cookhouse into the corridors, and filter under the classroom doors. The mind would become detached from the lesson, and stumble into a guessing game of 'What's for Dinner Today?' It helped to move the morning along agreeably.

HOME, SWEET HOME

Tea times at home on weekdays were invariably accompanied by 'Children's Hour' on BBC radio's Home Service. The stories of 'Toytown' with 'Uncle Mac' playing the part of Larry the Lamb in a suitably bleating voice, was a great favourite. The serialisation of some of Malcolm Saville's 'Lone Pine' books, set in the Shropshire hill country, had the imagination whirring, and led to the purchase of several of the books. The main meal of the day was usually consumed at mid-day, so that tea- time tended to be snack time. On Wednesdays, there would often be an individual steak and kidney pie made by Norgrove's, the butchers. A hole would be made in the top of the pie, into which hot 'Oxo' was poured from a small blue willow pattern jug. The pie, the 'Oxo', and 'Children's Hour' combined to create an atmosphere making tea time one of the day's most gratifying events.

The radio was a 'McMichael', quite a tall, wood-framed device that ran off the mains electricity supply. Some evenings, the boy would spend time fiddling with the tuner, causing a green dot to move about the rectangular dial in a 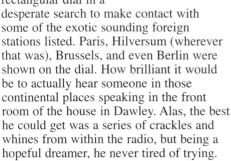 desperate search to make contact with some of the exotic sounding foreign stations listed. Paris, Hilversum (wherever that was), Brussels, and even Berlin were shown on the dial. How brilliant it would be to actually hear someone in those continental places speaking in the front room of the house in Dawley. Alas, the best he could get was a series of crackles and whines from within the radio, but being a hopeful dreamer, he never tired of trying.

The BBC Light Programme was a much easier 'kettle of fish'. Many winter nights were enlivened with such radio favourites as 'Have a Go', a travelling quiz programme presented by Wilfred Pickles (it actually came from Much Wenlock one week), 'Take it from Here' with Dick Bentley, Joy Nicholls and Bill Kerr,

'I.T.M.A.', with Tommy Handley, and 'Much Binding in the Marsh' with Kenneth Horne (a Shropshire man from Church Stretton), Richard Murdoch and Sam Costa. 'Much Binding' usually coincided with supper-time.   It's funny how certain foods can become synonymous with particular events. Consuming a bowl of 'Weetabix' still evokes memories of the typical 'patter songs' with which Murdoch and Horne concluded each programme. The taste of suppertime 'Weetabix' and the sound of Murdoch's distinctive voice still belonged to each other through many succeeding years. One night, after bedtime, the boy's mother shouted up to him that it had been announced on the radio news that his comedy hero Tommy Handley had died. He couldn't believe that somebody so apparently full of life could simply be snuffed out. Sleep was a long time in coming that night.

Life wasn't always a completely passive affair during the evenings, it must be said. On Tuesdays and Thursdays there would be some strenuous reading to be done, from comics such as the 'Dandy', and 'Beano'. The antics of such disparate characters as Corky the Cat, Desperate Dan, Biffo the Bear, Jimmy and his Magic Patch, and the boy with the magic lollipops, were required reading week after week. Sometimes there would be 'Film Fun', a comic dedicated to transposing such silver screen characters as Frank Randle and Joe E. Brown into printed form. On really energetic evenings, there might be board games of 'Ludo' and 'Snakes and Ladders', such as the boy's parents would also have enjoyed even in their childhood. During bouts of creativity, the boy and his brother would compete with each other to produce the best 'local newspaper', or cartoon strip in their drawing books. They might even try and produce the best 'cowboy films' using a small slate board and piece of chalk-- imagination was clearly a wonderful thing!

THE WEEKEND

Fridays have always been different from the other working days. You know you only have to survive Friday and then you will be released into the comparative freedom of the weekend world. In the boy's experience, once school was over for the week, a chain of events peculiar to the weekend would automatically swing into motion. In the late afternoon, 'Tall Will' Gregory (no relation to the author) arrived at the back door with a large, canvas bag slung over his shoulder. He ran a nice little part-time earner (nice so long as the weather stayed fine) by having a bulk supply of weekly publications delivered to his detached house in 'Old Vicarage Road'. They would then be sorted as appropriate and he, or a member of his family, would set off around the district delivering them to customers. Of course, this would be done after they had arrived home from their 'proper' jobs. At the boy's house, the 'Wellington Journal and Shrewsbury News', and the 'Sunday Companion' (a somewhat religious weekly) were handed over. This event marked the beginning of the weekend, so far as the boy was concerned.

On Friday evenings, the youngster was prepared to bide his time, thumbing through the pages of the boys' weeklies called 'Hotspur' and 'Rover' which he shared with his elder brother. He would do this while waiting for his turn to bury his head in the broad-sheet 'Wellington Journal'. It wasn't that the newspaper was full of riveting features (its front page simply consisted of columns of classified adverts.), but it was just an evocative symbol of Friday night, and the gateway to the weekend. It didn't matter whether he was reading the list of mourners at a local funeral, a brief report of a Whist Drive at Little Wenlock Village Hall, or the minutiae of the most recent meet of the Albrighton Hunt. The very fact of it being

Friday night reading made it come to life in a very particular way. The boy felt that those who didn't read the 'Journal' until Saturday or beyond were missing something rather special.

By contrast, the 'Hotspur' and 'Rover' were largely full of adventure stories very much for boys, including daring World War II escapades, and football stories featuring the likes of Roy of the Rovers and Baldy Hogan. They were entertaining, but for the boy, merely the 'warm up' act for the precious 'Journal'. As a small child, the boy had joined the Journal's 'Cousin Kate's Club', and had been thrilled to see his name in print, and to receive his personal membership documents. In his adult life, he had come to know the lady who had once masqueraded as Cousin Kate, and told her how thrilled he had been to be an infant 'playmate'.

Friday night was always bath night. There being no central heating, red-hot coals had to be carried on a short shovel from the main fireplace to a boiler in the bathroom. The boiler water was duly heated, and the bath filled with steaming liquid so that the ritualistic 'clean up' could begin. Finally, there was supper, and a communal tuning in to a radio programme from Wales called 'Welsh Rarebit'. There were Welsh comedians, soloists, instrumentalists, the Morriston Orpheus Male Voice Choir, and the 'piece de resistance' of the programme, the adventures of Tommy Trouble. E. Eynon Evans played the part of Tommy, whose weekly comic antics held the boy spellbound. Not surprisingly, the boy and his brother were soon off to sleep when bedtime arrived at the end of such an eventful evening. They slept contentedly knowing that the best day of the week - Saturday, lay in wait for them.

When the boy's mother was a girl, her Saturday morning rituals included cleaning out the fowl pen, and any other jobs her father thought she should do. After her father had been paid at Saturday lunchtime, she and her mother would often walk to Wellington for shopping, since goods were a bit cheaper there. By contrast, the boy's Saturday was almost recreational. Clearly, even by the late 1940's, a softer life style was creeping in.

On spring and summer mornings, the boy would be at his bedroom window by 7.30 a.m. with pencil and notebook at the ready. The name of the pre-breakfast game was recording the different types of vehicles passing along the main A442 road, a portion of which (two portions if you count a small gap between buildings on Dun Cow Bank) at Portley Flat could clearly be seen from the window. The page would be divided into columns with headings such as: LORRIES - VANS - MIDLAND RED BUSES - FORD - AUSTIN - MORRIS - WOLSELEY, and so on. The 'game' would end after forty-five minutes, the 'scores' totalled to reveal a winner, and one very contented boy went downstairs for breakfast.

Whereas the boy's parents would, in their childhood days, have been set some household task to do on Saturdays in order to relieve their over worked parents, the boy was largely free to go and play games with friends. His elder brother was however, required to visit the local butcher's in the High Street, and subsequently cycle down to his maternal grandfather's cottage near Dawley Church, supplying victuals to sustain the good man through the following few days. The mantle of this responsibility was later passed on to the boy, when he became a little older.

In the meantime, the boy and his pals were able to enjoy improvised games of cricket, and even hockey using a 'ball' ingeniously

made up of numerous layers of rubber bands. For a time, in response to the increasing need for pocket money, they ran their own 'wood business'. Each Saturday morning, a sack full of logs would be dropped at the home of one of the gang, by 'Perry and Brayne' of St. Georges. The boys then chopped the logs into small sticks, bundled them, using more elastic bands then loaded them into a hessian bag. The bag would be placed onto a flat, wooden truck that was proudly wheeled around the immediate area, so that the wood could be sold to certain customers. At one penny per bundle, the firewood was considered a bargain, and the resultant pocket money was put to good use in purchasing sweets (still rationed) and cinema tickets, or simply saved for future holidays.

On the wider front, at ten o'clock on Saturday mornings during the immediate post-war period, a commendable group of Dawley girls in their mid-teens would set off around the houses collecting 'salvage'. They would knock on doors and say *'Morning Mr./Mrs. So-and-So, any salvage, please?'* This became a regular occurrence for a few years, and residents would have their weekly supply of unwanted paper and cardboard at the ready, when the 'salvage girl' arrived. Into the canvas shoulder bag went the material, and the girl would stagger off to her next 'customer'. Each girl had her own regular itinerary, but they would all meet up in the High Street after nearly two hours of collecting. Together they would hump their brimming bags to the receiving point for sorting. The salvage depot was a yard next to Mr. Millward's half-timbered blacksmith's shop near the bottom of the High Street. This early exercise in re-cycling, was a valuable contribution to the country's gradual recovery from wartime austerity. For the girls involved, it was simply a source of satisfaction in a thankless job well done, since their efforts were purely voluntary!

Also in the aftermath of the Second World War, Malinslee had to get used to a brand new face, in the shape of a clock installed into the church tower in 1949. The clock, which still reliably tells the time to parishioners, and to travellers passing through on the way to Telford Town Centre, was put there as a memorial to those local men who lost their lives whilst serving in the forces during the conflict.

St. Leonard's church clock, Malinslee

Summer Saturday lunchtimes were a further landmark in the journey through this sprawling day of leisure. The boy recalls joyously working his way through a plate of sausages, potatoes, peas and wonderfully thick, brown gravy while the exquisite voice of John Arlott commentated on the Test Match against Australia, on the radio. The names 'Hutton', 'Washbrook', and 'Lindwall' just dripped from his tongue like honey and his tranquil tones were guaranteed to soothe even a housewife's nerves into a state of amity before tackling the chores of the afternoon. There could be no finer catalyst for the digestive juices than that, and for years the boy associated the sound of John Arlott with wonderfully thick, brown, Saturday gravy. Had the commentator himself been aware of that

small fact, he would surely have died an even happier man.

Summer Saturday evenings meant joint long walks in the surrounding countryside, in the company of a family who lived further down the road. A pattern developed whereby one week, the boy's family would knock on their friends' door, and the entire party would then walk in a southerly direction, and the following week, the roles would be reversed and everyone headed north. Throughout the proceedings, there would be much nattering and admiration of the scenery, or any other feature of interest that the group happened to stumble upon. The boy's particular favourite walk was the one that began with a descent of Doseley Bank. On a good, clear evening there were distant views of Benthall Edge, Brown Clee, rolling countryside above Coalbrookdale, and the wooded landscape of the Severn Valley towards Bridgnorth. The first siting of this rustic panorama never failed to cause a flutter of excitement within the boy's chest, and it set him up for enjoyment of the rest of the walk. The route also entailed passing beneath the tall, brick railway-bridge at Doseley, where the lads would compete to produce the loudest echo. There then followed a game of climbing through as many large drainpipes as possible, among the hundreds stacked up along the open pathway through Doseley pipeworks. At that point in time, Parliament must have been too preoccupied with post-war reparations to worry about new health and safety laws.

Eagerly cupped young hands would collect the icy water pouring incessantly from the Bath Spout's cast-iron channel. The reviving drink was always considered an essential requirement before attempting the next big challenge, a steep climb up the valley to the unmetalled by-way leading from Holywell Lane and the Stocking Farm to Horsehay. Across lumpy fields the ramblers then trudged, passing through Stoney Hill, then descending grassy slopes until the main road at Coke Hearth, Coalbrookdale was reached. Depending on the time, the party would either wait there, or walk down to Dale End in order to catch the No.904 'Midland' bus back to Dawley, in good time for supper and bed. Other Saturday evening destinations included the 'bluebell woods' near New Works, Old Park, and Madeley by means of the Castle Fields.

The Bath Spout

THE DAWLEY DIALECT

One thing you notice from quite an early age when growing up in Dawley, is that the local people have their own peculiar way of speaking. At least, many of them do, and it's almost as though there is a second language. Some citizens would speak 'broad Dawley' all of the time. The Dawley dialect was a corruption of 'proper English', and a Dawleyite would also clearly understand someone speaking to him in the correct manner. Some of the boy's junior school colleagues spoke 'broad Dawley' as of habit, although, curiously enough, they didn't do so in the classroom. The boy's maternal grandfather also spoke 'fluent Dawley' and nothing else, but did so in a way that was full of charm rather than sounding uncouth. The same could be said of many others for whom 'broad Dawley' was their 'natural language'.

What is 'broad Dawley' then, and how did it come into existence in the first place? It's doubtful whether anyone can fully answer those questions, there don't seem to be any written records tracing the history of the 'lingo'. We have already learned that for centuries Dawley was a rural, farming area, and that environment has contributed to the Dawley accent we know today. For example, you can still discern traces of a slight rural burr in the speech of some people brought up in the vicinity of Little Dawley. Pronunciation of the letter 'r' becomes more of an 'rrr'. As the cloak of industrialisation was eventually drawn over the Dawley district from the end of the eighteenth century, a hardening of the dialect took place. The language still included the 'thee's' and 'thou's' of earlier centuries. Somewhere along the line, the likes of 'thou knowest' became shortened to 'thee know'st', and 'cannest thou do it?' simply downgraded to 'coss't diew it?' As to why the word 'school' is pronounced 'schoowul', and 'pool' becomes 'poowul' is hard to fathom, but perhaps that's just down to the delightful eccentricity that is part of the Dawley character. Although some people claim there is a Black Country influence in the Dawley dialect, there are more differences than similarities between the two to suggest anything other than the uniqueness of 'broad Dawley'.

The trouble with growing up in the 1940's and 1950's under the influence of the dialect was that when you used it your parents would tell you off, making you feel you were not speaking properly. You grew up to regard it as 'bad language', almost as if you were swearing when you spoke it. Nevertheless, you quickly learned from those youngsters who unashamedly used it, and soon became fluent. Let's face it, without those natural exponents of 'Dawley speak' the dialect would have died out by now, and thousands of inhabitants would have gone through life without knowing it had ever existed.

Summing all that up, the dialect seems to be rooted in the archaic, rural language of the 17th century, or earlier, and coarsened by the industrial slang of the early miners and ironworkers. What does it sound like? Well, here are just a few examples with 'sub-titles' for the benefit of the 'uninitiated'

'Ow do, owd jockey -ow bist?'
(Hello old friend, how are you?)

'Dunna tek one, tek 'ontull'
(Don't just take one take a handful)

'I 'ope theet nock off, wut!'
(I hope you will stop it, will you!)

'Tek on theeself soft'
(Don't let it bother you)

'Wuts'd lake a tuthree chips?
(Would you like a few chips)

'Thee didstna/cudstna/wudstna'
(You did not/could not/would not)

Some individual words that often grace the Dawley dialect include -

'Nesh' (weak; unable to withstand the cold without wrapping up excessively), 'Cakey' (silly or foolish), 'puthery' (oppressive weather), 'mither' (to worry), 'gauby' (foolish), 'licker' (bacon fat).

We could go on, but perhaps the above will give a flavour of the vast and mysterious vocabulary that makes up the true Dawley dialect.

SEASONAL DIVERSIONS

The seasons brought distinctive pleasures to the boy's lifestyle. Winters, almost without exception, would bring at least one heavy snowfall. There were few things more exciting than the first snow storm. Looking upwards through the living room window at endless swarms of apparently black dots streaming from the sky, and seeing them transformed into tiny, white flakes which somehow piled up on the ground and covered it, was an annual novelty which never lost its fascination. Then there were the frosts. Some years, they were piercing enough to freeze the outside lavatories at school. No loos meant no school, so everyone was sent home for the day. On those occasions, the boy and his friends, having reported home to Mum first, would swiftly repair to the ice-covered Castle Pools, near Little Dawley. They would clamber up the grey clay bank overlooking the main pool ('The Dandy'). They would seek out and hurl large rocks down onto the icy surface, in order to test its thickness. Satisfied that even the heaviest rock had scarcely troubled the ice, the boys descended the slope armed with stout sticks broken from nearby bushes, and proceeded to spend the rest of the morning locked in an energetic game of ice-hockey, using a piece of ice for the puck.

Sometimes, the frosts would last for days, and by the weekend, the ice covering would be even thicker. There were Sunday afternoons when adults would come out to play in fair numbers, walking arm in arm across the ice as though they did it every week. Youngsters rode their bikes over the surface, weaving in and out of the groups of older people. Others, the kind who wouldn't trust a cup of tea until they'd seen someone else drink it first, stood admiringly at the poolside, enjoying the unusual spectacle from a safe distance.

In those days, it was fashionable in many homes to have an upright piano adorning the living room, and for the youngsters of the house to learn to play it. Winter nights were the ideal time for this activity,

'The Dandy' (Castle Pools), Little Dawley

although it went somewhat against the grain once the clocks had been moved forward an hour at the end of March. The boy attended lessons at the 'Chapel Street' home of Miss Nellie Lewis, for some three years. Despite this, he never fully mastered the skill of reading music. Instead, he preferred to memorise the pieces, once the teacher had played them through. Miss Lewis used to cycle daily to Shifnal Junior School, where she taught for several years. She would organise a Grand Concert annually, in which her piano pupils and a dance troupe from the school combined to entertain the good people of Dawley. The boy remembers participating at one such extravaganza in the Methodist Schoolroom, in 'Chapel Street'. His contribution was to play a bijou piece called 'Trotting Home'. It was so short, that he was instructed to play it through twice, so that the audience would not feel cheated. Needless to say, both trots home were performed from memory, the sheet music being used only for show!

The winter of 1946/'47 brought huge snowfalls, followed by prolonged heavy rain. The numerous fields of Manor Farm, which covered an area stretching from the parish church to Portley (now occupied by the likes of 'Manor Road', 'Webb Crescent',

and 'Windsor Road'), became seriously flooded. The people hadn't seen anything like it before. Boys being boys, our hero and his pals simply had to investigate the phenomenon for themselves. The boy had recently taken possession of his first pair of Wellington boots, and got the mistaken idea that the footwear was a guaranteed safeguard against the elements. Entering a field near the Gander Fields, the boys tramped through a huge sheet of deepish water that covered what had previously been one of their improvised football/cricket pitches. The boy was impressed with the sheer force of the water, as it pressed against his shins whenever he tried to move forward. It was as if the sea had suddenly come to Dawley - all you could see was water where previously there had always been grass. Battling with the tide seemed fun, as did the splurging of water down into the depths of the boots. What did it matter if his socks were ringing wet? They could always be taken off and dried out when the boy got home. The boys must have spent half-an-hour or more wading through the incredible mass of water in the fields. The boy's reward arrived a few days later, when Dr. Beatton diagnosed rheumatic fever, which kept the venturesome lad grounded for several painful weeks. The floods of early 1947 were not easily forgotten.

The 1940's were more or less the last decade when local amateur entertainment was universally popular. The boy remembers walking home from Sunday School, and noticing a small, hand written poster pasted to a telegraph pole. It advertised a 'Concert' at some local chapel venue, and featuring 'The Dawley Half-Wits'. The boy was intrigued, wondering just who those 'Half-Wits' were and exactly what sort of entertainment they offered. He little realised then that some twenty years later, when the group effected a 'come back' in the face of relentless competition from television, he would be invited to join them. In the company of Cecil Brown, Charlie Harper, John 'Wacker' Edwards and on one occasion, Ernie Highway (of musical spoons fame), he became one of the troupe, purveying a repertoire of novelty songs and corny sketches which had stood the test of time. The great news was that most audiences seemed to thoroughly enjoy it. The Old Folk's Rest Room, and church and chapel halls around the Dawley district were still the usual venues. Several local churches also continued to put on their own 'home made' entertainment, to brighten up the 'dark nights season', during the post-war years.

Later, there would also be concerts at the Horsehay Works Canteen (now the Village Hall) given by the Horsehay Works Dance Band, featuring Ron Phillips, Jimmy Tonks, Jack Whitehead, Harry Boycott (the former Brandlee organist) and others. Edith Walton of 'Hinkshay Road' also proudly displayed her young piano-accordian proteges in local concerts. Harold Gittens and the Seranaders was another ensemble on the local concert circuit. They often rehearsed at the home of the Garbett family in 'Portley Road', where the living room fairly shook with the cacophony of sound. With violins, piano, trumpets and drums going full tilt, the room was entitled to quiver just a little bit! It seems a shame that so much local talent goes to waste nowadays, while people generally stay at home to be amused by the small screen in their living rooms.

As far as commercial entertainment was concerned, the boy was an occasional Saturday afternoon visitor at 'The Cosy'. On those children only occasions, youngsters were fed a diet of cartoons, Lassie adventures, and knockabout comedy. It was a good way of spending a wet afternoon. On the way home, the boy

and his brother would call at Watts's bread and cake shop, to spend the remainder of their pocket money buying 'penny loaves' for tea.

On alternate Saturday afternoons, there would often be visits to the Bucks Head football ground in Wellington. To get you in the mood before leaving home as you wolfed down great spoonfuls of steamed jam sponge and custard, 'Come listen to the Band' would be wafting from the radio. Each week a different brass band would belt out stirring music, which somehow seemed to speak of the excitement of a visit to a football match. The boy, his brother and father would leave the house thus fortified and inspired, catch the 'Midland' bus, buy a packet of sweets at a shop near the ground, then settle down in the main stand to enjoy the game. The Wellington Town team was known as the 'Lilywhites' in those days, and wore white shirts and black shorts. The 'Lilywhite' heroes of that time included striker Hedley Sims, centre half Frank Childs, two Dawley men 'Ige' Lea (defender) and Norman Phillips (winger), and 'Smudger' Smith from Madeley. It has to be said, however, that when the boy's father took him to a Wolves match as a birthday treat, the writing was on the wall. The huge crowd at the packed ground, and the sight of the gold shirted Billy Wright leading Johnny Hancocks, Bert Williams, and the rest of the team onto the field to do battle with Tommy Lawton's Arsenal was simply something else. Nevertheless, in later years the boy was able to share his winter Saturday afternoons between the 'Lilywhites' and the 'Wolves' quite comfortably. It must also be said that there were occasional visits to the Council Field in Doseley Road, Dawley, to watch the local teams, Dawley Athletic and Dawley United play some of their respective matches. That was also to happen increasingly during the early 1950's.

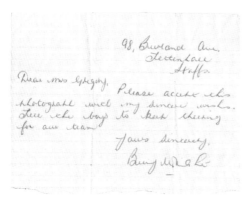

A letter of acknowledgement received from the great Billy Wright, during the 1940's.

The letter reads:

Dear Mrs Gregory,
Please accept this autograph with my sincere wishes.
Tell the boys to keep cheering for our team.
Yours sincerely, Billy Wright

The cinema played a more important role in the boy's life as he gradually progressed towards long trousers. There would now be weeknight visits to 'The Cosy' which provided a varied diet of films to suit all tastes, since the programme changed twice a week. The boy and his pals normally chose the comedy pictures, featuring the likes of Old Mother Riley (was she really played by a man?), and her delectable daughter Kitty. Then there was Will Hay (they particularly enjoyed the one where he was in charge of a runaway train), George Formby, Frank Randle, and Abbot and Costello. For the investment of 1/3d, you would be rewarded with two films. The 'little picture' was often a 'cowboy' adventure (later to be re-enacted by the boys in full, amid the gorse bushes on the Gander Field pit mound). Sometimes, there would be a gangster picture that seemed to contain nothing that would remotely cause a young person to consider embarking on a life of crime. It was simply an

entertainment, showing how good will always triumph over wrong in the end, and the evil-doers were always duly despised by the audience.

On winter Saturday evenings, the boy would regularly go with his mother and another lady to Wellington, to sample the delights of the town's cinemas. The 'Clifton' seemed to be their preferred venue. They always seemed to play 'The Skater's Waltz' there during the interval - not that that was the main reason for the visit - and the entire place had a 'proper theatre' feel to it, so that no matter what the film, a visit was always an enjoyable experience. The boy also remembers visiting the upstairs 'Town Hall' picture house in 'Market Street', to see 'This is the Army, Mr. Jones' (Mary Jones displayed the musical score in her shop window in Dawley, at about the same time). He also recalls seeing Alec Guinness starring in several roles in 'Kind Hearts and Coronets' at the 'Grand'. He liked visiting the 'Grand' because there was a particularly good fish and chip shop opposite. The bus journey home was always more enjoyable when you had a bag of chips on your lap. You normally travelled by 'Midland Red' bus but occasionally, Jackson's bus would be waiting when the 'cinema-goers' arrived at the 'Queen Street' terminus. On Saturdays, the trusty maroon-coloured 'Bedford' trundled sedately back and forth between Doseley and Wellington, its last run of the day being the one the boy and his companions would sometime patronise.

Wellington was also the scene of some much-enjoyed week night entertainment. During the late 1940's, a repertory company based itself at the Wellington swimming baths. One evening a week, the boy's family would make the bus journey to the town to enjoy a performance of a play by the group. The names of the various players became as familiar as the route numbers of the buses. The boy remembers eagerly scanning the programme each week, to see which of the team of actors were taking part in that week's production. He was also intrigued as to how the swimming baths could suddenly be converted into a theatre on performance days, and wondered whether there was any danger of the floor collapsing, and the entire audience becoming immersed in a little drama of their own. The quality of the productions was such that any thoughts of disaster were rapidly forgotten. It's interesting to reflect today, that the Kendal family involved in the Wellington Rep., included the young Felicity who went onto make rather a big name for herself in her adult years.

When the vernal equinox caused spring to return once again, the outdoor world beckoned youngsters to leave their winter hibernation and indulge in those activities which young people were supposed to indulge in at such a time. So it was that the shops began stocking up on marbles once again. A rash of impromptu games would break out all over Dawley, although admittedly there were particular patches of ground where the 'tournaments' tended to be held. In the boy's case, a grass-less area near the Gander Fields was a popular venue. Here, a circle and various horizontal lines were drawn by successive groups of players, as they prepared their pitches for the game. The contest was taken pretty seriously by most people amid cries of *'fat and fussy!'*, *'booths and lag!'*, and other incomprehensible exhortations from the players at appropriate moments in the game. These expressions and others meant something to the players, but would have stumped a foreigner attempting to master the English language!

One springtime activity the boy does not look back on with pride, was that of 'bird nesting'. Alright, so there were a lot more

common birds around at that time compared with today, and you simply tended to follow what older boys were doing, but the boy later came to loathe himself for having done so. The idea was to seek out, then rob the nests of blackbirds, thrushes and so on. Only one egg per person would be taken, but you pricked the two ends of the egg using a pin, then blew out the yoke so that the exhibits could be stored in a box lined with cotton wool. Lads would show off their respective collections, and try to outdo one another by seeking the eggs of less common species.

A less shameful activity was playing football in the same field (alongside the Gander Fields at Portley) where the carthorse that had the honour of nightly hauling Jack Hadley's druggan around the district resided. It was a big, dark brown, almost black beast that always had a well-groomed appearance. What's more, it didn't smell either - quite an achievement considering its occupation. It would spend its off-duty time grasping at the tall juicy grass around the field's perimeter, with its fearsome-looking teeth. This allowed the group of boys to re-enact the previous Saturday's football matches on the patch of short grass near the top end of the field. All would be well except that some evenings, the horse would suddenly be overtaken by a fit of unexplained energy, and decide to canter around the field using a random itinerary. Perhaps the thought of another night shift on the road sometimes got to him a bit too much. Someone would shout *'the 'oss 'as gone mad!'* Someone else would grab the case ball, and all the lads would scramble through a fence to safety before the thundering hooves could get too close. Fortunately, the horse didn't misbehave too often, and most games were played in relative peace. The father of the case ball's owner would charge each boy a penny a week for the privilege of kicking the inflated piece of leather. This went either towards the cost of having the ball repaired as necessary, by Mr. Jack Simmonds at his little garden workshop in 'George Street', or the eventual purchase of a brand new 'casey'.

In early May, the FA Cup Final would bring down the curtain on another soccer season. For the boys, this meant that the case ball would be replaced with wickets, and bat and small hard ball, enabling them to emulate the illustrious England cricket team, on their sacred little patch of ground, cart horse permitting. Maytime was the gateway to summertime, when so many activities took place to keep young children from getting under the feet of their parents. Sometimes parents wanted the children to be under their feet, however. The boy's father would take him on an annual hike to an old pit-mound at Deepfield. Small trees had long since clothed the grassy mound, and they provided a bounteous supply of 'pea sticks' from their slender branches. The two of them carried home an armful apiece, and the sticks were placed in straight lines in the rich soil of the vegetable garden, awaiting the eventual appearance of the sprouting pea seedlings. Potatoes, cabbages and carrots were among the other vegetables supplied by the garden each summer. Another evocative summer activity on those Saturdays when the usual evening joint walk wasn't on for some reason, was an informal picnic on Springwell Mound. The boy's family trudged to the hillock overlooking the 'Doseley Dodger' railway line, near Doseley crossing. After consuming their sandwiches, they would sit and wait for the evening train to appear on its way from Much Wenlock to Wellington. On a good night, the fireman would return their friendly waves, as the two-coach train approached Doseley Halt. The scene was not unlike the sort which now features on nostalgic, water-colour paintings of a by-

gone era you often seem to see in furniture stores these days.

Doseley railway crossing with the tree-covered Springwell Mound in the background.

Whit Monday, usually at the end of May, was one of those days when it seemed the entire population of East Shropshire had decided to climb the Wrekin - all at the same time! If you lived in Dawley, you would more than likely walk all the way to this popular landmark. That would entail hiking along lanes and through paths and woodland, roughly in the vicinity of New Works and Huntington, before miraculously emerging from dense woodland for the last leg of the walk to the 'Forest Glen' pavilion at the Wrekin's foot. You will already have slogged a few miles across country complete with food bag, and now you had to commence the steep climb up the hill itself. A sharp, right-hand bend in the broad track-way eventually led the walker up to the Halfway House. There, you could buy a bottle of 'Vimto' and sit at little tables both to consume it, and also get your breath back at no extra cost. Suitably refreshed, you would pay for a session on the 'swingle-boats' nearby, and try to swing higher than the people in the boat next to you. Then came the final assault on the Wrekin's summit. That was the point where you first realised just how many people had already laid their claim to a portion of the hill. There were scattered groups of folk busily munching sandwiches and guzzling soft drinks, along the entire route from the Halfway House to the hill-crest. It really was a unique and communal occasion. Those seeking the top of the Wrekin would press on, constantly thinking they had made it, and repeatedly finding that there was yet another ridge to climb before the peak was finally conquered.

Our boy normally visited the Wrekin with a group of fellows, some his own age, some who were older and looked after the younger lads. They would each carry with them a paper bag of some sort, carrying sandwiches and a bottle of tap water (hence, the need for the 'Vimto' at the Halfway House). The squashed sandwiches and tasteless (though welcome) water were consumed whilst sitting on the short grass near the top of the hill. Lots of other people were doing the same sort of thing, and there was a remarkable atmosphere of togetherness about the event, even though you may not have known many of the other folk who were up there. It was one of the big, local days out, an essential part of the community calendar. The 'Midland Red' ran a Bank Holiday shuttle service from the 'Cock Hotel' in Wellington to the foot of the Wrekin at the 'Forest Glen'. Despite the mass picnicking, there was rarely any litter to be seen in the vicinity - another sign of how times have changed. When the picnic was over, there was the obligatory ritual of climbing through the 'Needle's Eye', a precarious scramble through the narrow, rocky cleft between two huge boulders jutting out near the hilltop. The boys would then retrace their steps, tramping home for tea, having once again paid homage to one of Shropshire's best-loved landmarks.

Of course, Dawley had nothing to compete with anything the size of the Wrekin,

A view of the Wrekin.

despite its own somewhat hilly disposition. Malinslee represents the highest point of Telford, nevertheless. What the town did provide for energetic youngsters, was a scattering of former pit-mounds of various shapes and sizes, which had become suitably colonised with grasses and trees, and whose slopes became a natural playground for youngsters with fertile imaginations and the vigour to go with them. The boy's local little mound stood adjacent to the Gander Fields, where the flats at the top of 'Windsor Road' now stand. During summer holidays, the steep sides of the mound represented a kind of 'ski-run' as far as the boy and his chums were concerned. They would visit Woolley's the grocery wholesalers in the High Street, begging for discarded cardboard cases for use as 'vehicles' on the mound. Sometimes, each boy would flatten his box and simply lie face downwards on it toboggan style, so that he could race the others down the slope. The summer grass was always thin and parched on the western slope, so that after a few practice runs, the boys would have created an impressively slippery surface. The more worn the track became, the faster the journeys from top to bottom of the hill. The races were endless, but to introduce some variety into the proceedings, one of the boys would sometimes produce a large box that was still completely intact. He would then invite two other adventurers to accompany him inside the box, while two more were urged to close the lids and give the box a push. Down the 'ski-run' would hurtle the box complete with its heavy cargo. Sometimes it would simply zoom straight down the slope at frightening speed. Alternatively, it would somehow slew to one side during the descent then topple over, sliding on its side and giving the occupants an almighty buffeting in the process. Either way, careering down the mound on or in cardboard, was one of the joys of boyhood summers.

In good summer weather there was a host of escapist activity to be pursued. As every boy knows, you can't spend the entire summer holidays slithering down a grassy slope, however exhilarating it may seem. There are other important things for young lads to attend to. The Castle Mound on the way to Little Dawley was always waiting to be explored. The former pit-mounds of Dawley provided a perennial haven for generations of Dawley youngsters, and there was simply no time like the summer months for exploiting their recreational potential. The mound covered quite an acreage, and was generously arrayed with trees, including birch and elder. In all directions narrow pathways ran between the trees, and that was ideal territory for endless games of Cowboys and Indians, not to mention being Dawley's answer to Sherwood Forest. Re-enactments of scenes from the latest epic viewed at 'The Cosy', whether it had been a Western, a war film or a Robin Hood adventure, were carried out by the boys with considerable enthusiasm. There was also the challenge of building a 'tree camp' in the depths of the woodland. An elder would be the most likely specimen to use, since its branches were extremely brittle. The middle of the small tree would be removed to create a central cavern. Branches would be broken from other, nearby trees and placed

strategically around the gap to close it off. A small entrance would be created in such a way that it could be closed off again, when the campers were not in residence. What did the gang do inside the camp? Nothing, really, except take pride in the fact that it had been built using their own ingenuity, it was the first place they made for whenever they visited the mound. They would check it out for any signs of interference from an 'enemy' group, and it was where they planned the details of their next adventures.

Once, they discovered a sandbank at the far side of the hill, in which somebody had begun to dig a small hole. The lads responded to the challenge of continuing the dig so that a tunnel could be created. Taking it in turns to lie within the hole, they eventually succeeded in gouging out a passage to accommodate two young people at a time. That was fine until the inevitable happened, and the sandy roof began caving in. Fortunately, the two boys ensconced inside were able to scramble to safety before the entire underground passageway was reduced to a pile of loose sand. Naturally, that was one adventure that was not recounted to the boys' parents!

On a more relaxed footing, the adventurers would sometimes break suitable branches from the trees and produce 'fishing rods', also using a length of string as the line, and a hook made from a bent paperclip. They had also brought with them a can of small worms from the garden, and jam jars with improvised string handles. They would then descend the track of the old colliery tramway, sit on a rock, and try to persuade the minnow population of the largest pool to take a liking to the bait. Invariably it turned out easier to catch the fish by trawling the water's edge using the jam jars. The prize catches were carried home in the jars, to be shown off to the family. Despite using water brought from the pool, the boys could never understand why the poor fish rarely survived for more than twenty four hours at their new found home within the garden shed!

A moment of surprise excitement arrived when farmer Harry Price from Lawley (not the man who owned the lorries at Heath Hill) acquired the extensive land belonging to Manor Farm, 'Old Vicarage Road'. The fields were those through which the boy used to walk to Little Dawley Sunday School. Far from urging the boys to clear off his land, Mr. Price positively welcomed them. This was not so much to allow them to kick a football around, or re-enact Second World War battles, though he would certainly not object to those activities, but rather to enlist the boys' help in gathering the hay harvest. During holiday times, the boys would revel in their new found responsibilities, standing on the hay cart to receive and strategically place, as instructed, great fork-loads of the long, dry grass in correct order on the vehicle. A tractor would slowly trundle the large cart around the field, while men with names such as 'Jim' and 'Harp' tossed the hay in the boys' direction. The lads would also run errands for the farm workers, walking up to the High Street to purchase sandwiches and large bottles of 'pop' for the men's lunches.

For their pains, the boys received a shilling each per week, and a free ride on the loaded hay cart, as it wended its way towards Lawley. The load would be roped as securely as possible, and the boys were allowed to sit on the top, hanging onto to one of the ropes for grim death. Such things would never be allowed to happen now. For the boys it was an exhilarating privilege to be sitting atop a tall load of hay, as the tractor tugged it out of the fields, ran along Portley flat, struggled up the steep Dun Cow Bank, and with a sigh of relief continued triumphantly along the flat 'High Street'. The boys waved at people

they knew, just like Royalty being carried by the golden coach. They were tickled pink to be travelling the length of Dawley's main street in such fashion. At the bottom of 'Heath Hill', the tractor stopped to allow the boys to get off, being helped down by the workmen. With a wave, they watched the tractor and trailer begin to attack the climb over 'Heath Hill', and looked forward to its return the next day.

Needless to say, school holidays were much looked forward to. If the weather misbehaved, there would be 'Dinky' toys, or a small, clockwork train set to play with in the lounge using small boxes, or even thick books for the buildings of an imaginary town. There would be book reading, and the production of pretend comics and newspapers. Often, the radio would be playing in the background - the twice daily 'Music While you Work' featuring the likes of Victor Sylvestor's band, the Richard Kreen Orchestra, or Troyse and his Banjoliers was a regular favourite, its distinctive signature tune lodging in the brain-cells for the rest of the day. The lunchtime companion was 'Workers' Playtime', a sort of variety show on tour broadcasting live from some factory or other each week (the working population was really pampered in those day!). The fact was that such programmes were originally intended to boost morale and production during the war years, but in peacetime they proved so popular with workers and housewives alike, that the BBC kept them going for a while afterwards.

Being privileged to grow up during the late nineteen forties meant that you didn't miss out on some of the age-old activities which youngsters had enjoyed in earlier generations. For instance, there was 'pea-shooting', a rather dangerous occupation that involved fashioning your own 'pea-shooter' from a hollow stemmed plant, and ejecting dried peas, or even apple or orange pips at high velocity in the direction of some unsuspecting victim. Unsurprisingly, schoolteachers took a firm line with that sort of activity in the playground, especially as some victims sustained quite nasty facial injuries from the impact of the destructive missiles.

Horse-chestnut trees near Dawley Park would be raided in search of their autumnal seeds - or 'conkers'. The 'conkers' would be skewered, and a piece of knotted string threaded through in readiness for 'battle'. The 'conkers' tournaments would take place in the school playground, leaving a mess of broken seeds everywhere. There would be an elaborate method of scoring based on the number of previous victims a defeated 'conker' had gained. Some people soaked their 'conkers' in vinegar, or warmed them in the oven in order to create a tougher weapon. Some colourful language might ensue where the attacker managed to strike his opponent's fingers instead of the 'conker'.

Autumn's crowning glory came on November 5th. Most gardens sported their own bonfires consisting mainly of gorse chopped from bushes on the local pit mounds. For a few hours that evening, the air would be thick with bonfire smoke, and the entire area would be alive with the sight and sounds of countless rockets,

bangers, Jack Jumpers, Catherine Wheels and so on. Later in the evening, there would also be large, communal bonfires nearby on patches of waste ground, some of them would still be smouldering when children would be making their way to school the next morning.

Lots of boys wore tough, lace-up boots to school, and this footwear invariably came complete with short, metal studs. The tarmacadam playground provided an ideal surface for games of 'sliding'. Suitably booted lads would take a short run up, then slide down a sloping section of the playground one after the other, to see who could slide the furthest. At least it was safer than creating playground ice slides, which proved an absolute nightmare for those simply attempting to walk from 'A' to 'B' in relative safety.

More legitimate sporting activity took place when the school organised inter-school football matches against teams from such places as Coalbrookdale, Shifnal, Broseley, and the local Dawley National and Langley schools.

These then, were the boy's early growing up years. They were generally carefree, and a gradual preparation for the momentous period ahead during which his age would reach double figures.

Chapter Twenty Eight

EARLY 1950S ADOLESCENCE

Whatever else happens in a person's life, the teenage years remain the most evocative of all. In the boy's case, the start of the 1950's saw him reaching double figures, and thus the 1950's watched him passing through his entire teenage experience. Those are the years when your eyes are opened to a more expansive world, and there is a tendency to think that everything about your teenage years is fresh and new, and somehow more 'cool' than anything that has gone before. The reality was, however, that although new things were coming along all the time, as they must always do, growing up in Dawley during the 1950's also reflected much that had gone on in the district over a substantial number of earlier years.

Fairs and circuses were nothing new in Dawley. There had certainly been fairs temporarily encamped in 'Chapel Street' since at least the early part of the century, and people can recall the circus coming to town somewhat before World War II. At certain times of the year during the early 1950's, a travelling fair or perhaps a small circus show would decide to drop anchor in Dawley for a week.

'Studds Fair' and 'N.B. Davies Amusements' were the two most regular fairs to visit the town, and a patch of spare ground next to the 'Dun Cow' inn (roughly where the pub car park now stands), was the usual place where they, and any visiting circus, would set up camp. Naturally, the arrival of a fair was a pretty big event, preceded by a spate of advertising posters in shop windows throughout the district,

about a week ahead of the event. Children, some accompanied by their parents, would eagerly participate in the fairground attractions, determined to make the most of a week when the centre of Dawley was taken over with the clamour of 'all the fun of the fair'.

There would be swingle-boats, which soared higher than the ones on the Wrekin, so that those brave enough to ride in them were rewarded with aerial views of the town not normally possible. There would be side shows of 'Hoop-la', and 'Roll a Penny' both heavily weighted in favour of the showman. Those lucky enough to win, might carry home a goldfish in a bowl in the case of the former, or a bulging pocketful of pennies with the latter. There was air rifle shooting, and dart throwing for prizes that nobody ever seemed to win, such as giant teddy bears, or expensive looking glass ware, or a smart watch. There would be a coconut shy, and also a row of clowns' heads moving from side to side, and into whose open mouths patrons had to try and pitch table tennis balls. More excitement was provided by hobby horses on a large 'Merry-go-round', moving up and down and racing around at break neck speed. The young person in charge of the ride would often hop from one empty horse to another, collecting money from late comers while the roundabout was in motion. Sometimes, a hooter would give out several frenetic blasts as the horses gathered speed, and the deep-throated wail could be heard in the neighbouring streets.

Undoubtedly, the big attraction was the

'Dodgem Cars'. Popular music of the day would blare out from loudspeakers at the side of the dodgem track, advertising the entire show to people living in the vicinity. The dodgems were without doubt, the most scary and most potentially dangerous of the entire fairground offerings, and people often had to queue for the privilege of enjoying their unique thrill. As soon as the previous ride had ground to a halt, people darted across the oval track to grab one of the dodgem cars, often colliding with those who were trying to get back to 'terra firma'. When the money had been collected from the new participants, a member of staff turned on a switch in a little office, and the race was on. You had to put your foot on a cylindrical metal accelerator protruding from the floor of the car, in order to propel the vehicle forward. Electric power was conducted from the ceiling of the arena by a sparking metal taper at the top of a long, vertical rod attached to the back of the vehicle. The initial effect was startling, the car seemed to leap forward at an impossibly fast rate, so that there was little time to avoid hitting either another vehicle, or the rubberised sides of the track. Collisions were frequent and disorienting. There were always drivers whose prime objective was to give other drivers, or their passengers, an almighty fright by deliberately aiming their vehicle at them, and ramming the unsuspecting 'opponents' either head-on, or on the side. The really 'snidy' ones were clever enough to simply nick the back corner of another car, sending it in a helpless spin, right in the middle of the arena. Having said all of that, attendants were usually pretty quick to leap from the perimeter path to help the unfortunate victim, and deliver a swift admonishment to the offender. In his earliest experience of the dodgems, the boy would try to steer his car around the edge of the metal floor, but even this could be hazardous. Sometimes, a group of empty cars might be lurking along the sides, and

evasive action had to be taken. This might result in an unintentional collision with a moving car. Occasionally a novice driver might decide to drive in the opposite direction to everyone else, resulting in your being forced to swerve into the boundary wall. Since there was no reverse gear, you had to wait until an attendant came over and pushed you away from the side, using his hob nailed boots. If you were having a really unlucky day, you might get back on track again, just in time to be bumped by one of the aggressive types. It was all part of the game, for those who couldn't resist the lure of the dodgems.

When a circus was due to arrive in the early 1950's, the boy found himself in a fortunate position. Once again, posters were displayed in advance of the event, and the circus owners rewarded advertisers with two free tickets for one of the performances. The boy's aunt kept a small general store at 'Old Vicarage Road'. She willingly displayed a poster at the shop, and handed over the tickets to the boy. This meant that he and a friend could enjoy virtual ringside seats. Although circuses were never quite the boy's 'cup of tea', it always gave him a certain sense of satisfaction to be waved past the ticket office, and allowed to occupy one of the first couple of rows. In any case, much of the rear seating seemed to consist of a 'spider's web' of joined up planks of wood, with the ground clearly visible below - not a very happy prospect! The circus ring was a fairly small affair, and sitting close to it had its disadvantages also. The non-stop show relied fairly heavily on a tireless team of horses, several of them white, who came bounding around the ring's perimeter in a variety of formations, at the behest of a whip-cracking Ringmaster. No matter how well groomed and healthy they looked, there was always a certain smell attached to the horses, and sitting near the ring you became well accustomed to it, throughout the performance. Some light relief was provided when one of the white horses entered the ring, carrying on its back a little white dog that was wearing a tutu. Every act was interspersed with the shambolic escapades of a group of clowns, and the boy found himself looking forward to those raucous interludes, as comedy was something that especially appealed to him. Overall, it was an entertaining show, something completely different and for that, and the free tickets, the boy was always pleased to greet the arrival of the 'Dun Cow Yard Circus'.

ADVENTURES AT 'THE PICTURES' - AT HOME - AND ON THE SPORTSFIELD

Meanwhile, back at 'The Cosy', weeknight visits became more frequent as the boy grew a little older. The enterprising management had a superb ploy up their sleeves during the early fifties - the weekly serial. 'The Adventures of Kit Carson' was shown in fifteen-minute episodes on a particular evening, every week. The black and white film featured the daring exploits of the white-stetsoned cowboy hero 'Carson' exposing the nefarious activities of a moustachioed bad man named 'Kraft' (who wore a black hat) and his henchmen. Kraft had an underground den, which was reached through a trap door and a long flight of subterranean steps, just the sort of scenario to appeal to impressionable youngsters. The boy and his chums scarcely missed an instalment (unless one of them went down with mumps), so that it didn't matter what the main feature film was, the latest 'Kit Carson' episode was unmissable. Anyone too ill to attend an episode would be fully briefed by his friends at the earliest possible opportunity. Youngsters had become used to the idea of serials, through the BBC Light

Programme's 'Dick Barton - Special Agent' series during the late 1940's. Each weeknight between 6.45 p.m. and 7.00 p.m., millions of young ears across the country would be glued to the wireless, eager to listen to the latest developments surrounding the detective hero and his sidekicks 'Jock' and 'Snowy'. Needless to say, our Dawley heroes would enthusiastically discuss the previous evening's offering enroute for school, then re-enact it among the gorse bushes at a convenient, later opportunity. There was even a full length Dick Barton film shown at 'The Cosy'. That was a real 'red letter' night as far as the boys were concerned. By the beginning of the 1950's, like all good things, the Dick Barton series came to an end, to be replaced by something called 'The Archers'. The boys felt glad they had grown up with Dick Barton for inspiration. They pitied the poor children of the early 1950's, who would never know that pulse-enhancing Dick Barton signature tune at a quarter to seven every evening, and would have much less fun trying to imitate the 'adventures' of a family of farmers!

'The Cosy's' Saturday afternoon children's show eventually petered out, and some Dawley youngsters travelled to the 'Clifton' cinema at Wellington, to indulge in the Children's Club there on Saturday mornings. The 'Clifton' was a much larger, and more up market venue, with a balcony and smart electric curtains which parted automatically when the show was about to start. It attracted children from all parts of the Wrekin district. There was the usual diet of cartoons, Westerns, and adventure stories, and before the show began, all the children had to sing the Clifton Club's signature tune that was loosely based on a song called 'The Hop-Scotch Polka'. The boy and one or two of his friends joined the club for about twelve months, and enjoyed the Saturday morning escapades. Sadly, even if there was still a 'Clifton' cinema today, it's extremely doubtful whether such a club could exist. Sometimes, you feel glad to have been born at just about the right time.

A car park replaces 'The Cosy' cinema near 'Burton Street'.

The boy's sporting culture, and that of his contemporaries, was almost entirely based around the game of soccer. You played 'footy' in your backyard, you played it on little bits of nearby fields, you watched your local football teams, and as a special treat you might even be taken to watch the Wolves. It's no wonder then, that other sports, with the slight exception of cricket, simply didn't figure, and it took the power of television in much later years for any other type of sport, such as athletics, snooker, racing, tennis, etc., to get any kind of look in at all. There were school football teams playing regular weekly matches, but cricket games were somewhat thinner on the ground. On some Saturday afternoons, the boy and his friends might venture up to the Council Field in 'Doseley Road', to watch matches involving Dawley teams.

It's a curious thing that within a few minutes of watching your local team for the first time, your entire metabolism seems to absorb it into itself, it suddenly becomes your team. You quickly pick up

the players' names from the shouts of those around you, and 'bingo' - your life has swiftly acquired a completely new set of heroes. The first team that the boy watched was called 'Dawley United', and they wore pale green shirts and black shorts. Some of their players were so good that they were 'head hunted' by bigger clubs. Thus, Jack Tarr, Johnny Williams, Norman Phillips (a fifteen year-old winger), Gerry Smith and Les. 'Smudger' Smith all at some stage became elevated to the ranks of Wellington Town football club. Bill Aldred and Jack Butler even made it to Shrewsbury Town. Dawley United came into being in the 1930's, its predecessor being Dawley Town, who entered this life around 1932. That team (and their opponents) used to get changed in a back room at the 'Elephant and Castle' pub and later at a pub in 'George Street', both being in the centre of Dawley. The players had to troop all the way to Farmer Brown's field, near to where the Phoenix school now stands. That was about a mile from the 'dressing rooms', and the ramble must have worn the players out before they had even kicked a ball! Teams had figured in other parts of Dawley long before all that, of course, including at The Ley, and a field in Stirchley Lane, but this seems to be the first time an exclusively Dawley team had come into being. Perhaps the Dawley Town boys got a bit fed up with the fortnightly 'route march' to the field, and who could blame them, so when Dawley United came on the scene, they managed to acquire a pitch on the Council Field where once there had been a refuse tip. That windy venue with its impressive, distant views became the permanent home ground for Dawley teams from thereon.

Inevitably, in the early days of the club, the facilities at some of the away grounds were even more of a challenge than those at Dawley. At one rural pitch, the teams changed under a hedge. There were no line markings on the field of play, although there was a helpful notice on a tree warning of the presence of cow-pats. It must have felt like playing in a minefield! Having said all that, it also must be recorded that back at Dawley in wartime matches, visiting RAF teams preferred to get changed in the team bus. When you played away to RAF teams, not only did you have good and convenient changing rooms, but you were also treated to a good plate of pie and chips or the like, after the game.

For some reason, Dawley United became Dawley Athletic during the late 1940's, and initially, they played in Royal Blue shirts. A young Dawley man, Roy Pritchard, starred for the Athletic in its earlier days, and he made a big move to Wolves with whom he won an FA Cup winner's medal in 1949. Presumably as a 'thank you', Wolves then sent teams of young, up and coming players to do battle with Dawley Athletic at special weeknight matches. Those games drew the crowds, so that the collecting box carried around the touch-line by a committee member, was usually pretty full on such occasions.

In the early 1950's, the team changed its strip to black and yellow squares, and the new colour scheme seemed to bring about a further upturn in the club's fortunes, especially in the many cup competitions which abounded at that time. In one particularly victorious season, the trophies from the Bridgnorth Infirmary, Highley, Wellington and Wellington League cup competitions were triumphantly brought home by the Athletic. They probably had to invest in a new sideboard to accommodate them all! Most of the boys' 'Athletic Watching' was during the days of the yellow and black squares team, and they always stood behind the goal at the 'Chapel Street' end. This meant they could have informal chats with the home team's

goalkeeper. Over the seasons, a variety of men held that rather exposed position, including Don. Pitchford, Bert. Nock, Jack Martin (who later emigrated to Australia) and a chap named Milosovic who clearly wasn't a Dawley man at all. Most of the Dawley 'keepers wore a blue jersey. Most of them didn't mind a chat with the boys while the ball was at the other end of the pitch, except Mr. Milosovic who wore a green jersey and probably didn't speak much English anyway.

When the visitors' goalie was at the 'Chapel Street' end, the boys would try to distract him, especially when he was facing a corner kick, but it's doubtful whether their subtle efforts ever contributed to a goal for the Dawley team. Not that they needed much extra help, they always seemed a strong and capable team, and the boys were full of admiration for the home players who included the uncompromising little full-back Reg. 'Hacker' Rhodes, stalwart centre-half Ted. Tart, and centre forward Eric Houlston (who wore glasses and usually had a handkerchief stuck in the top of his shorts). Other players included Cotton, Smith, Bailey, and one or two recruits from the Army Camp at Donnington.

Dawley's younger element developed a team during the early 1950's, and the boy's brother and others were instrumental in forming a team known as 'Dawley Dazzlers'. They soon became successful in the Wrekin Minor League, and when the 'Wellington Journal' contacted one of the club officials to ascertain the team's name so that a league table could be published, the surprised committee man replied *'Oh, er, Dawley Dazzlers - I reckon'*. The name stuck for several seasons until at last someone decided that a more refined title would be appropriate, and they became Dawley

Rangers (or 'Reindeers' as some local wag referred to them). One of the Dazzlers' early triumphs was in a Shropshire cup-tie. They were drawn against East Hamlet, and this necessitated a journey to Ludlow - by far the longest distance the team had travelled. A coach was hired for the players and a handful of supporters, including the boy. A real ding-dong struggle ensued on the East Hamlet pitch, resulting in a drawn game with the strong South Shropshire side. The result was something of a moral victory for the visitors, and the coach journey home that early evening was punctuated with much excited chatter about the way the match had gone. Then there was a bout of rousing singing of such popular songs as 'My Truly Fair' and 'She Wears Red Feathers', complete with hand claps and lots of laughter. The team's home ground was on a farmer's field at Lawley, using a hen house as the changing room. For the important re-play against East Hamlet, the team managed to commandeer the Athletic's pitch at 'Doseley Road'. It was an evening game, and the visitors brought a considerable number of fans along with them. Once again, a tough game ended in a stalemate. The referee, a Dawley man, decided that extra time would be played even though the light was fading. By the second period of extra time, you could hardly see the half way line from the goal areas. When a Dawley player emerged through the gloom to plant a shot into the opposition's net with seconds to go, there was delirium in the home camp, while vehement protests came from the visitors and their supporters. It was a bitter end to an epic struggle, yet the referee was adamant that the result would stand. A devastated band of Ludlovians eventually went home in utter dejection, as they felt that a further re-play was in order. The memory of the two entanglements with the team from East Hamlet lived on in the folklore of the Dazzlers for some years to come.

The biggest change in the boy's life during the early 1950's was managing to scrape a free place at Coalbrookdale High School. The previous generation would have had to pay for the privilege of such an education. Suddenly this meant wearing school uniform, travelling to school by bus, having to do homework each evening (carrying it in a new leather satchel), and getting used to new classmates, most of whom did not live in or near Dawley. That was the backdrop to his life for the five years from 1951. He became a member of the lower school football team, in that eccentric position known as goalkeeper. His first match was 'away' to his old school at Pool Hill on a September Saturday morning. He, of course, walked to the Dawley school, and found it slightly odd to be lining up against the very team of lads he had been a part of only a few months earlier.

NEW HOME, NEW INTERESTS

On a snowy February day in 1952, the boy's family moved house from their abode in 'Portley Road' to a new council house a quarter of a mile away at 'Windsor Road'. On that day, he had the novel experience of eating his breakfast at the 'old house', and coming home from school in the afternoon to eat his tea at the new one. 'Windsor Road' was part of the large-scale development that eventually replaced just about every blade of grass on the former Manor Farm Estate. The boy had previously watched Irish navvies, and digger drivers cutting great trenches in the fields, which were to become the infrastructure of water mains, drains and sewers for the new houses. Then had come bricklayers from the Black Country, who chatted to the boys about football, and wartime exploits, as they skilfully constructed the shells of the houses and flats on land where once the lads had played ball games.

For years, a small pond had lain at the end of a long hawthorn hedge, in a field close to the grassy mound on which the boys had enjoyed their 'ski run' and other pursuits. Every spring, children would trudge to the pond, armed with jam jars to scoop up dollops of 'frog-spawn'. It was another of those annual rituals which children liked to follow, like bonfire building, and carol singing in due season. The pond never failed to provide an ample supply of the jelly-like substance with its little black 'eyes'. Children were forever fascinated by the yearly miracle of seeing the black dots developing little tails and legs, as they metomorphised into wriggling tadpoles within the jar. The only trouble was that the hapless little creatures soon died due to a lack of the right kind of nutrition. For the first few years at their new home, the boy's family was constantly disconcerted at the repeated flooding of their small back garden. Eventually, the local authority had a load of fly ash deposited in a hole that had been dug in the offending portion of garden, as part of the construction of a drainage system for the water. Only then did the 'frog-spawn pond' finally disappear forever.

A popular hobby at that time was the collecting of cigarette cards. Cigarette companies had long hit upon the ruse of enclosing little cards within the packets of cigarettes, containing pictures (often in colour) of famous footballers, athletes, motor cars, and other things of interest to children. The youngsters would then badger their parents to buy more packets than they needed, simply to boost the collection of cards. Trying to complete a set for a particular series of cards became an obsession with many young people. You could then send away for an album to store efficiently your prized collection. At the time of the property building at Manor Farm Estate, a brand of 'smokes' called 'Turf Cigarettes' ran a series depicting the

various classes of British steam locomotives. Since some of the boys had taken a keen interest in the noble art of 'train spotting', they were delighted at the prospect of collecting a set of the cards. As it happened, the various tradesmen involved in the building programme were pretty fond of 'Turf Cigarettes', so hunting for the discarded, empty packets among the rubble of part-completed buildings produced rich pickings for the collectors. The fact that the cigarettes themselves were probably contributing to eventual health problems for the smokers, was something which all concerned were oblivious of at the time.

Train spotting hit the boys like a disease during the early 1950's, and stayed with them for the rest of their school days. Once the mania got into the blood stream, every journey whether by road or rail, resulted in an instinctive craning of the neck in order to spot the number of any nearby railway locomotive. It was an enthusiasm that defied all sense, yet only those who became hooked on it could know that once sampled, it was irreversibly addictive, and not a little satisfying. There would be special days out to railway stations at Shrewsbury, Crewe, Chester, Wolverhampton, Birmingham and even London. Despite those excursions, the normal routine was to cycle to the main line railway-bridge near Dark Lane, and jot down the numbers and names of engines chugging along the Paddington to Birkenhead line. The boy recalls fields of ripened corn bordering one edge of the bridge, where now stand anonymous buildings within Stafford Park Industrial Estate.

When the boy became old enough to join the 'Boys Brigade', the Dawley Company had just folded when the Methodist Minister who had formed it, rather inconveniently left for some other part of the country. Some of the Boys decided to transfer to the 2nd Oakengates Company, and persuaded the boy and one or two of his school friends to join them. This happened about a year after they had started at the High School. After tea on Fridays, it was a case of get out the 'Duraglit' and white chalk, and buff up the uniform, ready for inspection at the weekly Company meeting. The pals met up and walked together to climb aboard George Smith's little Bedford bus, which stood waiting outside the 'Lord Hill' pub. At 6.45 p.m., the bus set off for Oakengates, circumnavigating the Webb Memorial, then rolling into 'King Street' and moving on to Lawley Bank, the Rock and thence to its destination.

'HIGH STREET', 1950'S VERSION

As the early fifties journeyed on, new delights and responsibilities joined the scene. The 'Eagle' comic made its debut, being delivered with the newspaper each Friday. The 'Eagle' revolutionised the world of comics. It had a spaceman, Dan Dare, as its cover-page hero, and his encounters with the cunning Mekon were a weekly 'must read'. Imagine the boy's surprise and delight on discovering that Frank Hampson, who drew the pictures for the Dan Dare adventures, came to live next door to his cousin in South London. Although he never spoke to the man, the boy would often watch Mr. Hampson surveying the stars through a large telescope set up in his garden. The comic would take much of the weekend to get through, as there were so many stories and features to be absorbed.

As for the new responsibilities, the boy eventually took over his elder brother's duty of cycling to Norgrove's butcher's shop in the High Street at about 9 o'clock each Saturday morning. The bike would be leaned against the window of a disused

adjoining shop, with no worries about its safety. Both the butcher's shop and the entire street became increasingly busier as the morning rolled on. In fact, the butcher's was usually fairly packed when the boy arrived, with customers occupying practically every square foot of floor space. The boy, not wishing to become asphyxiated, usually stood just inside the door, and slowly worked his way along the right-hand side of the crowd, hoping to catch the eye of one of the overworked staff behind the counter. Mr. Norgrove (senior) could be seen at a wooden bench in an adjoining room, expertly hacking away at animal carcasses with a fearsome-looking blade. Thwack! Bang! Clunk! The chopper incessantly laboured away. He really seemed to put heart and soul into it, stopping only to carry the fruits of his labours, a pile of chops or some other cuts of meat into the shop itself, before returning to start pulverising his next victim. The boy tried not to look at him too often, fearing that Mr. Norgrove might miss his target - but of course he never did!

The twenty-first century 'High Street' is closed to through traffic, a far cry from the congestion of the 1950's

Leaning against the wall at the right-hand side of the shop, the boy had a clear view of the fare actually on display at the window - including assorted trays of mince, tripe, liver, cartons of dripping, black pudding, and other tempting accessories. The 'big stuff' was mostly in the vicinity of the counter, including huge bundles of home-made sausages suspended from a hook like bunches of bananas on a tree. Mrs. Norgrove and her son Fred served in the shop, as did two lady employees - Mrs. Palin and Mrs. Jones, on such a busy day of the week. Whilst impatiently waiting to be served, the boy's eyes lifted from the tripe and black puddings to the pavement, now brisk with shoppers, and to the High Street itself with its steady flow of traffic, including the occasional 'Midland' bus pulling into the Market Hall bus-stop.

When at last he had been served, the boy rode part way down the street to Billy Taylor's cycle shop. The bike, and the shopping bag full of viands, could again be safely left outside the small shop while the boy went inside to pay off another weekly instalment on his new machine. On taking up his new Saturday duties, he was allowed to replace his earlier 'sit-up and beg' hand-me-down bike for a gleaming new, red and white 'Robin Hood' model velocipede, complete with three speed 'Sturmey Archer' gears. Mr. Taylor would duly count the money, then initial the boy's payment card to ratify the transaction.

A lot of people went into 'the Street' on a Saturday morning at least partly to have a conversation with people they knew. It was a real meeting-point for folk from all around the Dawley area, and fostered a community spirit that doesn't come as easily today. During the pre-supermarket days, the High Street shops would collectively cater for almost every shopping need. Just like his predecessors, the boy viewed the various shop owners as important personalities. They were part of

the fabric of the town whose names were well known to all.

At other times during the week, the boy occasionally visited Ron Weaving, the barber, (previously, Billy Smith had run a barber's shop on the junction of 'High Street' and 'Portley Road'), Frankie Bache (for kay-li suckers, and fireworks in season), Ball brothers (grocery), John Wooding (cheese and boiled ham), Lago (for a dish full of ice cream), the Post Office, Watts (cakes), Panter (greengrocery), Bembrose the chemist, Tommy Ayres (bread and cakes), Colin Evans (shirts and socks), Vaughan (pikelets), and Morgan the newsagent. The latter two were to be found in 'Burton Street'.

A visit to the barber's was almost as tedious as being in the doctor's waiting room, the main difference being that Ron Weaving relayed the BBC Light Programme through a small loud speaker on the wall. The boy's visits usually coincided with the 10.00 a.m. programme which featured popular tunes played on a theatre organ. It certainly helped to soothe the customer's impatience. When it was eventually your turn to sit in the barber's chair, awaiting your 'short back and sides' and self-consciously spying yourself in the large, facing mirror, Ron would anaesthetise you with some friendly conversation.

Clifford and Noah Ball's grocery shop had, for some obscure reason, blackened windows so that the interior was always illuminated by electric lights. At an earlier age, the boy had once disgraced himself by singing in front of the brothers, *'Mr. Wooding made a pudding, Mr. Ball ate it all, then threw the dish against the wall!'* Somehow, he never quite felt comfortable in that store during his early teens.

Watts's bread and cakes shop was a rather cramped affair, and had a wooden gate which led to the cakes displayed in the window. Various members of the Watts family served in the shop. If one of them wanted to retrieve an item from the window and the shop was full of customers, the person nearest the door would have to step outside in order to allow the server to get to the window display. The boy recalls a tall, dark coloured van with yellow lettering announcing that it belonged to Broadhurst the bakers from Northwich, Cheshire. The van regularly drew up in the vicinity of Watts's, and this might well have been one of the suppliers whose wares were to be imprisoned behind the Watts wooden gate. Either way, the vehicle was unloaded at one of the narrowest parts of the street, so that a passing heavy lorry or even a 'Midland Red' bus would be forced to mount the pavement in order to continue on its way.

Tommy Ayres created something of a revolution in the early fifties, by introducing to the Dawley public a new phenomenon known as sliced bread. Children who had been used to picking fresh warm lumps of 'proper bread' from loaves delivered to the door, were initially aghast, yet as we all know, the sliced bread idea really caught on in a big way. This new stuff was packaged in wax paper wrapping, and came from 'Champion' bakeries in Trent Vale, Stoke-on-Trent. This was the start of a brave new world so far as bread making was concerned. Having sliced bread somehow seemed 'cool', it epitomised the 'newness' of the fifties (just as jet aircraft, television sets and streamlined cars did), as opposed to the apparent 'ordinariness' that had gone before. So confident were 'Champion' that they were on to a winner, they installed in Ayres's shop window a small neon sign which bore the words 'Champion Bread

and Cakes', and the lettering magically changed colour from yellow to green to red in fairly rapid succession. Dawley had seen nothing like it before, and the technicolour advertisement was yet another symbol of the changing world. Sadly, it also marked the beginning of the end for the much admired local bakeries. To set Tommy Ayres's shop in its historical context, the premises had in an earlier life been Smith's the draper's. On Smith's demise, Tom Rowley of 'New Road', a smart-looking man with a thin, grey, military moustache, took over part of the shop as a gentlemen's outfitters, and Tommy Ayres acquired the other half for the bread and cakes business. Mr Ayres also had a dark green, probably 'Ford', delivery van for the benefit of customers living around the district.

Frank Morgan's news agency had the good fortune to be situated close to 'The Cosy', so his sales of sweetmeats must have been boosted considerably by groups of youngsters visiting this last oasis before reaching the cinema. There was always a strangely intoxicating odour in the shop, a sort of cocktail of the essences of chocolate, dolly mixtures and freshly arrived newsprint. You breathed it in as soon as you entered, and it somehow helped make the wait to be served that little bit less arduous. Sometimes, Mr. Morgan would be harassed by lads in ragged trousers, who tried to persuade him to hand out some 'freebies' from the array of sweets and chewing gum boxes on the counter. On one such occasion, Mr. Morgan broke off from serving a customer to ask of the nuisances, *'What dun yo want?'* *'Nuthin'* was the reply. *'Then tek it and go!'* ordered the shopkeeper, so that the urchins swiftly about-turned and left the shop as empty handed as when they had arrived. Frank Morgan was the nephew of Bob Briscoe who had in earlier years, run a fruit and veg. shop in the High Street. Perhaps shop keeping was in the family blood, but Mr.

Morgan's way of dealing with troublesome visitors was surely all his own!

Some of the other shops with which the boy made occasional acquaintance, also had interesting histories linking them with days now far off, and times which will never be seen again. Mrs. Jones's little fishmonger's premises had once been the fruit and vegetable shop of the redoubtable Bob Briscoe, who demanded only the best of fresh produce for his customers. For that reason, he journeyed regularly to the 'Crowgreaves' Farm at Sutton Maddock using horse and dray to lug the veg. to his shop. For her part, Mrs. Jones did especially well on a Good Friday, although the business generally thrived despite the proximity of Jarvis's fish, fruit and veg. shop on the corner of 'High Street' and 'Chapel Street'. Basil Lewis repaired shoes in a room above his newsagent's shop. Before Basil' s day, the shop had been the one owned by his Father (Jack), and before him by his Father Dockley, both of them being butchers.

The 'dark shop' belonging to the Ball brothers, had once been two shops. Noah Ball acquired the establishments of Billy Breese (confectioner) and Mrs. Prime the fish & chip lady, and joined the two buildings into one. The site is today occupied by the 'Supersavers Store'. Moule's cafe, sandwiched (if that isn't too much of a pun) between the original Post Office and Bailey the butcher, had earlier been 'bottom Darrall's', the grocer. An adjoining entry had been used to convey deliveries to the storeroom at the back of Darrall's shop. Panter's the green grocery, had once been Sutch and Gregory (cycles). One mysterious store that the boy never entered bore the name 'Melia's'. It was the last shop in the High Street before the 'Elephant and Castle' pub was reached, and therefore, just above the Market Hall, near the bus stop. It was yet another grocers, but

like one or two of its compatriots, didn't believe in window displays. In former days, a Mr. Timmis, a scout leader, had sold 'Meccano' sets and toys from the building.

The nice thing about all this is that, although traders came and went as the century progressed, the Dawley 'High Street' which the boy knew during the 1940's and 1950's, had remained the intimate and self contained shopping place it had always been. It not only supplied the needs of people from a wide area, but also provided an informal meeting place for the regular exchange of 'chit-chat'. It was a facet of life which had beguiled generations of Dawley people, but whose influence was destined to decline during the second half of the century. The development of Telford New Town was eventually to relegate Dawley 'High Street' to the status of mere 'local centre', a small cog in the vast wheel of a much more extensive urban area which had a huge, purpose-built shopping centre at its heart.

All is not lost, however, since the present-day Friday street market brings people into the street in considerable numbers on fine days. The traffic free environment allows groups of folk who have lived in Dawley all their lives, to stand around and chat in the street as Dawley folk have done for over two hundred years. People moving into the area due to the arrival of the new town have enhanced the numbers of Friday shoppers. They too, seem to appreciate the value of having somewhere outdoors to gather for a 'chin wag', as well as doing a bit of essential shopping. Admittedly, the place is a bit quieter at other times during the week, but it is hoped the traders will continue to make a reasonable go of it, so that the communal influence of the street can live on indefinitely. The narrow, winding road is still there, as are most of the original buildings. Long may people feel enticed into the present-day Dawley shops, because the place has a heritage far too precious to lose.

TYPICAL SATURDAYS

The next phase of the boy's Saturday led him to the former 'Great Dawley'. The 'Robin Hood' conveyed him on errands to his Grandfather's cottage, and his Aunt's corner shop. The cottage, was the top most of a short row of small dwellings originally built for workers in the nearby mines, probably in the late eighteenth century. The row stood on one side of a slight rise, which gave way to a further slope leading up to the gates of Holy Trinity Church. The winding lane had gloried in the postal address of 'Off Old Vicarage Road' for ages (although it had borne no such nameplate), until the name 'Hamilton Road' was imposed on it in the late 1950's. A nameplate to that effect was duly positioned at the top end. A handful of brand-new, semi-detached private houses were built at about that time, between the cottages and 'Old

Vicarage Road'. Harry Hamilton had been the vicar of Holy Trinity in the recent past.

He had also been a local councillor to boot, and it was surely right that a Dawley street name should keep the Scotsman's memory alive. The boy's grandfather was responsible for stoking the boiler at the church, and Rev. Hamilton would pay periodic visits to thank him for saving the congregation from freezing to death on cold Sunday mornings!

The brick cottage had metal ties running through it, which were fastened to iron brackets bolted into the exterior walls. The builders must have feared the possibility of slippage due to faulting underground. There were wooden ceiling beams in the parlour, and hooks in the ceiling for drying bacon joints. For years grand-dad had kept pigs in a sty at the top of the garden. A fattened pig would be slaughtered (amid shrill, distressing squeals), hung and quartered by an expert on the premises, to provide a generous harvest for the family and others. Perhaps the room's most striking feature was the fireplace, which occupied about half the width of the room. The grate was the middle compartment and had vertical brass bars at the front to stop the burning coals from falling to the floor. Underneath, was a fairly deep chamber for catching the ash. For some reason, Dawley people called this the 'esshole', which doesn't sound very nice, but is probably a corruption of 'ash hole'. The grate's companions were an oven on the left-hand side, whose door was inlaid with tiles of a dull red colour, and had a black cast-iron knob. If you delivered a pre-cooked meal to Granddad, he would immediately place the plate into the oven to keep the food warm for later consumption. On the right of the grate was a cast-iron sort of settle, on which pots and pans would temporarily be housed, until required for use. Smoke from the fire rose up an enormous opening and into a large, brick chimney breast. The boy often looked at the opening, and imagined that in earlier days, the chimney sweep's boy would have been sent up there to carry out the job of relieving the chimney of soot. It certainly seemed big enough to get a small person up there.

Auntie's general store formed part of an old house that stood at the junction of 'Old Vicarage Road', 'Harp Lane' and 'New Road'. The customer area was probably the smallest part of the shop. This was because the small store, as was often the case with outlying shops in those days, stocked such diverse merchandise as sweets, cakes (in glass cases), cough mixture, 'Express Powders', hairnets, canned fruit and vegetables, trays of fresh eggs, vinegar (in a barrel with a wooden tap on it), custard powder and goodness knows what else. For good measure, a metal tank in the small yard outside contained paraffin for dispensing into cans brought to the shop by customers. Despite the proximity of other such stores in 'Finger Road' and at Portley Corner, Auntie's shop was never short of customers - some of whom stopped off there on the way to or from Dawley 'High Street'. Such little shops provided an essential service to the population living within a quarter-mile radius of their hallowed precincts. People could buy from them many of the things they needed day by day, and folk could also gather there for a natter and a gossip before continuing on their way. As with the High Street, they were places where people who knew each other well, could regularly meet to buy and talk, and they helped to oil the wheels of a genuine community atmosphere.

The hire-purchase boom of the late 1950's and 1960's enabled people of modest means to obtain their own motor cars for the first time. The car would take them to Dawley or Wellington or Oakengates and even Shrewsbury, where all the shopping could be done in one fell swoop. It was the beginning of the end for most of Dawley's out of town little shops. The boy's Saturday visits to Auntie's shop culminated in his being give the freedom to choose any item of confectionary on display. On most occasions, he requested a bag of pear drops. The sweets were stored in one of numerous, large jars containing boiled sweets and toffees on shelves near the counter. Many of the jars bore the label of 'Old Betty Plant'. Old Betty Plant appeared to live in Stoke-on-Trent, and the jars of sweetmeats were ordered through a visiting traveller, then delivered periodically to the shop by van.

Once he had fulfilled his duties, the boy would join forces with a few friends, still making use of the 'Robin Hood' bike. They would either pedal off to the railway-bridge near Dark Lane for some train spotting, or in a less energetic mood, simply ride to Portley Corner, remain seated on the saddle placing one foot on a low stone wall for support, and watch the traffic go by. Some of that traffic was predictable - the convoy of 'Ribble' coaches (summertime only); a small dark green van bearing the name 'Owen's,which delivered pies and cooked meats from its Wellington base to little shops such as Mrs Durnall's on Portley Corner, and the boy's Auntie's; and a blue 'Bedford' bus whose rear informed you that it belonged to Bert Box of Bridgnorth (it conveyed workmen back to the Bridgnorth area, presumably from Sankey's at Hadley). Occasionally, there would be a surprise package in the Saturday procession. One day, the boys blinked as a coach with darkened windows passed by, displaying a placard in the rear window announcing that it was carrying the Johnny Dankworth Orchestra complete with vocalists Cleo Laine and Roy Holder. *'Fancy them cummin' through Dawley!'* the boys remarked. They watched to see if it stopped at the Town Hall on Dun Cow Bank, but it just carried on up the hill and into the High Street, doubtless on its way from one gig to another at much more prestigious locations.

On some winter Saturday mornings, there would be school football matches to be played,and on alternate Saturday afternoons the boy and the inevitable group of friends would watch Wellington Town play their home matches. 'Midland Red' would convey them to the 'Cock Hotel' bus stop in Wellington, from where they would walk to the ground. It was always fun hanging around outside the main entrance, watching the home players arriving in their ones and twos. The match would be watched from the terraces amid much banter from the crowd, and often not a little abuse directed at the referee and visiting players. Most of that abuse came from adult supporters whose repertoire of censorious comments was a source of great entertainment to the boys. It was almost as important a post-match topic as the incidents of the match itself.There would always be a fleet of ('Midland') buses waiting for the returning fans at the end of the game, and they all passed through Dawley. There was never a problem for the Dawley contingent in finding their way home again.

On occasional summer Saturday afternoons, the boys would walk to Horsehay and Dawley rail station, and await the branch line train to Wellington where they would enjoy a train spotting session. Having completed its climb from Doseley Halt, a tank engine pulling two coaches would come huffing under the railway-bridge, and glide gratefully along the single platform where it stopped for a well-earned rest. On resuming the journey, the train never seemed to get up much speed, since there were several stations a short distance

from each other on the remainder of the route. Soon after leaving Horsehay and Dawley the 'dodger' passed between high embankments alongside Spring Village and Horsehay Common, before plunging into a short tunnel beneath the A442 road, near Heath Hill. There were stations at Lawley Bank (some distance from much of the housing) which also had a level-crossing, a mysterious non-place called New Dale, then Ketley Town, and Ketley where the line crossed the busy A5 road. Soon after leaving the latter station, the train joined the main line. It was time for boyish heads to bravely, yet dangerously, peer out of opened carriage windows, to see whether there was a main line train approaching from the opposite direction. At Wellington station, the boys would be able to watch at close quarters express trains to London, Bournemouth, Aberystwyth, and Birkenhead. There would be lengthy, clanking goods trains, local trains to Shrewsbury, Stafford, Crewe, Coalport, Much Wenlock and Wolverhampton. There was an engine shed with simmering tank engines standing near the up platform. An afternoon delighting in such edifying pleasures seemed the ultimate in adolescent recreation at the time.

1950'S RADIO SHOWS

If you asked a person of the boy's parents' generation in Dawley whether they listened to the radio at home in their younger days, the answer would invariably be *'No, we didn't have a radio in those days'*. Although national radio stations had been going for about a couple of decades before World War II, it seems that ownership of a radio set was chiefly the province of wealthy people. Some folk dabbled in crystal sets, even assembling their own, but the results were often spasmodic and unclear. The war was the event that caused many ordinary people to save up and buy a 'wireless', as they were often called, not so much as a form of entertainment, but an essential and more immediate way of keeping up with events in the alarming theatres of war. Some of those wirelesses were powered by something called an 'accumulator', a large, glass vessel which contained acid and was linked by wires to the radio set, acting as a sort of battery. Before too long, the accumulator would run out of energy and need re-charging. It would have a handle on the top, and it was a fairly common sight to see someone carrying an accumulator up to the High Street, so that the device could be brought to life again. Presumably, most people kept a spare, so that there was no interruption to their listening. Leighton's shop, near the Market Hall entrance, specialised in re-charging accumulators. The shop was under one of the arches close to the Market Hall clock, it was the next door neighbour of Mary Jones, but you turned left instead of right to enter Leighton's. In time, accumulators, which were something of a nuisance anyway, became a thing of the past, and Leighton's eventually ceased to trade there.

The upshot of all this is that by the time the war was over, most households possessed a radio set of one sort or another. The set stood on a table in a corner of the lounge at the boy's home, and became a valued source of news and amusement, way beyond the war years. The boy's generation was thus the first to grow up in an era when such home entertainment was available to the masses. It soon became indispensable. During school holidays, the boy tuned in each morning at nine to 'Housewives Choice'. That was a record request programme in which guest presenters such as Jack Train, Mr. & Mrs. Elrick's wee son George, Roy Rich and others would charm the ladies during the reading of their messages and playing of their record requests. Interspersed among the regular favourites featuring the likes of Richard Tauber, Anne Zeigler and Webster

Booth, and ballet music would be the occasional popular tune of the day. The 'pop charts' were first established in 1952, and you could find out from looking in music shop windows the ten tunes whose sheet music copies were currently selling best, and their order of popularity. Copies of the songs and tunes would be purchased by local bands and, of course, people who had pianos and other instruments in their houses. Some of those early 'pops' such as the 'Cuckoo Waltz', and 'Get out of here with your boom-boom-boom' seem rather tame by today's standards, but this was the beginning of something big. The world was soon to be conquered by the 'pop' culture, and the boy's generation was in on it from the start.

Most people didn't own a record player in the early fifties, so you had to just hope and pray that your favourite tune would crop up among the more predictable fare on 'Housewives Choice'. As mentioned in Chapter 27, the boy's junior school organised a coach trip to Rhyl as a reward for the pupils' efforts at a musical concert in a packed school hall, during the early 1950's. On a particular, sunny Friday morning during the summer term, two or three coach loads of children set off on this unique outing. To the boy's amazement, his coach had a radio with speakers placed intermittently around the interior. The boy had become entranced by the sound of Les Paul's Guitar. The American entertainer had experimented with multi-track recording technology, and had a string of popular hits in the early 50's. He was way ahead of his time, and his techniques were to be used extensively by others in later years. Soon after the coach had left Dawley his favourite Les Paul record called 'Goofus' came on air, and this set the tone for a memorably enjoyable day out from school.

Morning after morning during school holidays, the boy would listen intently to the record programme whilst washing up and watching people passing by on their way to and from the High Street on their daily shopping expeditions. They had to be daily expeditions because people didn't have fridges, relying instead on a cold pantry shelf to keep perishable food reasonably fresh. When the programme was over, it was a case of getting the trusty bike out of the garden shed and going to see if a few friends were willing to form a 'posse'. They would then make one of those celebrated bike rides around the district, discussing the records played on that morning's show as they did so. 'Pop' music was a phenomenon denied the boy's parents' generation who must have feared that society was going downhill fast, especially when they were politely asked to be quiet whilst a favourite record ran its three minute course on a radio programme. Things got even better around 1954, when the BBC had the brilliant idea of devoting the 9.00 a.m. slot on Saturday mornings to children's requests. Soon, thousands of children were tuning in to listen to 'Children's Choice' (later called 'Children's Favourites'). The initial presenter was none other than Derek McCulloch, nice old 'Uncle Mac.' from the weekday 'Children's Hour'. You were safe with Uncle Mac and he even allowed the occasional 'pop song' to be played in between the staple diet of 'The Runaway Train', 'The Good Ship Lollipop', 'The Big Rock Candy Mountain' and many other perennial requests. A lot of the recording artists were American, and some also featured in Hollywood films. Somehow, the Saturday morning programme conjured up images of that vast and magical country lying a few thousand miles across the enormous Atlantic Ocean. The boy's generation grew up to revere American popular singers, instrumentalists and film stars as if they were in a 'Premier League' of their own, and towering over anything that Britain could produce.

Listening to the programme and watching even more shoppers in transit to and from the High Street, became the normal beginning for the boy's Saturday mornings. On certain weeknights, there would be an adult request programme called 'Family Favourites'. On Sunday mornings at noon, came along a ninety minute blockbuster called 'Two Way Family Favourites', when presenters in both London and Cologne, Germany, would link-up Service Men (many of them National Service Men) with families and sweethearts at home. That programme was a fertile source of the latest 'pop' records, and a regular 'must' for the boy. He was even allowed to keep the programme switched on during Sunday lunch. He considered that the sound of the weekly record request show, combined with the taste of roast beef and Yorkshire pudding, and the sight of a persistent procession of thirsty men sloping off to central Dawley pubs for a lunchtime drink, regularly created one of the most evocative sequences of the entire week.

TELEVISION VERSUS THE LOCAL CINEMAS

In 1953, the gulf between the rites of passage of the younger generation and that of its parents was pushed even further apart. The Coronation of Her Majesty Queen Elizabeth II caused many ordinary families to invest in one of those new-fangled devices called television sets. Television had been invented as long ago as 1926, and it had been possible to watch TV programmes in Britain from the late 1930's. Nevertheless, until 1953, a television set had been pretty much the exclusive play-thing of the rich. As the Coronation drew nearer, more sets were appearing in the shops, including Kendall's of Dawley, and more people were tempted to splash out and get one, and be among the first people to actually watch a coronation ceremony from the cosy comfort of their own living rooms. The sets had small, usually nine- inch, screens and the pictures were black and white. Some sets were quite tall and free standing, while others were more bulky and stood on the top of a sideboard. In early May of that year, the boy had been delighted to watch the 'Stanley Matthews Cup Final' on a neighbour's set. In earlier years, it had been possible to follow the progress of the Cup Final whilst playing with friends in the road outside their homes. Practically every household would listen to the match on the radio, and since every living room window was open because of the warm weather, you could walk up and down the road all afternoon and hear Raymond Glendenning's graphic commentary, no matter where you stood at any given time.

The boy was completely bowled over to discover that a few days before the Coronation in early June, his own family was about to acquire a TV set. It was the bulky stand-on-the sideboard type, and instantly replaced the fireplace as the focal point of the front room. On the great day, relatives, friends and neighbours who didn't have a set, were invited to watch the proceedings on the newly attained apparatus. The gathering was as exciting in its way as a family Christmas party. When the big event had disappeared into history, households were still left with their new TV sets, and the radio got pushed into the background (except, of course, for 'Family Favourites' and 'The Goon Show'). Regular TV performers quickly became household names, as familiar as those of the many radio favourites entertaining people earlier. TV wasn't wall-to-wall in those days and there was only one channel (BBC). You had to wait patiently at tea -time for the 'Test Card' to finally disappear, allowing a genial announcer's face to welcome you to the evening's viewing, without the aid of a cue card. Children's programmes would get

the evening off to an interesting start, followed by the news and a magazine programme. From time to time during the evening, there would be an Interlude, presumably while everyone at the studio was enjoying a relaxed coffee and a fag. The boy's favourite Interlude featured an endless team of Shire Horses pulling ploughs across a huge field. It was so soothing that it was a shame it had to come to an end. Along would come another programme such as George Cansdale holding, or trying to hold, a variety of unusual animals and reptiles before the camera's obtrusive gaze. It was all live TV, and occasionally, some exotic snake or other would escape from its box (or Cansdale's grasp) and make itself acquainted with reels of electric cable around the studio.

Saturday tea times were famous for the tales of 'Billy Bunter', played by Bridgnorth born Gerald Campion. On Saturday evenings, there would be Television Music Hall, or Henry Hall's Guest Night, or Cafe Continental - all purveying variety acts of various sorts - which were eventually to ruin a good deal of live theatre. The thing was, TV got people talking, not so much while the programmes were on, but next day - before Sunday School started, on the way to day school, in the queue at the butcher's, on the 'Midland Red' bus, at the work bench and so on. The world was changing, and every TV viewer knew it.

At first, the cinema fought back, and introduced the wide screen known as cinema-scope. Both 'The Royal' and 'The Cosy' at Dawley got themselves wide screens, the one at 'The Cosy' seemed almost as wide as the building itself, which didn't take a lot of doing. Although it often took about a year for a new film release to reach Dawley, the big films of the day always played to full houses when they did arrive - especially on Saturdays. The likes of 'From Here to Eternity', 'The Greatest Show on Earth' and 'The Black Shield of Falworth' really packed 'em in at Dawley's cinemas during the early fifties. Not all the films were in cinema-scope, but eventually the twin attractions of wide screen and 'technicolour' seemed to take the local 'flicks' to new heights.

'The Royal' still stands but is now a bingo hall.

Nothing in this life can be taken for granted, however, and from the late fifties, the economic boom (and with it, hire-purchase) helped 'joe public' to obtain cars, bigger TV's, vacuum cleaners and fridges, with a consequent effect on people's life styles. ITV arrived in 1955, and the small-town cinemas were looking down the barrel of a shotgun. By the 'swinging sixties', 'The Cosy' had been demolished to make room for a car park, and 'The Royal' remained standing, but in turn succumbed to the lure of Bingo. Two bastions of twentieth century Dawley folklore had effectively disappeared forever, and only those who had been regular patrons could know just how much had been lost by their passing.

GETTING AROUND

The same phenomenon was eventually to take its toll of the local public transport system, but at least in the early 1950's, it was still possible to experience the idiosyncrasies of the area's bus and train services at first hand. The 'Midland Red' dominated the Dawley bus routes, and included service 905 to Dawley 'Lord Hill', 907 Lawley Bank, 920 Little Dawley via 'Finger Road, and 921 Little Dawley via Doseley (the latter two running only on Wellington Market days, which were Thursdays and Saturdays). The service 897 passed through Dawley on its way to Madeley and Ironbridge, 904 went to Much Wenlock via Horsehay, 909 to Kidderminster via Madeley, Ironbridge, Broseley and Bridgnorth, and 919 to Bridgnorth via Sutton Maddock. At one stage, there was also a service to Kemberton. The Birmingham and Midland Motor Omnibus Company ('Midland Red' for short) was thus the 'official' bus service of the entire area and beyond. In the boy's early years, the buses were petrol driven, and were a distinctive shade of orangy red, with white roofs. When a bus was parked on even the slightest gradient, the conductor had to shove a heavy, metal shoe behind one of the front wheels in case the vehicle decided to show contempt for the handbrake's properties. Gradually, diesel buses began to take over, again usually having white roofs, although some were red all over. Later, the conventional design with the engine at the front was replaced piecemeal with 'box shaped' all red buses, with the engine hidden underneath. On the older buses, the conductor had to fix a destination board into two brackets at the front outside of the vehicle, announcing the location in blue lettering on a white background. The board would simply be reversed for the return journey. The service number was indicated at the front by a series of metal number-plates, placed in order by the conductor into a black box, which could be opened and closed by the turning of a knob.

Walter Hart, who kept a couple of 'Bedford'

buses in a garage at the bottom of 'Chapel Street', ran a market day service from 'Finger Road' to Wellington. This well-liked man somewhat short in stature had a reputation for driving slowly. He also ran excursions to the seaside and other places of interest. Of course, it may have taken a while to get there, but Walter's genial personality saw to it that passengers never got fed up with all the travelling. When Walter Hart decided to pull on his hand brake for the last time, his coaches were taken over by local haulier Jack Ashley, whose garage was near the top end of 'Chapel Street'. Apart from works and local services, Ashley's used the coaches for excursions, including Sunday evening Mystery trips, and also took fans to football matches at Gay Meadow, Shrewsbury.

Other private services were operated by brothers George and Ted Smith (Dawley to Oakengates via Lawley Bank and the Rock), Darrall's of Malinslee, and Jackson's (Doseley to Wellington on market days). The railways were still alive in the area during the 1950's. Branch line trains would depart from the bays at Wellington station, for Coalport and Much Wenlock respectively. Local people called them 'dodgers', and to Dawley folk the Coalport train was 'The Stirchley Dodger'. The London Midland Region of British Railways operated the line. A black tank engine making a deep-throated sound, would pull a couple of pre-war maroon coaches through Hadley, Oakengates, Malinslee (really Dark Lane), Stirchley and Dawley, and then to Madeley Market, and the terminus at Coalport.

The Western Region (formerly the Great Western Railway) ran the Much Wenlock service. It was to continue into the diesel era, finally closing to passenger traffic in July 1962. 'Horsehay and Dawley' station lay in a sort of gully, so that you had to descend quite a steep slope to get to the single platform. Rhododendrons clothed the embankment opposite, lending a rural air to this far-flung outpost of the Great Western empire. Above the embankment were some goods sidings, chiefly for the benefit of the nearby Horsehay Works, although other goods were sometimes also received and despatched. One track went out of the sidings, crossing 'Bridge Road' to get into the works. Some of the company's smaller girders would be despatched by rail on low-loaders, although the larger ones would have annihilated any train passing in the opposite direction, had they been transported in that way.

A FAREWELL TO BOYHOOD

If there was one year that encapsulated all the good things of the early 1950's, the boy's early teen years, it had to be 1955. For a start, the weather was remarkably good for almost the entire period from spring to autumn, the summer months being particularly sunny and warm. You don't get too many years like that in Britain, and it meant that the boy and company were able to get out and about in the Dawley area to a greater degree than usual. Once, on a 'Goon Show' programme at the time, the character 'Eccles' gleefully declared *It's good to be alive in 1955*', and it certainly was as far as the boy was concerned. It turned out to be a wonderful last full year before leaving school. There was an appreciable snowfall in February, but by April the weather had settled into a fairly reliable pattern of pleasant sunshine. In their more mischievous moments, the boys, on seeing an adult male walking along the pavement would shout from the safety of a nearby field, *'Mr!'* When the man inclined his head in their direction, the playful lads would sing '--- *Sandman, bring me a dream* ---' as if really singing the opening words of a 'pop' song of the time, all along! As a result, nobody was able to chastise them, because the whole performance might just have been innocent from the start.

There was great excitement on the Council field when the Pool Hill School Senior Football Team won the Wrekin Schools Senior Shield. A crowd much greater than the one which usually watched Dawley Athletic, lined the four sides of the pitch to roar on their respect favourites on a warm, sunny, April evening. Whenever the action on the pitch slowed down, there were always the exquisite, distant views of Benthall Edge and Brown Clee to feast your eyes on under clear spring skies. It had been a memorable evening, which provided a fitting curtain raiser to the 'light nights season' just beginning.

During the Easter holidays, there were bike rides to meet up with school friends from other parts of the area, especially Horsehay. There, a host of youngsters banded together to play an informal football match on a sloping, green field at 'Woodhouse Lane', where 'Forester Close' now stands. There would also be further bike trips to the main railway line near Dark Lane, for train spotting. During the summer term, quite large groups of lads from central Dawley would congregate on the field at Portley Flat, for nothing more harmful than games of football and cricket. Sometimes, fixtures would be arranged so that a team representing Portley would play their counterparts from 'The Finger' or 'Webb Crescent', and a few spectators would even stand and watch, whilst leaning on the wire fence at the side of the main A442 road. On one occasion, a big hit by a youthful batsman narrowly missed the back window of a passing 'Midland' bus, and the soaring cricket ball ended up in a cottage garden on the opposite side of the road.

At school, pupils were showing an increasing interest in the weekly 'pop'

charts, since 1955 was a vintage year so far as early 1950's, pre-rock and roll 'pop' music was concerned. The boy listened even more avidly to 'Family Favourites' and 'Children's Favourites' in the hope that some of the year's hits would be featured. 'Unchained Melody', 'Cherry Pink and Apple Blossom White', 'Earth Angel', 'Cool Water', and Slim Whitman's record-breaking 'Rose Marie' were among the host of tunes constantly buzzing through the boy's brain throughout the long, baking summer. The climax to the summer term at school embraced a Summer Fayre, Sports Day and a Summer Evening Concert in which the boy sang in a large school choir on a particularly balmy July Friday evening.

The field at Portley Flat where informal games of football and cricket were played. In the background is the site of the 'druggan depot', and the pine-covered Paddock Mound.

Then it was all gone, and the summer holidays were under way. With so many days of warm sunshine, that last summer holiday of the boy's school career was the most evocative of them all. Any place seems tolerable in warm, sunny weather, and in a strange sort of way, Dawley in the drenching heat of summer, 1955 felt even more special to the boy than it had at any time. In July and August, the buildings of

'High Street', which had seen more than 150 summers come and go, were lit up by the hot sunshine so that the old, dull brickwork appeared to take on a perpetual sheen, as if newly polished by a giant hand. The people ambling along the pavements appeared always to be in a good mood, such is the energising effect of constant, bright sunshine. They were keener than ever to stand around in small groups to talk about this and that, and, of course, remark upon how lovely the weather was.

The boys would often cycle around the district observing the likes of Lawley Bank, Old Park, Hinkshay, Stirchley, Aqueduct, Little Dawley, Doseley and Horsehay all of which lay basking in the blazing sunlight, and as the Goons had remarked, it really did feel good to be alive in 1955. When not feeling so energetic, the lads would simply sit on a patch of short grass in their usual field at Portley. They would discuss important issues such as the latest Test Match, bikes, steam trains, female classmates, and the number of weeks during which Slim Whitman had been at the top of the Hit Parade. A succession of hot, lazy summer days has a way of making life seem unrealistically bright, and triggering the senses so that you find yourself dreaming of wider horizons. Money was not particularly plentiful in the mid fifties, but in the summer heat of 1955 the boy found his thoughts straying beyond their normal confines towards supposedly more exotic places than Dawley. Images of the U.S.A., the islands of the Caribbean and Pacific, and the far distant lands of Africa, New Zealand and Australia illuminated his imagination as if suddenly falling from a school textbook. He had seen glimpses of such places in films at 'The Royal' and 'The Cosy', on television nature programmes, and, of course, in Geography lessons. He would surely never see such faraway utopias for himself, but felt that they also would be lazing in the same prolonged, hot sunshine to have settled so insistently over Dawley during the summer, and that seemed to bring them a little bit closer to his grasp.

The family holiday that year was spent on the south Devon coast, just as late July was giving way to early August. One particularly hot afternoon, some members of the family (the boy included) went for a cooling drink at a seafront pavilion. As glasses of chilled orange squash were slowly being consumed at table, the melodic strains, of the theme from 'Moulin Rouge' poured from a wall-mounted loudspeaker. It was one of the most evocative tunes of the entire early fifties. The boy sipped and listened, and his thoughts wandered involuntarily back to Dawley. The events of the recent spring and summer days at home came drifting through his consciousness as if part of a carnival procession. The snow-balling in February, the football final at the Council Field, the 'Mr. Sandman' game at the Portley field, the 'pop' music enjoyed on the radio, countless bike rides, fun in the sun with friends both at school and at home, train spotting trips and so much else came flooding through the brain in a gentle cocktail which touched the senses. Perhaps things would never be as perfect again. Being fifteen seemed to be about the best age anybody could be when such a glorious spring and summer reigned, and there surely wasn't a better place than Dawley in which to have enjoyed such a wonderful time. Those were the boy's feelings, and nobody was going to deny them.

High summer moved languidly onwards and gave way to an Indian Summer, so that the remarkable spell of warm sunshine floated on and on into September and October. It even made returning to school a slightly less painful process than usual. Late autumn rains eventually accompanied the year towards the Christmas season. For their main Christmas presents, both the boy and his brother were given their first portable radio sets. Now the door was open for late-night listening in the dark silence of the bedroom each evening. You had the continuous 'pop' music of the commercial station Radio Luxembourg at your fingertips. Everywhere you went in the house, you could take the radio with you. You were the master and the radio did your bidding, wherever you happened to be. Your parents had never known such liberation as this!

On Christmas night 1955, as the boy's grandparents were leaving the family party, the front door of the parental home was opened to reveal a raging snowstorm. The storm had stealthily got under way unnoticed while everybody inside the house had been enjoying the good food, party games and conversation at the blazing fireside. There was a covering of a few inches when the grandparents set off for home, chaperoned by the boy's father. The snowfall continued into the night, creating an exciting end to Christmas Day -

provided you didn't have to venture outside. Boxing Day was fine and sunny, and, of course, everywhere was plastered with white. Suitably clothed in wellies and winter coats, the boy and some friends went on a walk of discovery. Nearly a foot of snow covered the ground, and the fir - trees on the Paddock Mound had become thickly draped in glistening whiteness. In the bright winter sunlight they looked truly beautiful, engagingly resembling a Christmas Card scene. The rooftops of cottages and houses at Portley also enjoyed a thick layer of snow, as did the empty roads, including Dun Cow Bank and the deserted 'High Street'. A year that had brought such a long, hot summer and so many youthful pleasures was about to say farewell with the most exquisite finale winter could muster. Beyond it, lay the year when the boy was to take his 'O' levels, leading on to the unknown world of work. 1955 had been the last full year of 'freedom', those days of innocent growing up in a place the boy loved - a place whose endearing character had been indelibly shaped by its long and engrossing history.